MW00337655

JUST LOVE

JUST LOVE

The Essence of Everything

A COMPILATION OF TALKS

SRI SWAMI VISHWANANDA

The words spoken in this book contain everything, the entire universe. They describe a Love that has been addressed before – after all there is essentially nothing new to add to the wisdom of the Holy Scriptures of both East and West – yet the way this Love is addressed is new. They are expressed by someone who not only knows about the all-pervading, all-life sustaining Divine force that forms the creation of the Universe, but who is completely one with it.

His message is simple: Just Love. Yes, just love. Love is all there is. Love is all you have to do. The rest will take care of itself. Those who have inner ears will hear. The words are like a sweet love song that if you allow it to touch you – will change your life forever. Because it will change you, and make you want to become again that which you already are, always have been, always will be - just Love.

JUST LOVE

PREFACE

JUST LOVE is a collection of talks as they have been expressed by a fully realised soul to enable each and everyone to attain the Divine Light in a simple way. JUST LOVE is all one needs, nothing else.

More than five years have passed since Sri Swami Vishwananda's public mission began on 13 June, 2005. Much has happened since then which is beyond description and human comprehension.

The Divine game of creation and the identification with only a limited part of the whole is always repeating itself and is a never ending story. But the story of how we are taken back from the limited realms to our home inside the Divine Mother's womb is ever new and truly original. The Divine never repeats itself in this. We are now being offered once more a new, fresh and playful opportunity to embark on a journey back home.

Everything Swami describes is about the unchangeable bond of Love between Creator and Creation. He says in a child-like way: "All I know to talk about is Love. I don't really know anything else." Swami's talks most often are expressed before or during a Darshan event, in which he distributes blessings to each visiting guest. He usually sings before and after he talks, as a Love song to God conveys more than a thousand words. He also begins and ends his talks usually by addressing the audience with "Jai Gurudev", which literally means "Victory to the Guru within", a beautiful acknowledgment and reminder of the fact, that the Divine resides in everyone.

Whereas before he began his public mission in June 2005 he displayed a kind of shyness when speaking in public, over the years he developed into a powerful speaker. His words are not formed out of thought, as many who have witnessed him speaking will confirm, but seem to come straight from the highest realm. Those who are present in the room, often feel like he's talking to them directly. His words seem to address each person in the audience individually. While the words themselves fade away over time in the weak memory of our mind, the profound impact on our heart has a lasting effect. May you, the reader of this book, be touched in the same way.

Since "Blossoming of the Heart", an extensive compilation of stories by devotees sharing their experiences with Swamiji, JUST LOVE is the first major book written with words directly from Swami. It is the first in a series of works that will appear in the future. While there was a smaller booklet with talks released in 2006, the larger compilation now being published allows us to free ourselves from dates and to see the connection between the overriding themes. While Swami's message is essentially always the same, his way of expressing it changes from place to place, from time to time, and from situation to situation.

There is always a special aura of joy and playfulness accompanying even the most serious of topics thus softening their intense impact. When listening to him one often has to laugh or smile, one relaxes, opens up and lets the transforming effect of his energy enter one's own sanctuary. Swami speaks with great simplicity and in a particularly charming Mauritian way.

When transcribing the audio and video recordings we tried to accurately convey what was actually said. Now this may sound like an easy thing to do, but it is more tricky than one would expect as there is the element of the filtering through one's own ego. It is astonishing to see how quickly the mind's alchemy can get in the way of what was really said and transform the original quote into something else. Luckily we have audio and video recordings to back things up. One can only imagine how in past times the original message of a master got distorted, twisted or even lost over time. Thanks to modern technology and the internet, this has changed.

While it is lovely to hear Swami live, on Youtube, on DVD or on CD, it is also – besides being practical – soothing and calming to the mind to hold in the hands the silent messenger called a book. It helps to direct one's sense organs within and allows one to enter into an inner dialogue with the master.

There you will once again be encouraged – in your very personal way – to find the Kingdom of God, directly, without interference from anyone. You will learn again what you already know. The Kingdom of God is made of one thing only: Just Love.

We kindly thank all who contributed to bring this book together, and we sincerely wish for its content to reach the hearts of as many readers as possible. May they reconnect with the Love within and then spread it to their Loved ones and beyond.

Springen, Germany, 15 December 2010
S.K. on behalf of the Publishing Team

JUST LOVE

JUST LOVE

LOVE

Just love!
Love is the greatest worship.

Sri Krishna

YOU ARE THE CHILDREN OF GOD

Darshan, Mumbai, India, 10 February 2006

Dear all children of God, I address you as children of God, because this is your true identity, this is who you really are. Beyond all religions, beyond all castes, beyond all colours, you are the children of God. God loves all of you equally. It's not because I'm a Swami that He loves me more or that He loves you less. The point is that I have Realised His Divinity and you all have not yet come to the point of realising it. You know about it deep inside of you, because you are born with it. You are called to Realise it.

Religion is one path. It's a disciplined way that helps to go from the outside to the inside, but it doesn't stop there. Very often, humans start by praying, but they get stuck, they get stuck only on the form that they're praying to. They don't cross over, they don't really want to realise who they are in reality. As long as there is not this want of realising, it's difficult. You really need to want it, to want God. Then He can give Himself with dignity.

Humans have many wants, don't they? They want this; they want that. The wants never finish. One want comes after the other. As long as the mind is focused on the outside, as long as the mind wants the material, as long as the mind says that you are just a human being, you are just a mere human, you will be that. You have to reach the point where you feel Love for God, where you say that the material world is not the ultimate of everything, because all other wants will never finish. You can desire a nice car and the moment you have it this desire goes away. Then you have desire for another thing and when you have the other thing another desire will come and so on and so on.

When you feel deep inside of you that you are unsatisfied, that you can't satisfy yourself, you keep desiring. The desires keep coming, the wants keep coming, pain keeps coming, suffering keeps coming and misery keeps coming. As long as there is want in this material world, as long as there is want of the limited things, of course, there will be misery. Who wants misery? Does somebody really want misery in this world? Nobody wants misery, even somebody who is committing suicide. Why is this person committing suicide? Somebody is committing suicide to run away from misery. Someone is praying to God, and praying from morning to evening, meditating. Why do you think this person is doing that? To go out from the misery that is in this world. So, the goal of it is to attain happiness, to attain eternal bliss and this is what mankind is here for. The rest is just secondary. But nowadays, people have placed God in the second, even third position, while expectation is shining beautifully – number one! Misery dresses itself so beautifully that it can make you get trapped in it. The moment you get trapped in it, She is happy. *Maya Devi* is very powerful, because She traps everything. Everybody gets trapped in it.

Even saints get trapped in it, but they know their goal. The yogis, the *sadhus,* the persons who are enlightened they know their goal. They know what they want. They know what is real, what they desire inside of themselves. This is what is real: to know what you really want, what your heart wants, to listen deep inside of you, to be free from the misery of this world. I don't mean that you have to die. You can become a *jivan mukti.* You can live in this world but, at the same time, not be part of this world. Then you can have happiness, you will discover it, you will enjoy it, you will know about it.

For that, there are many ways. There's prayer, which helps to calm the mind. There's *bhajan* singing, which gives you bliss; you can lose yourself in it, you develop *bhakti* inside you. But still, this cannot be fulfilment. It's through meditation that you can really come to the point of complete fulfilment. When you do prayer, when you sing *bhajan*, you lose this aspect of witness to the outside, when you lose yourself and forget about everything, forget even about you being the body, you see that you have become One – with eternity, with God. You have attained your own realisation. This is how great saints and great prophets have taught mankind about it. One of the most beautiful aspects of *bhakti* is Meerabai. She was so much into it, she forgot about herself. She forgot about her body. She forgot about her mind. That state is only Eternal Bliss. This is the soul itself.

The true Self of man is *Satchitananda*. *Sat*: Being. With *Sat* - Being, only existence as a mere human and without realising the *Chit* and *Ananda*, you can´t come to the point of complete realisation only with this one aspect. You can´t come to the point of realisation only with one aspect, you cannot come to the point of realisation with two aspects: *Sat* and *Chit*. *Chit* – Consciousness – and then there is *Ananda*, which is Bliss. We call that *Satchitananda*. So human being is the body, the mind and the soul (which is everlasting) and also *Satchitananda*. God has made the human being such a precious vehicle. It is very important that you look after it. It is very important to enjoy it and to be happy with it, to respect it, to realise that it is the temple of God. It is in this temple that God is dwelling. It is in this temple that God can make humanity advance and realise itself. Without this temple it's very difficult.

How many lives does mankind have to take to achieve a human birth? 84,000 species you pass through. And then, when you have this body, you keep making the mistake of running away from realisation, from realising God-Consciousness. As long as you keep running away from it, as long you will be coming [back here]. God loves you and He wants you back with Him. He wants you to realise that you are with Him all the time and that He is with you all the time. Then the light, which is deep inside of you, will shine! Love will shine. If you ask God "God, make Your Light shine through me", can He refuse that? He can´t refuse you anything. Whenever you pray to Him, He can´t refuse you anything. He is here to give. Only you should know how to receive it. When you receive something, very often you keep your fingers open, so when the Grace comes, it drops through and goes.

Whenever you experience the deepness of Love inside your heart; whenever you sit down for prayer, *bhajan*, or meditation; and you don´t feel pain, you don´t feel happiness, you don´t feel hot, you don´t feel cold but you feel a joy, which you can´t even express, treasure it. The word that we can put to this is bliss, but still this word is limited. The only thing I can tell you is just experience it, live it! You can´t express it with words. And this is what you have to be at all times.

> You are the temple of God. God dwells inside of you. You will realise this Love for yourself. You will know that He is here inside yourself, sitting here all the time.

When you become equal toward the outside, by knowing that everything and everybody is One, you will love everybody, you will love, firstly yourself. As I said before, you are the temple of God. God dwells inside of you. You will realise this Love for yourself. You will know that He is here [inside yourself], sitting here all the time. In this great country, many saints; many *Avatars* have walked through and still there are so many great *Avatars*, great saints and *sadhus* here. All of them are working for peace, in their own way, to help people. How blessed is this land!

So, in one way, I have come to help you, to give something, which is very simple, for attaining this state of Bliss. It's through meditation actually. We breathe every day so many times. How many times do we realise how important this breath is? Not many, because it's so normal, isn't it? It's a routine; it happens automatically. So if you really want to realise God, try to meditate. I will show you a very simple meditation that you can give to anybody, will you do it?

A guided meditation

- Try to sit straight. Your spine should be straight.
- If you cannot sit on the floor, sit on a chair.
- First of all, I will ask you to take a normal breath, breathe normally, a few times.
- Now that you have breathed, concentrate. Close your eyes and focus on the third eye. Use your creative power now, because, as I said, you are a child of God. As God is the Creator, you are the creator also. With your creative power, the power of creation that God has given to mankind, to all of you, create the *OM* sign, or any divine sign, the cross, the crescent, any sign that you feel close with. Create it on the third eye.
- Now, listen deeply to your breathing. Listen to it. And breathe *OM*. Take your time. Do it in a relaxed way.
- Breathe slowly *OM* in and breathe slowly *OM* out.
- Keep your focus on your *Ajna chakra*, on your third eye.
- After some time you will feel that on the third eye it is a bit ticklish, like something is working. Go deep into it. Let this vibration go down the spine: from your head to the base *chakra*. Let it flow.
- Breathe OM in and out. Let the *OM* sound vibrate on all parts of your body. (for a few minutes)

- Now, reduce the size of the *OM*. Bring it back to your third eye.
- Bring it to your heart. Let it stay in your heart. Let it vibrate in your heart.
- Chant *OM* loudly for a few minutes.

By chanting *OM* or meditating on *OM*, you draw the vibration of peace, joy and happiness.

This vibration helps humans to achieve their Real Self, let's say, to realise the pure Consciousness of God within oneself. You can even feel it, when you say it. When you say *OM,* and it vibrates, let it vibrate on the solar plexus. All the power of creation, the whole universe is present deep inside you. Let it vibrate in each cell of your body. Every time you have a little spare time, sit down and just breathe *OM* in and *OM* out.

Yogis meditate for a long period of time and if you go very close to them, you can feel their bodies vibrating, you can also hear the vibration of OM coming from some of them. So use your creative power inside of you, that God has given you, that you have been born with, create the sound Om, chant it and let it vibrate to the outside. Firstly, it will be mechanical; it will be with your mind. Secondly it will come from your body; finally it will reach your soul deep inside of you. This will happen just by chanting the sound of OM.

So, try always to listen to your heart, because it is through the heart that God talks with man. It is through the heart that you will know what is your way, what is your path in life. Follow it. Don´t doubt it. The heart is very powerful. Try your best to listen to it and follow it.

THE ESSENCE OF GOD´S LOVE

Darshan, Bari, Italy, 28 April 2006

It gives me great joy to be here in Italy. What I really want to talk about is the Love of God, which is present inside you; the gift that God has given to you; this Love, which is without any limit; this Love, which is without any condition; this Love, which is free and without any expectations. We are all bound by the truth that we are children of God. In all religions, wherever you go across the Earth, whatever tradition it may be, they will all tell you that God is Love and that Love is God. We all talk about God, but we don't know God, we don't have an image of Him. Of course, there are different aspects of the Divinity. But one thing that we can do is to feel God and that's how we can know that He is with us all the time. To feel Him continuously and to enjoy Him at every moment, we have to become part of Him, we have to realise this unity.

Firstly, the unity starts with our mind, then with our heart and with our body. When the body, mind and soul are united together, you will experience the Divine without any limitation. Actually, this is the main aim of man: to realise his oneness with the Divine. When you realise it, you become Divine. The question is how to do that? There are many ways to realise the Divinity within oneself like there are many rivers that flow to the same ocean. The main thing is to find the simplest one. The more simple it is, the more you feel free in whatever path you are on. That is the best way. I can't tell you that in this way you will Realise God and in that way you will not Realise God. God is sitting deep inside the heart of man so you just need to focus your mind on your heart and try your best to feel Him at all times.

So the best way is to start loving, without any question, without even thinking of loving, without asking yourself: "how to love"? Train your mind to focus on God, train your mind to focus on your Self. Take any Divine Name, take any Divine aspect and keep chanting the name until you Realise that you are one with this Name. It's not a Name apart from you, it's the Name of your own Self.

The more you think of yourself being human, like many people think, the more you become human, but the more you think of yourself as being the Spirit, being part of Divinity, the more you will become the Spirit and Divinity. You think that you are just this body and very often you focus only on the body, so what happens? The more you focus on the body, the more you have pain and the more you are miserable, because the reality gets covered, becomes overshadowed. And when this reality gets covered, of course it brings pain. This body will go back to earth and it will go back to the same five elements it used to be. But if this is the reality, if the body is the only reality, then where is God? Where is the Divinity? This great energy that makes the body work, that makes the body act, is the Spirit and it's who you really are. If you were the body, would you still be alive even after death? Whereas being the Spirit,

> **The more you think of yourself being human, like many people think, the more you become human, but the more you think of yourself as being the Spirit, being part of Divinity, the more you will become the Spirit and Divinity.**

you live eternally until you become completely One with the Divine. Work for this reality. Work and love God. Whatever you do, every action, every thought, focus your mind on doing it for God. Love God in everybody and everything around you. And when you love, love one hundred percent. Try to not doubt this Love, because when you doubt it, even a little bit of doubt, stops your advancement.

LOVE IS OUR TRUE NATURE

Darshan, Cisternino, Italy, 29 April 2006

It's so lovely to have all of you here. You are all here for one truth and this truth is Love; this Love, which is equal to all mankind; this Love, which is present deep inside each one of your hearts and which is waiting and wanting to come out and express Itself. But so often there is a blockage, a wall that stops you from loving unconditionally.

When you realise that the only path is to Love and to be in Love continuously, you realise how much God Loves His creation. The same way that God Loves, the same way you can also Love. All other kinds of love are secondary, because mankind is here to become this Love. But to become this Love, you will first have to overcome many obstacles, because mankind thinks that Love, God, is something apart from them.

Whenever you pray, you pray towards the outside. You say that God is there, on the outside and you are apart from Him. You should really stop separating the Divine from you. It doesn't matter in which way you are praying, but if you talk with God, you talk with your true Self inside of you, so do it from within.

There is one major factor that stops mankind from achieving that: it is the mind. But the mind can be overcome by chanting any Divine Name. You see, if you practice it regularly, it becomes easier to focus the mind. When you are singing *bhajans*, your mind is not troubling you, because when you chant your mind is busy and it becomes hard to think and for the negativity to take over.

So by chanting the Divines Names wherever you are, whatever you are doing, you keep your mind fixed only on God and this will help you to open up your heart. Chanting the Divine Name is the most efficient way of controlling the mind. Look at any religion. Christianity has the rosary or *komboskini*. Hinduism has the *japa mala,* and Muslims have the tasbih. So the name of God is very important and it's very easy and very simple. Why complicate it? Why try to complicate things when God has given us the easiest thing? By chanting His Name, you feel so close to Him.

But it doesn't stop here. It's like when you know there is a treasure somewhere. You know the place, but will the treasure come out if you just call "Oh my treasure, come out, come out, come out!"? The treasure will not come to you, but you will have to dig down. There are lots of stones and a lot of earth that you will have to get rid of before you will get this treasure. It's the same on your spiritual path, there are lots of things that you have to get rid of before achieving complete oneness with the Divine.

That doesn't mean that God is far away from you. He is here all the time and He is waiting, telling you "wake up and make yourself realised", because you were born with this realisation. It's just that all this dirt from the mind is limiting the Self. Cross over this, chant the name of God and be in Love with God, because He is the only one that can really Love you unconditionally, He is the only one who really gives to you without expecting something in return. Try to achieve this Love and to become this Love. Try to realise how much Love you have inside of you and then spread it. Love can't be kept. Like that, you become an instrument of the Divine and He reflects through you, He acts through you. And then you realise what your mission is.

BECOME A LOVER
AND THE BELOVED IS ALWAYS WITH YOU

Darshan, Budapest, Hungary, 29 July 2006

It gives me great joy to be with all of you. We are all here because of our spiritual path, because of our spiritual way – this way to the heart, this way to realisation, God-Realisation.

Most of you probably know that the main aim of this life is to *know thyself*, to realise the completeness of who you are in reality. In this search, you can travel to India, to America or everywhere around the world, but all the searches on the outside have a limit. The search brings us to different places and we meet different people, but still we are incomplete. We say, "God I have left heaven to realise it here. Whatever I'm doing, I'm doing it for Thee. Wherever I go, I'm just looking for Thee."

All your searching towards the outside is of no use, because at the end you realise that He's always with you, deep in your heart. God is always with you. It's like an ocean where you have lots of precious gems. To get them you have to dive into the ocean and go deep inside. So God lies deep in the heart of man and with your mind you have to dive deep within your heart, because of all the waves of illusion.

To achieve this Divine state you have to really Love God. You have to start, firstly, to love yourself. You love others, everyday you say to somebody "I love you," but how many times do you say to yourself "I love myself?" It's easy to love others, but some say that it is difficult to love oneself. But I will say "No, it's not difficult." See, when you love others, you see the goodness in them, but when the point comes to love yourself, you see all your negativity.

Stop looking at the negative. Look at the positivity within yourself. When you start looking at this positivity and start thinking about yourself positively, you will dive deep inside this ocean. Then your heart will open up. Know one thing, when you become a lover, the Beloved is always with you - all the time. But you have to become the lover. You have to be madly in love with God the same way you are madly in love with your partner. When I say madly in love with your partner, I mean for some time, because it usually doesn't last long.

So you have to really understand what Love is. Even in a normal relationship, you forget

> Know one thing, when you become a lover, the Beloved is always with you - all the time. But you have to become the lover. You have to be madly in love with God the same way you are madly in love with your partner.

about everything when you are in love. At the beginning, all goes well. After some time, it becomes such a routine and then you get fed up. But the real Love, which you have inside your heart, you will never get fed up with, because that's what you are made of. That is what each cell of your body is made of. You just need to realise it and say to yourself "I am part of God and I'm made in the image of God and I'm with Him and He's with me." When you realise this Oneness you become this Oneness. I'm telling you it's not difficult. If you practice your meditation, sincerely, every day, you will achieve it. If you love sincerely, you will achieve it. If you serve sincerely, you will achieve it. But it's up to you to do it. The sincerity with yourself will be the sincerity that you will give to the outside. You have to become an instrument of God and you have to become an instrument of this Love. You have to become a *jivan mukti*, a Realised, Enlightened soul, right now! There should not be any time wasted. Spirituality is simplicity. Practice it and you will achieve it. But the main thing is Love. Love will guide you on the way of devotion, *bhakti*. Through devotion your eyes will open. Even realisation will come to you through devotion.

I would like to do a little meditation with you-a very simple one.

A guided meditation

- Take a few deep breaths and, when you breathe out, drop your shoulders. Release all the pressure from your shoulders.

- Close your eyes. Focus your concentration on your third eye. And there, with the power of creation that God has given you create the *OM* sign or any Divine symbol or aspect - the cross or any symbol you feel close with. And concentrate all your attention on this point, on this aspect.

- The mind will think; let it think. Don't try to stop it; don't use force to stop it. But don't hang onto this thought. In the same way it comes, let it go.

- Focus on this Divine aspect and, with your ears, listen to your breathing. Listen to it carefully. You will hear, when you inhale - if you listen properly - you will be inhaling *OM* and the same when you exhale, the sound will be *OM*.

- After some time, you will feel a pressure point where you are concentrating.

- Let it expand. Let this energy expand, covering your whole head.

- Let it expand to your upper part of your body - your arms, your chest and your back.

- Let it expand to the lower part of your body - your legs, your feet.
- If you have any pain or illness, focus on that point. Let it vibrate.
- Now, focus on the heart. Let the *OM* vibrate in your heart.
- Expand. Let it vibrate more and more, at the same time, choose the image that you created, that you like, and let it go inside your heart.
- Come back to yourself.

You see this form of visualisation is very simple for practicing anywhere you are. In place of thinking or talking of things that are of no use, learn to sit quietly, keep the mind busy, but keep the mind focusing on positivity.

BE ALWAYS SIMPLE AND LOVING

Darshan in Mafra, Portugal, 13 April 2008

It's lovely to be here and to sit with all of you. Love is the most important thing and we each have to become an emissary of that Divine Love. And to become an emissary of that Love, we have to realise, firstly, how important it is, because it's only through Love that the world will change. It's only through Love that peace and harmony will be restored. Love has many aspects and one of the aspects is harmony and another aspect is unity. That's why at the bottom of the Bhakti Marga logo, you will see that there is Love, Patience and Unity. Firstly, these three basic things are not on the outside, but are within us. If we want to give Love, we have to become Love. Like Sri Krishna said in the Gita: A true *yogi* first realises Me within himself, then, he realises Me as an extension of the Self everywhere. Christ also said, "Love everybody as you love thyself."

Love is very important in each person's life. You know how important it is. Without love, nothing works. When you go to work, you need to love your job. You love your children, your husband or your wife, you always love. In everything that you do, there is Love. Even if it is not on a big scale, even on this small scale, Love is present everywhere, but we can increase this Love, we can make it stronger. Like the story of Krishna's flute, we just give ourselves. Be like that, [empty like a flute]. Be in the hands of God. May you be ready always to be His messenger, His tool, to spread His Love. As Christ said to His disciples, "What I am doing, you all can do much more." You just have to believe it and if you believe without doubt, it will happen. You need faith like a child, because when you look at a child, a child doesn't question its mother's word. If a mother says to her child, "Listen, my dear, that boy is your brother." The child will not say "Yes, mother." or "No, mother." or "Why is it like that?" He will just accept it, because the mother has said "Yes, this child is your brother", because she knows it! This confidence in the mother, you know, is there! And that confidence you should have.

Yesterday during *darshan* I was holding a little baby. It was so sweet to look at how the child was. She came to me, I wanted to give her candy but the moment she turned to the mother and looked at her, she didn't even want the candy, she just wanted to go to her mother. It brings me great joy to see this surrender, you know. Then I said to the people 'Imagine if the whole world would be like that, if they saw the Reality and knew about God, knew about the illusion, they would let go of the illusion and run towards God-Realisation.' It was really great to see that the child didn't bother about the sweet or the chocolate, or anything! No toys even mattered to the child, because the mother was the most important.

> When we do something with our heart, the simple things that we do will give us joy. So be always simple and loving.

That's why whenever we do things, it comes to a point where we lose satisfaction, because whatever we do on the outside, which is just material-centred, has a limit and it is finished after some time. When we do something with our heart, the simple things that we do will give us joy. So be always simple and loving.

It was lovely to be here with all of you.

LOVE JUST KNOWS HOW TO LOVE

Darshan, Jyväskylä, Finland, 8 August 2009

Note: Swami started by singing with the people and then began his talk.

When you sing, let it come from deep within you, not just outside. This is the power of sound. And to make it more powerful it has to emerge from deep within. That's why when you say *OM*, you don't just say *OM* from the throat, otherwise there is no vibration into it. When you chant *OM*, you chant from deep within you, from the micro cosmos that you have inside of you.

That's what it is said in the *Vedas*. They talk about the micro cosmos, which is deep within humans, where the Divine is seated all the time. That's why, also, when you sing, if you want to make it more powerful, let it emerge from deep within you and you will have more power. That's why when a lion roars, he roars from deep within. You never see a lion roaring very softly from the outside. That's why he is the King of the animals. The roaring of the lion is so powerful that it sometimes shakes even the Divine! When Narasingha Dev appeared on Earth and roared, even the Deities in the Heavens got scared of it. And it's the same if you want to wake up the Divine, which is sleeping within your heart, call His Name. Of course, one will say "We don't really need to shout to call Him", but He is lying down in your heart and He will enjoy your call.

Why do we sing? Why do you think that people, when they sing, are in such a great joy? They forget about everything and go deeper. Why is it? It's because when we sing the power of mind is less in action. We are deeper into this Divine energy, because all the vibrations are cosmic energy. There is one technique called the *Nada Yoga* or *Nada Kriya* that explains the power of sound. And with this technique, you will see that all the sounds emerge from the vibration *OM* and everything is vibration. Our life itself is a vibration.

What is life? Life is Divine. And how many people know what life is? How many people know this Divinity? How many people know how precious life is? Once you realise what life is, you will see life in a completely different way. Life is not just working, eating and sleeping, like people very often think. People enslave themselves in work. They enslave themselves in eating. Most of the time they don't eat properly. They enslave themselves in just sleeping. Life goes on and when the time comes to leave this life, then they realise "Oops, I have missed something." When they look back and see how many opportunities they had of realising the beauty of life, they regret because they realise how many opportunities came to them on their way so that they could realise themselves, so that they could realise how great is this gift of life that God has given and yet, they wasted it!

Again, I ask the question: What is life? Life is love. The Divine is far away from the mind because it is very difficult for the mind to understand the Divine. Until you have really cleansed the mind completely, until you have really purified the mind completely, it is quite difficult to understand the Divine. Life is Love and Love, of course, is Divine. Love is God. But the feeling of Love, that's what life is all about, to realise this great Love, not just this partial love when today we say "I love you" and tomorrow "Who is that person?" Life is not that love, but the Love that is beyond expression, this Love that is unconditional, which is in everything around you. That's what life is.

Have you ever sat down and looked at nature? Have you ever felt nature? That Love which is burning inside of you, that life which is inside of you is everywhere. If you analyse the truth around you, if you analyse the beauty around you, you will realise that we are all linked together by one thing, which is Love. And it's beyond the religions, it's beyond the colours, it's beyond your status on the outside. It's beyond the duality that is in your mind, because Love doesn't know any duality. Love just knows how to Love. And Love doesn't expect anything. We express this Love every day. Some do it consciously and for some it happens unconsciously. Of course, I am talking about Divine Love because the love that we expect from people we are always conscious about. When we love someone, we always expect something, because this is human love and human love has a limitation. It's, also, an expression of Love, because there is the Divine inside, but it doesn't last for long. Why when you are in love, in the beginning, it's very beautiful and you don't see anything wrong in the person that you love?

You know the expression "love is blind."We say love is blind, because the love with expectation - it doesn't matter whether it is for somebody or for something - blinds you. You don't see anything. You see only the object of your expectations and it is where all your attention is focused on. But all the objects that you put your attention on, all the objects of desire, all the objects on which you project certain qualities of love are limited. There is limitation into them. You feel this great love, but after one year you ask yourself, "How did this love begin? I used to love that person, but now I don't feel that love for that person?" Why is this? This happens in everybody's life, doesn't it? But yet, even with all these expectations, we always come back to love. Love never finishes. When you love somebody, you start with love, but with time, it diminishes. Then what happens? You fall in love again. You *fall* again in love! Know that word very well: you *fall*! And, as long as you fall, you will never rise. You have to rise in love! The way to rise in love is to find your

Self, to realise your Self, to realise the greatest gift that God has given you. Of course, some people will say "Yes, it's easy to talk about it, but it's difficult to practise it." But Love is there! There is no point in saying that it's difficult or it's easy. It is there already. It just needs time for you to look at it. And when you take time, through your spiritual practice you will realise the beauty of Love, the beauty of life and you will know why you are here. And once you have opened this fountain, this tap of Love, Love can just flow, nothing else.

In your spiritual practice, whatever path you are on, whatever *sadhana* you are doing, why are you doing it? It is to realise your Self, to realise God inside of you, to have God-Realisation, because God-Realisation or Self-Realisation will not come to you just like that. It needs effort from you. To realise this great Love needs effort from you. You need to say "Yes, I want that. I want to feel myself full again." As long as this desire inside of you doesn't awaken, as long as you don't take the first step, it's difficult. Very often people say "Yes, I love everybody." If you just sit down and say "I love everybody" it will not happen.

Love doesn't know any duality. Love just knows how to love.

Christ said, "When you have pearls do not give them to the pigs, because they will not know the value of them. They will know according to their own state of vibration." And this is the same. You have the greatest gift, the greatest treasure inside of you. Realise it! Let it not be that when life is finishing then you say "Oops, I have wasted my life." The time is now. Awake! Let your Self be awake!

Do you want peace? The world has always been calling for peace, but the peace will happen only when *you* change! Until you change, there will not be peace. There will never be unity until you change yourself. It starts always with you. One can say that it's selfish, but from selfish you will learn to become selfless, because once you have realised what you have inside of you, you can't keep it for yourself. You will have to give it, you will have to help people.

Once there was a doctor who took his job very seriously. He was very satisfied whenever people came to him and got healed. He was very happy about it, but his happiness had always only a short duration, so he was always wondering "Why is it that I can be happy, but, yet, it lasts a very short while?" You know about this kind of happiness, no? Then the doctor went to Ramakrishna, an Indian Saint who lived in the 19th century, and told him "Ramakrishnaji, tell me how you Love. I feel this love, but it doesn't last for long."

Ramakrishna answered to him "My dear doctor, I know that you help people and that you feel this love, but know one thing: your love is based on how much you get as payment. So go and help people. It's not that you should not take money. Take it, but once a week give free consultation. You will see that this love inside of you will grow more and more." And, of course, the doctor practised what Ramakrishna told him. After a few months he came back to Sri Ramakrishna and fell down at his feet saying "My Lord, I have done what you have told me and I'm the happiest person. Now, I don't do this selfless service only one time a week, I do it two or three times a week!"

Love always sounds selfish because firstly, you give to yourself, then you give it to others and it becomes selfless, unconditional. Because as long as there is expectation in it, as long as there is want in it, there will always be limitation. So find this Love inside of you. Feel this Divine Love inside of you. Feel it in the plant kingdom and feel it in the animals. Then you will see that there is perfect unity and that you can also create unity. But, firstly, be good with yourself.

A guided meditation

Now, we will do a simple exercise. I love to do this little meditation.

- I ask you to take your hand and place it in front of your heart chakra - not on, but in front.
- Feel each beat of your heart.
- Focus your attention on your breathing. Listen. God has given you ears, so listen to your inhaling and exhaling. The more you listen to your inhaling and exhaling, the more the mind will get calmer and calmer.
- And, at the same time, feel the vibration emanating from your heart to your hand and from your hand to your heart.
- Relax yourself. Concentrate on your breathing and on your feeling.
- When you are inhaling and exhaling, just inhale and exhale, without a pause in between.
- Now, place your hand on your heart, without any pressure. If you can, feel the millions of thrills going through your heart.

That's Love. If you felt it, this is what I am talking about. If you have not felt it, keep practicing it. Once you have felt it inside of you, look and touch a plant, touch a tree and you will see how life flows, hold an animal and feel what is going through that animal. Then you will know what life is and you will realise your Self not in a limited way, but in an unlimited way. You will realise the cosmic you!

KRISHNA,
MANIFESTATION OF DIVINE LOVE

Krishna Janmashtami, Springen, Germany, 13 August 2009

You all know that tomorrow is Krishna *Janmashtami*. Actually, it's not really tomorrow, it's today night, in the middle of the night. Krishna's birthday is celebrated on the eighth day after *Rohini Nakshatra*. So this night is a very special night. Originally, in ancient times, Krishna *Janmashtami* was celebrated on the 11th of September, but today, the 13th of August, is the day when the astrologers calculated that Krishna was born. In some places you will see that they celebrate it on the 14th, in some places on the 15th, but actually it's this night the real *Janmashtami*. I said on 11th of September, because, if you calculated it according to the ancient calendar, the old Vedic way, it would fall on the 11th of September. So, today is the end of the *Rohini Nakshatra* and it is a very special day, because we are celebrating the Appearance [of Krishna]. I am not saying birth, even when *Janmashtami* means taking birth, because He [Sri Krishna] has never taken birth. Even His birth is just a manifesting of Himself. He was ever present and He is ever present. When we say that somebody is born, it means that there is

> He has never taken birth. Even His birth is just a manifesting of Himself. He was ever present and He is ever present.

41

also death, there is an end, but The Lord who is without beginning and without end, how can we say that He is born? If He is born, He has to die. Then, there is an end. But Him, who is without beginning and without end, He can't be born. It's just a manifestation of Himself, an Appearance that the Lord Himself chose to manifest.

You all know the story of Krishna, how He was born, so I will not tell the whole story, again. It is said in the *Gita* about His plan to manifest Himself *"Yada yada hi dharmasya glanir bhavati bharata abhyutthanam adharmasya tadatmanam srjamy aham"*, which means that whenever there is a decline, whenever there will be anything terrible happening in the world, He will manifest Himself. Of course, the Lord always manifests Himself, but in the minds of the people they want a big manifestation, a *'bang'*, but He is everywhere. So Mahavishnu, Narayana, took this form to help Mother Earth, because Mother Earth appealed to Narayana, saying to Him, "Help me. I am suffering so much. The demon Kansa is terrorising and hurting me." Actually, it's not hurting directly Her, but the people. The Lord answered to Her, "Yes, I will manifest Myself. I will come." Then He chose the right time and manifested Himself into the womb of Devaki. He was born in a prison. The mother and father were locked there, because an *Akashvani*, a celestial voice, had said to Kansa that the eighth child of Devaki would kill him. Of course, everybody is scared of death. Even Kansa, who was a great and knowledgeable devotee of Shiva, was scared of death, because death was unknown to him. This is because whenever we look at death, we look at our limited self. Kansa was so scared that he wanted to protect himself. He didn't want to be killed. He didn't want to face his own death.

Now that I am going into the details of the story, it's better that I tell you the whole story. In the story, Devaki and Vasudeva were in love and they got married. On their marriage day, Kansa, who was the brother of Devaki, was happily bringing his newly married sister and brother back to his place because she was his favourite sister. But, as they were going, they heard a voice from the sky that said, "Kansa, you fool, what are you doing? Don't you know that the eighth son of your sister will kill you?" Here you see the number 8. People who do numerology know very well how important is the number eight: it's the number without beginning or end.

Now the *Akashvani* had said to him that the eighth child of his sister would kill him, of course, that enraged him. So at that moment, he wanted to kill his sister, because he thought "no sister, no death". But Vasudeva stopped him and said: How can you kill a woman? All the people will say that you are just a coward. Of course Kansa, who was very arrogant and proud of himself, didn't want that, so he said, "Okay, I will imprison you!" Then Vasudeva answered to him, "Yes, imprison us and every time she gets a child, I myself will bring that child to you, then you can do whatever you want with that child."

So Kansa imprisoned them. He imprisoned also his father, because the father would be against him. Then he invited all his demon friends to come and rejoice with him that he had become a king. Every year a new child was born and every time Vasudeva brought the child to Kansa who, without any mercy, would kill the child, but the seventh child of Devaki disappeared. When Devaki was pregnant with the seventh child, the child miraculously disappeared from her womb and appeared in Rohini's womb. So in the night Rohini was sleeping and the next day she found herself pregnant. It's scary, isn´t it? Matajis, what would happen if you would wake up tomorrow pregnant? So, the same way, Rohini was shocked, but she accepted it. She was old, but she got pregnant, so it was something miraculous and she accepted the Will of God. Then they told Kansa that Devaki and Vasudeva had lost their child. Kansa, was so happy, saying "Look, the child was not even born yet, but he was so frightened of me that she lost it." He didn't know, of course, that the *Shakti* was transferred to Rohini. Actually, it was Adishesha, the bed on which Mahavishnu lies down that got manifested and took the form of Balaram.

Then a few months passed and Devaki got pregnant again. Here you have to understand that it's not in the same way that you all are thinking when I say that Devaki got pregnant. It was not in the way how normal people got pregnant. You see, after she lost her seventh child, Kansa tied Devaki to one part of the room and Vasudeva to the other side of the room and thought that, in that way, the eighth child would not be born and so could not kill him. He was thinking that Devaki, would get pregnant in the normal way, not knowing that it was the Lord that would manifest Himself. But even though Devaki and Vasudeva were tied to the different corners of their jail room, Devaki became pregnant with the eighth child. And the night when the child was born, at the very moment the child was born, the prison room was filled with so much light. The chains were unlocked and all the guards who were guarding them had fallen miraculously asleep. And when the child was born, Devaki and Vasudeva saw the true form of Sri Krishna, which is Mahavishnu, with *Shanka, Chakra,* and *Gadha,* standing in front of them. Then Mahavishnu said to Vasudeva, "Take the child and bring him to the other side of the river where there is Yashoda and, when you get there, exchange the babies. There is another baby, a girl, there; you should take her, bring her here and you should leave your child there."

When Mahavishnu was in front of them, they could remember all of their past lives; they could remember everything. They could remember why Mahavishnu and they were there and why the Lord would have to manifest Himself through them, now. It was because, after Rama disappeared, in one of their past incarnations Devaki and Vasudeva had been a king and a queen who had wanted so much to have God as their child. They had done penance for thousands of years and Mahavishnu was so pleased with them that he promised them: Whenever I will incarnate myself next time, it will be through you. Of course, because of the *Maya Shakti*, they had forgotten about everything, but the moment they were in front of Mahavishnu, they could remember everything and who they had been.

So Vasudeva did according to what Mahavishnu said: he took the baby, put Him in a basket and carried Him out of the prison. All the guards of the jail had miraculously fallen asleep and there was nobody stopping them. Vasudeva entered the water of the Yamuna carrying the baby and, as he was going deeper and deeper into the Yamuna River, Yamuna wanted so much just to touch the feet of the Lord. And the moment the feet of the baby Krishna touched the water of Yamuna, she became very calm. Also, it was raining so much that Sheshnag, the serpent god, even came behind to cover baby Krishna.

After Vasudeva crossed over to the other side of the river, he saw Yashoda and Nanda, her husband, sleeping and. Yashoda had just given birth to a baby girl, but she didn't even know it – such is the manifestation of His Maya. So Vasudeva quickly exchanged the babies. He took the baby girl with him and left baby Krishna there as Mahavishnu had asked him to do. Then he crossed over the river to the other side and everything became normal again.

The next day, when they all woke up in the prison, the guards heard the cry of the baby and they rushed to the King and told him, "Kansa, your sister has had a baby again." Kansa rushed quickly down to the prison, opened the door and said, "Give me the baby." At that moment Devaki answered to him, "No, my brother. It was said that my eighth son would kill you, but I didn't get a son, I got a daughter." Hearing this, Kansa calmed down. Then he started to think: Why did the voice say that it would be the eighth child? But this is a girl, how could a girl kill me? Then his mind started to reason a bit and he said to himself "What if this is Vishnu Maya? What if it is Vishnu Himself in that form?" With that idea in mind, he took the baby and said, "Yes, I will kill this baby." He took her and he was going to throw her on the wall, the same way like he had done with the other babies, but at that moment, the baby flew up and changed Her form to the form of Durga, Maha Shakti. Then She laughed at Kansa saying "You fool. You want to kill me? You can't! The One who will kill you is born already. Count your days!" So Kansa was really, really scared at that moment. He rushed back to his sister and said to her, "What have you done? Tell me."

But, of course, Devaki and Vasudeva could not remember anything, because Mahavishnu had covered them again in *Maya*, so that they wouldn't remember anything that had happened during that night. Vasudeva had even forgotten that he had taken the baby Krishna to the other side of Yamuna and exchanged Him with Yashoda's and Nanda's daughter. And, now, they heard that when Kansa had wanted to kill that baby girl, she had flown up and taken the form of Maha Shakti and warned Kansa. Of course, Kansa was not that stupid. He knew that if Maha Devi had said that the Lord had already manifested Himself and that he had to count his days, he would have to try everything possible to find and kill the baby.

From that day on Kansa started his great killing. He killed all the children who were born around that time. He sent demons all around to terrorize the people who were praying, so that they would stop praying. And his demons were very successful everywhere where he would send them. There was only one place, Gokul, where when he sent a demon, the demon would not come back but would get killed there. Then Kansa started to think "Why in all other places where I have sent the demons, they were very successful, but only in this one place the demon got killed and didn't come back?" Like that he understood that the Lord had had to be in that place – in Gokul.

When Nanda and Yashoda woke up and saw the baby, Krishna, it was a great surprise for them, because they were both very fair skinned and when they looked at their child they saw that He was so dark. But they were so happy that they had a son. And this child was so special that whoever would look at Him would automatically be in love with Him, because He was the personification of Love. So, of course, they had a big party for the occasion, they were so joyful. Everybody came to Yashoda and praised her, saying "How blessed you are, Yashoda, that even at your age, you could bear a child!" (because she was well-advanced in age). "This is surely the Will of God. And look at the child, He is just so charming, so loving that nobody can go away from Him."

So as I said before, Kansa had sent many demons that were killed one by one by Krishna. The first demon that he sent was Putana. I will say how blessed she was, because even if she was a demon, she took the appearance of a mother. So Putana took the appearance of a girl who would roam around singing. Wherever she would go, she would feed every baby that she found with her breasts filled with poison. Of course all the children then died. So, finally, she arrived at the place where baby Krishna was. She could enter the house because Yashoda didn't stop anybody from coming to her house. So everybody could come in and go out as they wanted. So Putana, also, came in. She was looking for the right moment to feed the child, then she took the baby, went to one corner with Him and started the breastfeeding. But this child was different. All the other children had died, but this one kept drinking and drinking all the poison out of her. He was even taking all the life from her.

Blessed was she, you know. We can say that Putana was very lucky to feed the Lord. This was because in one of her lives she had been a *yogini*. She had done so much *tapas*, so much penance. She had, also, done penance to become the mother of God, of Narayana, but because of her karma she could not. But He is so merciful that

He said: It doesn't matter. Your wish will be fulfilled, also. So this time she took birth as a demon and, of course, when Krishna was there, He drank from her. But He drank everything, the whole of her surrender, the whole of life itself. This is how He is, you know. And this is how Putana was. She was fully surrendered. Many other demons came, one after the other, trying to kill Krishna, but they were all completely unsuccessful. At the age of sixteen, Krishna went to Mathura and there Kansa got killed and you know the rest of the story of Krishna.

Seeing the beauty of the Lord, we ask ourselves how did all the people in His lifetime feel when they saw Him? What did they feel? What did the Gopis feel? How was it for the people of Vrindavan to be near Him? We have read several stories about that. We read how beautiful it was, how great it was, but yet we ask ourselves "Why not now? Why, when we pray so much, nothing happens?" You, also, would like to feel and experience this Love. You, also, would like to be so much in Love with Him, but yet you find it very difficult, don't you? Why?

If we look at ourselves and we look at the people in Vrindavan, there, whatever they were doing throughout the day, Krishna was the main important thing in their lives. Their minds were so much into Him. Whatever they were doing wherever they were it was just for Krishna. They would cook for their own family, but in their mind, it was for Krishna. They would wash their clothes and, in their minds, it was for Krishna. Everything was for Him. They were so much surrendered that their every breath was Krishna. If every breath of theirs was the Lord Himself, of course, the Lord was present inside of them at all times.

But nowadays, when you are working, how many times do you think of God? Only when you have time, because when you are working, you are fully concentrated on your work. And the little time that you have left, what do you do with it? You worry about how to make the work better. When you do your spiritual practice - let's say, when you are doing your *Atma Kriya* - you concentrate so much on the breathing, you concentrate so much on reciting the Name of God. Why? Why do we do all our spiritual *sadhana* ? It's because we know that there is something greater, that our soul wants. We want something, but, yet the mind doesn't understand it too much. We try to understand with the mind and we always want things to be how we want it to be – our way.

But what is our way, actually? It is *His* Will even if we always think that we have a free will. Once somebody asked a saint "Do we have a free will?" The saint said "Well, you have a will, but it's not free." It's like a cow: the cow is tied with a rope and is given only a certain radius to go around. The cow is free, but it is free only within a certain radius. And such is also the will of man. And the rest is His Will only. But within this little radius which seems *so* big, we like to make ourselves feel greater than anybody else, don't we? We like to make ourselves even greater than the Lord Himself.

This reminds me of Narad Muni, the messenger of God, who was cursed by Maha Vishnu, who had said to him, "Narad Muni, go to Hell! You are doomed! Go away." Narad Muni became very quiet and said "My dear Lord, as you have told me to go to Hell, can You please tell me where it is?" Maha Vishnu said, "OK" and with His *Shakti*, He manifested a chalk and He started to draw. He said "Here is Heaven and, then, He drew Heaven. And here is Hell and He drew Hell." Seeing that, Narad Muni became very happy. He approached the drawing, jumped into the drawing and started to roll in the place where Hell was. Maha Vishnu was very amused and said "Narad, what are you doing?" Narad Muni answered Him "Well, You told me to go to Hell, didn´t You? Here I am. I'm rolling myself in Hell." Then Narad Muni continued, saying, "You are the Lord of everything. When you say "This is Heaven", of course, it becomes Heaven. When you say "This is Hell", of course, it becomes Hell.

When you sent me there, I went there. Even if it is just a drawing, it is Hell for me, I can feel it." Maha Vishnu was very pleased with him and He blessed him.

This shows us also, our own limitations, the limitations that our mind creates. We could be free, but our mind doesn't let us be free. We could see the Lord everywhere, but our pride always stops us. We could Love Him, but our expectations are always there too. When one lets go of these three things, one will be really, fully into Him. Above all, He is the manifestation of Love. He is the manifestation of who we are, all of us. In Him Love is manifested in the outside, in everything that He expresses, in every action of His. But in humans it is manifested deep inside, because we don't let it out. We are scared of it. We are scared of our true Self. We are scared of what we have inside, but yet we crave for that. We want it. We are always looking for it everywhere. In whatever we do, in whoever we meet, we are looking for this Love. But it's not on the outside. It's inside of us. The representations of the Lord beautifully decorated in some temples are good because they enable us to concentrate and to focus ourselves, but firstly, He is born within your heart.

Then one will ask "But why do we have to concentrate on Him outside? Why can't we concentrate on Him inside?" With all these things covering you, all these expectations, this anger and fear, it's very difficult to concentrate on the unmanifest form of the Lord, on the Love of God inside of you. That's why He has given His outer forms for us to concentrate on them. It's like when someone learns to shoot. First they start to shoot at big things, no? And the more experienced and concentrated they become at shooting, the smaller things are given to them to shoot at. So it's the same thing: as long as you have a mind, which is very active, always jumping around, you need something to focus on; on the outside. When your mind is calm through your *sadhana*, then you will be able to concentrate easily on the Lord inside of your heart. So chant the Divine Names.

Focus on His form first and through that, at the end, He can show you that He is inside of you.

Krishna is Love Incarnate. Now, on His birthday, ask Him to be born inside of you. Ask Him to manifest Himself inside of you. He never refuses anything from anybody. If you sincerely ask for that, if you sincerely ask Him for Himself, you will see that He will give you Himself. That's what Meerabai asked for and she received it. When all the saints have asked, they have received, because they were sincere towards themselves. They were sincerely asking the Lord "Give me Yourself." And it doesn't matter how long it takes, because you know that He can hear you. And in His own time He will come and manifest Himself.

RADHA, DEVOTION INCARNATE

Radhastami, Springen, Germany, 27 August 2009

When you came here today, you probably noticed that we are doing the prayers for Radharani. Even Krishna, here, is dressed like Radha today because it's actually Radharani´s Appearance Day and we celebrate Her manifestation on Earth. It is Krishna Himself in the form of Radharani. Maybe you have notice that we always put Rhada first, and then Krishna. We say *"Radhe Krishna, Radhe Shyam*, because She is the *Shakti* of Krishna. She is the One who gives power to Krishna. One could say that Krishna is God, so why does He need power? But Love - which is Krishna, which is God - is useless without devotion. So in this form, in the form of Radha, He manifests Himself as *bhakti*, which is pure devotion. What is this pure devotion?

We all have devotion: we pray, we do our work every day and this is, also, called devotion, but pure devotion is complete surrender. This pure devotion, which Radha had for Krishna, even though She was separate from Krishna, even though She was separate from the Oneness – it was just to teach us what surrender is. Actually, Radha represents all of us, the creation, the manifestation. She symbolizes the Love, the example. She symbolizes the *bhav*, the complete surrender to the Will of God. It's not about Her own will, but the Will of God, the Will of Krishna. That's why it is said that She is the only true devotee and we all have to become like Her. The manifestation of the Lord Himself into Radharani is to show us how to love unconditionally, how to have such faith that even a storm will not uproot you.

Nowadays we talk about faith. But the moment something happens and doesn't turn out the way people want, what happens? They are uprooted already. Faith is like this: you have to become like a huge tree when a storm comes, the branches will blow, but the roots are so anchored into the earth that the tree does not come out. That's how faith has to be. And that is what Radharani teaches to us. In Her Life there were not only joyful times, but She transcended the joy and the pain.

We all want bliss, don't we? We all want to attain the Divine, but yet we hang onto things. We say that we want to love and we want to do God's will, but in our mind we always think "Yes, I want to do God's will, but I want to always be happy", because in the mind of man, what he sees as happiness, is bliss. That's what he thinks! But the transcendental happiness that is called real bliss is beyond the happiness that you say with a big smile "I am happy", because when one is in bliss, one doesn't know happiness or sadness. It is difficult to comprehend it with the mind, because your brain can only understand whether you are happy or sad, or you are happy-sad, but transcending these two is *Ananda*. And that's what our soul is longing for.

There is one *bhajan* that I always sing that says "For love one can do anything." Isn't it like this? But Love is sacrifice, you know that? Are you ready to sacrifice your all completely for that? How many of you are ready to sacrifice everything, completely? Truly! So, that's what faith is: complete surrender, even in the smallest things you are completely surrendered to the Will of God, and whatever you do, you remember the Divine, wherever you are, you remember the Divine, in that way, you will transcend everything.

People always ask for something and, of course, God will always give. But there will come a point where there will be no need to ask the Divine for anything, because it will be given to you before you ask. The more you are surrendering to the Will of God, to the Divine – not surrendering only in your mind, but also surrendering here, in your heart – the more there will be no difference between you and Him. That's what Radharani transcends, She transcends the duality to show that there is no differences between Her and Krishna, to show that there is no difference between we humans and the Divine. The only difference is that we are limited with our mind. We see the difference, we see the duality, but in the higher realms they don't see the same way we see. They have a hierarchy, they have their own jobs, their own duties to do, their *dharma* to do, but there is no judgement like we always have.

> There will come a point where there will be no need to ask the Divine for anything, because it will be given to you before you ask.

Through our *sadhana*, through our spiritual practice, what do we do? We transcend this duality. We focus our mind, so that we can stop thinking and start acting in the Divine way. Still, when we say Divine Will, we mean, always, whatever is good, whatever is creative, but the more we are surrendered, the more this duality will disappear. And we will see that all is alike.

There was once a Saint who was passing by the Kali Temple in Dakshineshwar. He stopped and stood for a moment in front of the temple and as he was looking at the temple, the whole temple started to shake. Ramakrishna was there, looking at what was happening. Then He said to his nephew "Do you see this *sadhu* who is dressed with not so nice clothes, like a beggar? Did you see what he just did? Can you go and find out who he is?" So, the nephew ran after the *sadhu,* and when the *sadhu* saw him coming, he started to run, also. The nephew continued running after the *sadhu* and finally, he caught him and said to him "I want to be your disciple!" The *sadhu* answered "What? I don't want you. Go away" and started to walk away very fast. But again, the nephew of Ramakrishna ran after him, took hold of the *sadhu's* feet, and said "I will not let you go until you take me as your disciple." Then the *sadhu* said "Ok, get up. Look there, do you see those two rivers?" There were two rivers flowing. One of them was very filthy and dirty and the other one was very pure and clean. Then the *sadhu* said to him "I will accept you when these two rivers seem equal to you."

Do you get it? The moment your mind is completely surrendered to God, there will be no judgment. There will be only pure Love. As long as there is judgment in the mind you will see the difference. When a big storm comes, the tree of your faith can get uprooted as long as you see the difference, so work on your faith. Ask Radharani to give you the gift of faith, so that nothing can move you, no matter what. This kind of faith is not only told of in the *Gita*, it is not only in the Hindu culture, but it's in all religions. All the great Masters from all the religions have taught that. That's what Christ said, "Build your faith on a stone, where the wind will not blow it away." It has to be like that. When faith is strong, the Love will be much stronger, because when you have complete faith, you are the Lover. And when you are the Lover, the Beloved will always be with you.

> Even if you don't know Him with the mind, you know Him with the heart. You all know Him, because you are part of Him.

So, strive for that! Work so that Love can fully grow in your heart; so that your mind can fully be into the Divine; so that the Divine can reveal Himself to you. Even if you don't know Him with themind, you know Him with the heart. You all know Him, because you are part of Him.

TRUE LOVE IS EVERLASTING GIVING

Darshan, Prague, Czech Republic, 23 August 2009

It's lovely to be here with all of you, especially on this very special day, which is *Ganesha Chaturthi*. This is the day when Lord Ganesha was created. In the Hindu tradition it's a very auspicious day. I guess that you all know Lord Ganesha, don´t you? He is the elephant-headed God. In the Hindu tradition we have a lot of Gods, but all of them form the One, which is *Paramatma*. And amongst all of them, Ganesha was given the task to remove obstacles.

He is the One who removes all the obstacles from ones path. That's why when we start any prayer the first prayer that we offer is to Lord Ganesha. Why do we pray to Lord Ganesha first? We pray to Him to remove the obstacles. Where are these obstacles? The greatest obstacle is the mind of man. We pray to Him to clear our minds so our prayer will be successful, so our prayer will be heard. Like I said, Ganesha is the remover of obstacles, the One who clears the mind. That's why the name Ganapathi, Lord of the mind, Lord of the *Ganas*, which are present in the mind, is given to Him. When your mind is clear, you will see how easily you will love.

The more one is in the mind, the farther away the Divine will be.

What do we want to realise on our spiritual path? We want to realise our unity with the Divine we want to find the Divine, we want to find our true Self, but obstacles are always there. People meditate, but yet, the mind is so strong. As long as one doesn't let go of the mind and have it under control, one will always be a slave. One will always be under the rule of the mind. The more one is in the mind, the farther away the Divine will be. Actually, each part of you is the Divine but the mind stops you from everything, stops you from loving. All of you love, don't you? What is this love? We say that Love is sacrifice. In this sacrifice, are you ready to give yourself, your all, completely? How many among you are ready to give yourself completely? That is lovely if you can answer yes, but be truthful towards yourself.

I will tell you a small story. I tell this story often, because I find it to be really lovely. Once there was a teacher who said to one of his disciples "My dear disciple, it's time for you, now, to find God fully, to fully Realise your Self."

Actually, that's what we are here for. In Hindu tradition, we have four questions in life that we ask: Where do we come from? Who are we? Where are we going? And why are we here? There are only these four questions. It's that simple. If you have an answer to these four questions, you are fully realised.

So, the *Guru* said to the disciple "Now it's time for you to fully realise your Self, come!" The disciple said "My dear teacher, I love you so much, but you know, my wife loves me so much and she will be really unhappy." Then the Guru thought for a while and said "OK, my dear. If you really think that she loves you that much, take this pill." He gave him a pill and said to him "Next Monday, before you go to bed, take this pill. When you have taken this pill, you will appear dead to the outside, but you will hear everything." The disciple said "OK, let's try it."

So on the Monday he took the pill at night and went to sleep. He was supposed to get up early the next morning, so when his wife saw that he was not getting up, she wondered what was wrong. She pushed him, saying "Hey, get up!", but got nothing, no reaction. Seeing that something was wrong, she started screaming and wailing. She was wailing so loudly that all the neighbours came to see her. All the family came and soon they were all crying "Oh, why have you left us?" The wife threw herself on her husband's body and said "Oh, why have you left me alone here? I should have left together with you. We are here for each other." Big crying was going on. The son of the man said "Father, why have you left us?" And the mother of the dead-appearing man said "Oh my son, I should have died before you! You are so young! You still had your full life in front of you. I should have gone earlier than you." So the wailing carried on like this.

Finally, the *Guru* came and asked "Why are you wailing like this?" They said "Oh, he has left us." Each one said their father, husband or son had left them. Then the Guru said "I see that all of you love him so much! You were just saying that you should have died in his place, so I have a solution. I have a pill here. This pill is such that whoever takes this pill will die in his place and he will be revived." The *Guru* turned to the wife and said "Respectful mother, you were just crying that you should have died in your husband's place, no? This is what a good wife would do. You love him so much. Here, take this pill." At that moment the wife stopped crying. She said "Why are you saying that? I have little children. It is his bad luck that he died. I can't do that." The *Guru* turned to the mother and said, "Mother, you were just saying you are old, so you can take the pill." The mother said, "Well, you know, it's his *karma*. I can't do that. I still have my grandchildren to look after, my children to look after." The Guru tried with everybody, but they all said the same thing. Then he took some water and threw it on the man's face. The man woke up and was looking at everybody, seeing that, although they were expressing great love to him, in the time of sacrifice no one was there for him.

Christ said "A true friend is ready to sacrifice everything." And, actually, Love is that sacrifice. If you truly Love, you will sacrifice everything. Until you have come to the point of really feeling this kind of Love inside of you – and you have to be ready – all the other kinds of love will have expectations. Very often what we call Love, is just passion or desire. Today you love that person, tomorrow you love another person, but in one year you don't even remember who these people were. Real love is deep inside of you, it's your true nature, it's who you are in reality. The Divine is not far away. He is inside of you. He is consuming you every day, little by little. You just need to calm your mind and introvert yourself. So see how much you are truthful towards yourself and how much you really, sincerely want the Divine.

Real Love is deep inside of you, it's your true nature, it's who you are in reality.

True Love is everlasting giving, without expectation. We do our *sadhana*, we do our spiritual practices, only to attain this Love, so that it may become unconditional. In the state of Unconditional Love, we realise the unity with the Divine. Then we can say that we are really in Love. As long as it's here in the mind it is very difficult. Christ said, "Love Thy God, with all Thy mind and Spirit." The mind has to be fully on the Divine. The mind has to transcend the limitations and transform itself. This is, also, why we pray to Lord Ganesha, "Help us to remove all the barriers, help us, to transcend the limitations, so that we can be ourselves", because our true Self knows no judgment, no difference, no pain, no hatred, no jealousy and no anger. Our true Self is in constant unity. He is each one of us. And that's true Love.

The ancient Greeks said 'know Thyself and you will know everything else', and that's true. Once you know yourself through your practices, you will know everything, because everything is linked together and Love is that which links everything. Life is very precious, you know. Life is actually, the most precious thing that one has. So, don't waste it. Don't waste time. God has called you to the spiritual path and it's for a reason. Take full advantage of this life and realise your Self.

THE LANGUAGE OF THE HEART

Darshan, Brazil, November 2009

So, like I said before, I am really happy to be here. I have travelled around everywhere and I have been to many places, seeing different cultures, different languages, but there is only one reality: the language of the heart, which is Love. Love is a language, which even the limited words that we express, can't express; it can be felt only. It's a language that the mother understands. When a newborn baby comes on earth, it doesn't speak. It's a heart-to-heart communication and this heart-to-heart communication is the true language. This is the language of love, the language of your soul. Life without this language, life without love is of no use. Even if someone doesn't feel Love, there *is* a degree of love in him otherwise nothing would exist. A life without love is like a land, which you can till as much as you want, but it will never be fertile. The life with a *little bit* of love, that's what we call joy.

There are two kinds of joy: the one where we find joy in things and the eternal joy, which is deep within ourselves. One joy is with limitation and the other joy is without limit and only the wise one goes for the unlimited joy. We are all called for that, but we are confronted so much with our limited mind, with only what we can *perceive* or understand. And then, we see our limitation and we say "Is that it? Is that life?" No, it's not.

What is life? What is the purpose of life? I am asking you. You know I heard that in Brazil people are very alive. What is life? To love thy neighbour and the evolution of the spirit, both are very good answers from you, but actually, what is the spirit?

So, what is the purpose of life? The purpose of life is to realise who you are. When you have realised that you are a drop in the unlimited ocean of love, life's purpose will be fulfilled; because in that ocean, a drop is not the same as you understand, but it's One with the Oneness. The evolution of the soul or, like it was said before: Love thy neighbour is difficult until one realises this Love within. You can say "Swamiji, you are talking about Love, but yet I don't know what Love is." Yes, you don't know it with the mind. You can't understand it with the mind, but deep inside of you, all of you know it. You are here to realise this through your spiritual practice. You practise daily? I hope so.

> When you have realised that you are a drop in the unlimited ocean of Love, life's purpose will be fulfilled.

What is practice? It's to remind yourself of the Divine continuously in whatever you are doing. That's yoga. If somebody just meditates and prays on the outside only, without realising that the Lord that they are praying to is seated inside of the heart of each being, then it's of no use. Realising *first,* through meditation and through your prayer, that the Lord is not on the outside, but is inside of you, you will then see Him shining in everybody. Until you realise that there is no difference, you will always see the limitation.

You know about Mahavatar Babaji? He is a Master in India. Actually He is about 5,000 years old and still alive. He is my *Satguru.* You can see sometimes some pictures, some drawings of Him where He looks very strict, actually. But I tell you, He is such an expression of Love that it's difficult with words to express it. Even the word love is limited to express this Love. And as He said to me once, if He achieved that, everybody can.

A few days ago I was in Israel. I was there trying to feel how Christ felt. Of course, you know that the Church preaches about a Christ who is strict and severe, where you always have to be serious and unhappy, but actually it was completely different.

All the great Masters have taught about Self-Realisation, about finding this eternal happiness – not on the outside, but within you. Because, with the happiness that we run to on the outside, we will always 'bang' our head. We say that something can make us happy, but the moment we get that thing our happiness changes into something else, because we didn't find this real happiness that is within us. And once you have found this real happiness within you, you can express it. You can share it. But one has to *really* want it. How many really want that, sincerely? And what will you do for that? Anything?

The easiest way is to help others, because what opens the heart, what makes Love easy, is to share the Love, to help others and to see the happiness in somebody else. That's what makes the journey within much easier, because you see, when we say "Let's sit and meditate," what happens? The mind is very busy; so we just have to learn to calm the mind. And how do you calm the mind? First, to calm the mind, chant the Divine Names. It's like giving the mind a toy to play with. When a baby is very nervous and screaming, what do the parents do? They just give the child a game. The moment the child gets the game the child will start playing and remain quiet.

The same is with the mind. If the mind is active, if the mind is jumping like a monkey, give the mind a game to play. And don't give the mind a game that has a limit, but give the mind an unlimited game. Give the mind Divine Names. The more you chant the Divine Names, the more you become the Divine Names, the more the mind ceases to trouble you. Once the mind ceases to trouble you, it will be much easier in your meditation. So, when you help others, you see this happiness, you feel this happiness and with the Divine

Names you will realise that you are serving the Divine. This helps you on your spiritual path.

But I will give you one simple way of calming the mind, which is through the breath–the gift of life. You can go on, you can live without food, you can live without drinking, but you can't live without breathing. That's what Christ said: Give us our daily bread–the bread of life, which is the *Prana Shakti*. In all spiritual paths, wherever you go, in whatever culture, they have the controlling of the breath. So we will do together now one easy way of controlling the mind.

There are many ways of controlling the mind. Some are very easy and some are very difficult. So, which one would you like? The difficult way or the easy way? So, let's do it. The mind flow is always running ahead. Even when I tell you to sit for meditation, where has your mind already jumped? It's already thinking "Oh, how will it be?" Sometimes you are sitting here and you are already in America so fast is the mind. That's why we say "It's jumping like a monkey from tree to tree." So to hold this monkey, to tie it up is very important. Otherwise, you will never be free. You will be like this monkey. So try to sit straight for the good flow of energy inside of you. Leave your eyes open.

You see, when I say to meditate, the first thing people always do is to close their eyes. It's a trap. The moment you close your eyes, your mind jumps. First, before doing this technique to calm the mind, let's see in one minute how your mind is. OK? Close your eyes and observe your mind for one minute. Tell me, without being ashamed or being shy, in this one-minute's time where you were? Did your mind run outside? Did you travel around? Were you far away? Were you very far, like India? You see, we can travel so fast, even faster than lightning is the thought of Man. So, let's try this easy way of calming the mind now.

Meditation:

- Sit straight. Inhale deeply and exhale deeply, continuously without any break in between.
- If possible, put your hands in the *Hridaya Mudra,* which is the *mudra* of the heart.

Take the middle and ring fingers and join them to the thumb. Bend the index finger and touch the base of the thumb with the fingertip. The little finger stays straight up. This is called the Heart *Mudra*-the *mudra* that opens the heart and awakes the Love inside of you. It's one of the most powerful *mudras*.

Do you know other mudras? The *Gyana Mudra* is famous. It is for knowledge. The Heart *Mudra* is very important and is, also, very good for people who have physical heart problems. It helps to heal. For people who feel pressure, it helps to heal them. And for people who have a heart that can't love unconditionally, it helps them to love unconditionally. Simple, no? It's a flow of energy. So put your hand in the *Hridaya Mudra* and inhale and exhale.

- Close your eyes. Focus on your third eye and listen to the sound of your inhaling and exhaling. The inner sound is the cosmic sound of OM. (5 minutes)
- Now bring all your focus in your heart and slowly open your eyes.

So this is one technique to calm the mind. Of course, you will not get the effect just by practicing it once. You know you have to practice it regularly. So, if you want to Realise your Self, focus more on what you have here inside of you. You have a great treasure. Each one of you is special, each one of you has special duty, *dharma*. And pray that you realise the purpose of your incarnation.

That's why we pray: *Asato ma sat gamaya, Tamaso ma jyotir gamaya, Mrityor ma amritam gamaya.* The sages have always chanted this *mantra*, which means: From untruth to truth, from darkness to light, from mortality to immortality. This is who we are. When we put limitation, we are always in the *untruth* of ourselves, because we don't see the reality. We are always in the shadow. That's why we ask that the shadow of ignorance be removed and that we are in the light, in the wisdom of the Divine; so that our mere mortality is transformed into our immortality, which is our *atma*.

THE GREATEST FORM OF WORSHIP

After Darshan, Brazil, November 2009

(Note: Sri Swami Vishwananda is practising some bhajans with a few of his devotees)

Do you know the meaning of the song *Choti Choti Gaya*? It's like: "Little, little cows, little, little boys." Around Krishna there were always little *gopas*, you know? The cows, the boys, He was a cowherd, you know? *Choti Choti Gaya* means: "little, little cows."
(Singing) "Little, little cows, little, little boys. Little is my sweet Krishna. Little is my sweet Krishna. In front, in front is the cow. At the back are the boys. In the middle is my Krishna. In the middle is my Krishna. Cows are eating grass, boys are drinking milk and Krishna is eating *makhan*," *(Swami explains)* buttermilk.
(Singing) "Black, black cows, white, white boys." *(Swami explains)* And Krishna, who is in the middle of them, is like dark-blue-sky colour. He's like a dark-coloured cloud.
(Singing) "Little, little anklets and little, little garlands." And Krishna is playing the flute. "Little, little girls and little, little boys are playing in the Madhuvan", *(Swami explains)* the forest of Vrindavan. *(Singing)* And Krishna is dancing the *Ras*.
(Sri Swami Vishwananda starts to sing with his devotees another bhajan: Sabse Oonchi, Prema Sagai)
I will say *Sabse oonchi* and you will say *Prema sagai*. *Sabse oonchi* means: "What is the greatest form of worship?" And then you say: "Love is the greatest form of worship." *Prem* means: Love. *Sagai*

means: worship.

You know, this *bhajan* is one of my favourite *bhajans*. It's all about Love. It describes the Love that Krishna had, that God has for humans. That's why it says: "What is the greatest form of worship?" And then you say: "*Prema sagai.*" Love is the greatest form of worship. Love transcends all the barriers that we put up. Even the mind can't comprehend Love, because it transcends all.

And then you say: "*Duryodhana ko mevā tyāgo.*" Duryodhana was a King in Krishna's time. You know, at that time, there were the good ones, who were Arjun and the Pandavas and there were the bad ones always fighting with them, who were the Kauravas and Duryodhana was their chief. Duryodhana invited Krishna to eat and of course as a king, he would give Him the most delicious food, but Krishna refused it. Instead He went to Vidura. Vidura was Krishna's uncle, but he was very poor. And there, Krishna ate the simplest food – just rice and other simple food. And He was very happy about that. Why? It was because of the Love of Vidura. Duryodhana had everything, had all the luxury, but he didn't have Love. It was just for pride, to show off. Whereas Vidura, in his simplicity, his humbleness, he was full of Love. And Krishna went there because of that Love not because of the food.

> Love transcends all the barriers that we put up. Even the mind can't comprehend Love, because it transcends all.

Swami sings: *Jūṭhe phala sabarī ke khāye.*

Sabari was a great devotee of Rama. Rama is one aspect of the Divine. In the time of Rama, Sabari everyday would collect fruit from the jungle and she would wait for Rama, since her youth. She would wait until Rama came to eat the fruit. So every day, she would bring fresh flowers and she would bring fresh fruit and wait for Rama. And she would chant all day: *Ram, Ram, Ram, Ram, Ram, Ram*. Eventually she grew old; she became a very old lady. Nearly all her teeth fell out. She became so old that Rama finally came. When Rama and Lakshman were on the way to Lanka, they passed by the cottage of Sabari and they saw this old lady with just two teeth in her mouth, who was waiting for Rama. When Rama came, she was really joyfully welcoming Him. She put Rama on the seat there, because every day she would write with fresh flowers the name of Rama. So when Rama was there, she opened up her heart so much. Her heart was so full with Love. Rama was with Lakshman, who is His brother, His younger brother.

Jūṭhe phala sabarī–jūṭhe: jujube is a fruit. I don't know whether you have it here. So, she would first taste the fruit, whether it's sour or sweet. She gave Rama only the sweet ones to eat and then Lakshman said "Oh, my goodness, how can you eat this?" And Ram said to Lakshman "You would not understand that. This is between the *bhakta* and the Beloved, the Lover and the Beloved, it's the love, the soul connection."

That was the Love that Sabari had for Rama. So Rama would eat it, because of that Love. That's why we say: *Jūṭhe phala sabarī ke khāye | bahu vidhi prema lagāī*. That means: "He would feel great joy by eating that fruit."

Swami sings: *Rājasuya yajña yudhiṣṭhira kīno | tāmai jūṭha uṭhāī*

There was a great fire ceremony, where all the kings and everybody, all the sages were sitting, but there was nobody to serve them. So when they finished eating Krishna helped to clean, to pick up the rubbish. Why? It was because of the Love for Yudhistira – the leader of the Pandavas. Then, during the war of *Mahabharata*, Arjuna didn't have anything to offer to Krishna, apart from his Love. But out of this Love that he had for Krishna, Krishna accepted to be the charioteer and ride the chariot for Arjuna and that's the greatest Love that binds the soul to the Divine.

In Vrindavan, Krishna did the Ras, the dance. When He was dancing with all the girls from Vrindavan, He was the only One. That shows that in the Love for God we are all passive. He is the only active One. We all crave for that Love, whether you are man or woman, it's beyond that concept. You crave for the Universal Love, which is the Love that is seated inside your heart, the Love that you are.

Swami sings: *Sūra krūra is lāyaka nāhī*

Surdas is saying "Lord, I am unworthy of that Love. I don't deserve that, but yet you have shown me Your mercy."

Sūra krūra is lāyaka nāhī | kaha lag karau baḍā. "So He is the merciful one."

Surdas was a great poet, actually. He was blind and he would sing the Name of Krishna and he would sing the Name of God, dancing around everywhere. When he was small because he was blind, nobody wanted to play with him. One day he heard some people singing the Name of Krishna, so he started following them and started singing. And then he would sing, but of course, the group of people didn't want him. So they cast him aside and then he started to sing by himself.

So Krishna, God, revealed Himself not on the outside, but inside of him, in his heart. So he would see Krishna inside of him, constantly. He was going everyday to a temple and there, although he was blind, he would describe how the Deity was dressed because in the Hindu tradition every day when they bathe their statue, they dress the statue nicely with new clothes. So, everybody and even the priest was thinking "Oh, my goodness, probably he is just pretending to be blind." So one day they didn't dress the statue at all. They left the statue naked and then he sang "Oh my Lord in your nakedness, You are even more beautiful than with clothes." And such was his Love for Krishna that Surdas was one with Him.

One day Krishna appeared to him and gave him his sight back. He could see Krishna. Then Krishna said "Now you can go; you can see."

Then he said "No, my Lord, I don't want anything. No, what I would like you to do is take back the sight. I have seen You. I don't want anything else. I don't want to see this world."

This song is about the Love that we have for God. Worship is not about the prayers, it's not about what we utter as words, it's what we express with our heart, it's the Love and Love is not quantity, it's quality.

THE GREATEST FORM OF LOVE

Darshan at Shree Peetha Nilaya, Springen, Germany, 14 February 2010

Two days ago we celebrated *Shivaratri*, the Night of Shiva. Today, in the West, they celebrate Saint Valentine's Day. It's the day where all the people who love, not only lovers, but who love in general, they express themselves to say "I love you" or whatever. We have been singing *Radhe, Radhe,*and Radhe is Love itself. As it is mentioned in the *Gita:* Only when one develops Love, as Radha has for Her Beloved will one attain the Beloved. Which means, like I have said, only when one develops the ultimate Love for God will one reach the Divine. And how is one to develop this Love?

You know very well that love is from the heart. And you all know about it, no? You know that your heart is full of love, but yet, often you find it difficult to express it. You find it difficult to let it out. It's because, in your mind, you are so limited by the barriers that you create. You are so limited by your own limitations. But if we know that love is seated in our hearts, why don't we keep calling it? Let it out!

It's like if you go to my place and you know I am inside the house and you need me badly. What would you do? You would knock at the door; you would keep knocking. If there was a bell, you would keep ringing the bell. You would go around the house and try to find a way to get my attention. Am I right? You would do that. If this urge is really there, you will do anything for it.

It's the same thing with this Love that is present inside of you. But very often people say "I want to feel it, but if I don't feel it in a month's time, finished!" But it's not like that. Real love or normal love - love is love, whether it is for God or for somebody. We start by loving what is nearer to us, what we can see, what we can hold and this will lead to the Higher Love. That's why when two persons are in love, at the beginning, of course, there is a great love. But this love can grow more and more if one let's it grow.

It is the same thing with the Love for God that you have inside of you, if you let it out. Like I have said many times, you have to be persistent. It is seated inside; the Divine is seated inside of your heart. The real temple is not outside of you. It's here, inside of you, and it's where the real Lord is seated. The real church, the real mosque, is here, in you and all of you know about it. Whether you have felt Him or not, in the mind you know that God is seated in your heart. And the mind, the power of the mind is so strong. You know that, no? When you worry about little things, you can make the worry huge. It's the same thing with Love. If you know that the Lord has a small place in your heart, you can also make yourself know that He can have a big place.

> The power of Love is the only thing that conquers everything. If you want to conquer God, conquer Him with Love.

And as you know very well, the power of Love is the only thing that conquers everything. If you want to conquer God, conquer Him with Love. If you want to achieve Him, you will achieve Him only with Love. But the Love has to be pure and purer. It's not by saying "OK, I have been to the centre here, I have been to the *ashram*, I have been to *Shivaratri*, so my Love is pure." It's that *you* have to make that Love pure *inside* of you. You have to train your mind to become positive. When your mind is positive and you know that the Lord is seated within and you keep calling Him, there is no chance that He will not reveal Himself inside of you.

There are so many stories in which even criminals have changed. During *Shivaratri*, I was telling the story of Suswara, how he was a big criminal, but through Love, through devotion to Lord Shiva, he changed. In the same way, everybody can change. This is the connection that the *Atma* has with *Paramatma* and this connection is not a connection of just now. Now you are limited to the body. Each one has an individual body and each one thinks of himself or herself as separate. But you are the *Atma* and what is the *Atma*? It's part of *Paramatma* and this *Atma* one day, whether it's in this life or in a hundred lives, will go back to its Source where it comes from. There is no chance that it will never go back there, but it's up to each one whether to quicken it or not. That's the free will that God has given. You can quicken your way to the Divine and realise Him or you can just sit around and make it longer, which many people like to do.

But everybody, in the end, will reach the Divine, because the essence of your Self is only Him. And only through this Love, when this Love really gets awakened and becomes like Radharani's Love, then there is no chance of not attaining Him. So, as today everybody is expressing love, keep expressing it not only today, not only because of Saint Valentine.

Saint Valentine came only in the year 269. Love existed much before that. Now, everybody is saying "Happy Valentine! Happy Valentine!", but why do we say, "Happy Valentine?" Who was Saint Valentine? How did he become a Saint? You all celebrate Saint Valentine, no? OK, it's commercial, but apart from the commercial side of it you express the love, no? Of course, nowadays it has changed, it has become very commercial. Some clever people have commercialised it like everything else.

But you see, in the *Bible* there is one verse that says "A real friend is the one who is ready to give his life for his friend." Saint Valentine was the Bishop of Terni, in Italy, and actually, to protect a couple, He gave his life. He accepted being killed as a martyr to protect this couple. And as He was dying, He said "Whoever will remember me on that day, I will pray to the Lord for them, so that Love shall grow inside of them, so that they become a true friend." This is the story, in short, of Saint Valentine, the one who gave His life to protect Love, which is considered as the greatest form of Love.

So, let love rejoice inside of you, not only today, but always. And may you, by the grace of Radharani, become like Her. Like many other Saints, not only Radharani. Among all the Deities who love the Lord, you will see that there is an expression of this Divine Love. If they could do it, we all can do it, also. If saints have achieved the Oneness with the Divine, be strong and say yes, you can and keep nagging the Lord inside of your heart until He opens the door and says "Here I am; what do you want?" And be ready, when He asks you what you want, to know, really, what you will ask Him.

THE COURAGE TO BE ON THE SPIRITUAL PATH

Darshan at Prague, Czech Republic 25 August 2010

I'm happy to be here with all of you and I'm very happy that we have Swami Satya Narayan Das from Vrindavan here. He's the founder of Jiva Institute. Later on Swamiji will talk a little bit. I'm happy to see that everybody was clapping this time and also trying to sing. It's about the self-confidence inside of you. So, today I will talk about self-confidence, also, about self-respect.

Often, [we wonder] when travelling around and looking at how people are, how people live, in different parts of the world and also, how far along spirituality is. It's a bit sad, actually, because people long for peace, people long for happiness, people long to be free; but, yet, when you see how they live their life you may wonder "Will they ever be free? Will they ever be happy? If you ask the question "Will they ever be happy the way they live?" the answer will be, "No." Imagine how lucky you are, to be here and to sing the Divine Names, how lucky you are that God chose you to be on a spiritual path. But it doesn't end only here. Very often I've seen people on the spiritual path, very shy, very shy to say that they are on this path. They are shy to say that they love God. Well, if you are shy to say that you are on a spiritual path and you love God, where is the self-confidence in it? Where is the faith in it? Where is the faith in yourself? You should never be afraid to say that you love God, because this is the thing – He is the only One that you can love, really.

It's only by being true to yourself, by being sincere to yourself, that you can really change something. Like that, you don't only change yourself, but you change other people, also. People are scared of the spiritual path, because they see the limitation of the outside. If spiritual people limit themselves by being scared of the outside, well, it will not help. It will not help others to change. Like I said last time, become an instrument of this Divine Love and if you become an instrument of this Divine Love, you have to spread it. You have to make a difference in this world, not only in your life, but, also, to your surroundings.

That's how the Disciples of Christ spread the message of Christianity, the message of Jesus. They were not scared, even though they were persecuted. Christ had said to them, "In my name you will be persecuted, but blessed are those who really go till the end." So, it's the same thing for each one of you who is on the spiritual path, or the searching path, if you want to make a difference in this world, don't be scared.

> You should never be afraid to say that you love God, because this is the thing; He is the only One that you can love, really.

Actually, don't be scared to be yourself. Only by being yourself will the Divine radiate through you, will the Divine work through you. And here, if you close yourself and reserve yourself, if you say "No, I'm shy. I'm scared of telling somebody that I'm spiritual," what are you making yourself? You're making yourself weak not strong. There's lots of work to do.

There is much love inside your heart. Don't close it. Don't restrict it. Open your mind; fill it with the Divine. When your mind is open, your heart will automatically reflect this love. To attain God, is not difficult. Some will agree and some will not. Some will say "Yes, it is easy" because they have the self-confidence that it is easy, they remove all the barriers of difficulty, and of course, it is easy, because these barriers, you created. As you created them, you also can remove them, because God calls all of you. So, don't be shy and don't close yourself, don't restrict yourself, don't put these barriers to your Self. You are an instrument of God; you want to attain Him. Limitation of the mind is your own limitation.

This reminds me of a story of two frogs. There was once a frog that grew up in a pond and all his life he stayed in this pond and for him this pond was his world and was very great. One day a bird was flying above with another frog on his beak. This frog was from the sea and he fell in the pond. So now there were two frogs together. The frog from the pond said to the frog from the sea "How is it, where you come from? How big is your pond?" You see, because he thought his pond was the biggest one, he started to ask, "Is your pond a quarter of mine? The frog from the sea answered, "No, bigger" So the other frog asked again, "is it half the size of my pond?" and again the frog from the sea said "No, even bigger than that" Finally, the first frog asked "Is it as big as my pond?" and the frog from the sea said, "No, it's also bigger than that!" Hearing that, the frog from the pond started to argue "How can you say that your pond is bigger than mine? It's impossible. My pond is the biggest one!"

So, this is the same as when you limit yourself. You forget that inside of you there is an even greater thing and to realise that, you have to have faith. You have to have trust. Faith and trust together will reveal this vastness, this greatness inside you, and then you will realise that this greatness is only God and that He is the only one that pervades everything, and not this I, not this ego, this pride. You will realise that only through His Grace you are everything, but you have to take the first step. Without you developing your self-confidence, it's difficult. And you can develop the self-confidence by doing your *sadhana*, your spiritual practices, by chanting the

Divine Names. And the more you chant the Divine Names, the more the self-confidence and the more joy and happiness will be inside of you.

So remember, this joy has to be spread. If you want to change, to make change in this world, don't close yourself. Open. Open your heart to love, Unconditional Love and this is who you are. Don't forget that you have a soul and don't limit yourself. You have a soul and you have to realise your Self. You have to go closer and closer to the Divine. And the more you approach the Divine, the more you will see the Divine will bring Himself much nearer to you.

There was a Sufi saint who said, "I have made three mistakes in my life. The first mistake I made was when I started my spiritual path, when I started my search, I thought it was me who was approaching the Divine. But, actually, it was the opposite. The Divine was, long before I started, on His way towards me. The second mistake that I made was that I said I loved Him very much, that my love was beyond comprehension. But, in reality, my Love is just like a drop in His vast ocean of love. And the third mistake I made was when I said I had attained Him, because it was not me who attained Him but He who made it possible that I attain Him."

So, it's the same thing for each one of you who are here. It's not you, but it's through the Grace of God, through His Grace, that you are here. It's through His Grace that you can act, that you can love in this world and only through His Grace will you realise and attain Him. So, be ready always; be ready whenever He will call you. Make yourself ready for Him -this is within your capacity to do- until, finally, you realise that it's only Him.

ENDLESS LOVE

Darshan, Steffenshof, 2 May 2007

The *bhajan* we sang expresses the Love that the devotee has for the *Satguru*, the Love that the devotee has for the Divine. This Love is single-minded Love. This Love is a Love where the devotee doesn't expect anything, apart from the Lord Himself. And, in this Love, nothing can move the *bhakta*, no matter what comes! When Meerabai was singing for Krishna, people would say "She's crazy", but this didn't change her faith, this didn't change her Love. She was so concentrated; her mind was so focused and one-pointed towards the Lord that nothing could move her. It is said that devotion has another name: one single-pointed mind. If your mind is completely focused on God, you will have Him.

It's like a fisherman in his little boat. He throws his line and tries to catch a fish. He's so concentrated on the float, wondering when the fish will eat the bait. When the float goes down, he will pull the line and he will get the fish. The fisherman is so concentrated on the float that, even when someone comes near and says "Mr. Thomas, can you show me where Mr. Paul is?" He does not listen. He ignores it one time, two times, three times! So finally, the person searching for Mr Paul starts to go away. And the fisherman, in his concentration doesn't hear anything. He doesn't bother about what is around him. He's so focused and his concentration is only on the float. Even if people shout, he will not hear anything. After he has caught the fish, put the fish down and cleaned off his

sweat, he will finally say to the man "Hey! Why were you shouting?"
But, of course now, the other one will ignore it, because he had
been shouting, and asking the same question many times and the
fisherman ignored him. But finally, he returns again to ask "Tell me,
now, where is he?" Then, the fisherman shows him the way.

You see, when one is concentrated, when one is focused on God,
when one is in deep meditation, one is not affected by anything
around, by any noise, by any touching. Even if a snake is crawling
on you, it will not affect you, because you are calm and your mind
is on God. Whereas, when you have fear, when you start panicking,
what happens? All these things disturb you!

People sit in meditation. You see them very deeply in meditation,
I mean on the outside, they seem to be in deep meditation but in
fact, they are wondering what others are doing and listen to them,
thinking, "In my quietness I can listen to what my neighbour is
saying." Is that concentration? No, it's not. When your mind is
focused on God, it has to be only on God. No matter what happens
around you, don't bother about it.

It's the same thing as when a fisherman is concentrated on the float.
It's the same thing when people who like football, when they watch
their favourite team play, nothing can move them from the front
of the TV. Or ladies, when they like to watch their beautiful series,
they are focused, one-pointed and, at that point, nothing can
move them from their seat. I tell you, when you look at these men
watching football, you can pass in front of the TV and still you are
invisible, they can only see the TV! I tell you, if such concentration
as this would be on God, how beautiful it would be! But it's sad,
man's concentration is just for some time. They're concentrated on
petty things, things that have limited joy. The eternal joy is waiting
for you but you put your mind somewhere else.

Focus on the true joy that you have inside of you. Focus on the Love
of God that you have inside of you. Focus on the Divine, which

is present inside of you, and focus in a way that *nothing* on the outside can move you. No matter what comes, nothing can move you! Christ said it, "Build your faith on the stone. Make it strong that no wind can move you, that no wind can destroy this. Become a pillar of this faith." This kind of concentration you should have so that when you're focused, when you sit down for meditation, you don't hear anything, you don't think about anything, only about the Lord, only Him, nothing else.

> Surdas, looking at Krishna, said, "My Lord, my eyes have seen You now. Make me blind, again. I don't need to see the world, because I have seen You, I have seen everything."

Of course, at the beginning it will be a little bit difficult. Your mind will wander. It's the same thing when you watch your movie or you watch your football and you're all excited, wondering if your team will win, no? So, at the beginning, there will be some agitation, but afterwards, when you concentrate, when you try really your best, it will be easy. And it will be very, very easy for you to concentrate. It will be very easy to detach from every feeling from the outside and only attach to the Lord, which is seated inside your heart.

When you sing the Name of God, close your eyes and let yourself be drawn into it. When you sing the name of Krishna, just see Krishna in front of you. When you sing the name of Devi, see Shakti in front of you. When you sing the name of Jesus, see Him in front of you. By focusing your mind on the Divine, by placing the holy image in your mind, you conquer the mind. You conquer the agitation of the mind and, when it's focused, the *Satguru* deep inside your heart will guide you. So, when you sing, close your eyes and visualise.

What I will sing next is the greatness of Love. The greatest prayer that exists is Love. So when I sing *Sabse Oonchi*, then you say *Prema Sagai*, meaning: Love is the greatest prayer. This *bhajan* was written by Surdas, one of the devotees of Krishna, one of the greatest devotees of Krishna. He was blind and The Lord appeared in front of him and asked him "Surdas, what do you want?" Surdas, looking at Krishna, said, "My Lord, my eyes have seen You now. Make me blind, again. I don't need to see the world, because I have seen You, I have seen everything." Such was his Love and that was what he wrote about, what he expressed in his singing, the greatness of the Love of the devotee to the Lord, to the *Satguru*.

In this song, it is said: *Duryodhan ko mevā tyāgo sāga vidura ghara pāī*. Duryodhan, was the cousin of Arjun and he offered to Krishna lots of gifts, lots of delicacies, but there was no love in whatever he was offering so Krishna categorically refused everything, because the Lord is craving for this Love, the Love you have inside your heart. He doesn't want anything; He has everything.

In the Psalms, God told David, "Whatever you are offering to me is already mine. Do you think if I need something, I will come and ask you? I will just take it! The mountain I created by my will. The birds are flying by my will. The fish are in the sea by my will. You, you are yourself, by my will. Do you think I need something from you? I just accept this Love, the sacrifice of this Love."

(Then, the song continues): *Jūthe phala sabarī ke khāye bahu vidhi prema lagāī*. Shri Rama took the fruit that Sabari was giving to Him and ate it happily. Before giving the food to Sri Rama, she had waited her whole life for Him. Every day she would chant Ram's Name continuously. Deep inside of her she knew that one day she would meet her Rama. Deep inside herself she knew that Rama would come to her one day. Every day she would prepare everything. She would prepare the flowers. She would prepare the place for Rama. She would go in the forest and pick all the wild fruit that she could get and bring them. Waiting for Rama, she would keep chanting Rama's Name. When Rama, on the way to Lanka to get Sita, passed by Sabari, Sabari was so happy! She was giving these fruits with so much Love to Rama, but first she chose the sweetest ones. She would offer only the sweet ones to the Lord. She ate a piece from it and then gave it to the Lord. Lakshman, who is the brother of Rama, said "How can you eat? This lady doesn't even have teeth and you are taking the fruit and eating it?" Then Rama said "You will not understand this. This is the Love between the Master and the disciple; this is the Love between the *bhakta* and the Lord" and this is the Love that He accepted from Sabari.

Rājasuya yajña yudhisthira kīno tāmai jūtha uthāī Out of Love for His devotee, the Lord forgets that He is the Lord. When Yudishtira made the great *yagna*, He served the people Himself. Krishna went and served everybody. Then He Himself picked up the leaves on which they were eating, showing that there is no difference between the Lord and the One inside of you; to break all difference in the mind of Man, to show that He is bound with this Love, which is inside of you. He accepts to forget that He is the Lord. God accepts to forget that He is God and becomes the servant of His devotee. And such Love one has to cultivate; such Love, such devotion, such calling one has to have inside the heart. And when you have Him, you will have everything.

Aisi prīti badihī vrindāvana gopina nāca nacāī. Krishna demonstrated such Love, such humility, in Vrindavan, where He would dance with the *gopis*, He would dance with the shepherd, He would dance with the cows. He showed such Love that He didn't limit Himself for Himself, but He limited Himself for His devotees, He limited Himself for everybody to enjoy Him.

Sūra krūra is lāyaka nāhī kaha lag karau badāī. Surdas said to the Lord "Lord, What have I done to deserve such grace and how can I make this Grace more and more? How will I expand this grace?" And the Lord looked at him and smiled to him and said "My dear

Surdas, Love! Only by Love one will reach me. Only when one has selfless Love, will one realise me. Only when one has selfless Love, that one will become One with Me. Develop such Love and I will be always with you".

THE PATH TO THE DIVINE

Darshan, Poland, May 2007

It is lovely to be here with all of you. I know that it might be difficult for you to sing the *bhajans*, but I hope that when the musicians sing some Polish songs, you all sing very loudly and expressively because I know you are all lovely people and you all have *so* much love inside of you. When you love people, you always express yourselves, no? So, as you are all lovely people with so much Love inside of you, you should, also, express this Love. God's Love is not to be kept quietly or hidden inside the heart. It has to reflect through you; it has to reflect through your face. It has to reflect through you yourself and one of the easiest ways is to sing, also to dance.

Nowadays, people like to go to discos. I don't say it's bad; it's good. It's a place to express oneself, but often there is not a positive energy there. When you dance, you don't always dance in the right way. And, of course, when you return from a disco, you are always tired and the first thing that you will do is to go to sleep. Whereas, when you dance for God, when you chant the name of Hari all the time, when you dance in His glory, of course, you also do get tired, because you have a physical body, but what happens? It is so intoxicating that you will always want to dance in His name and the more you dance the more energy you will have.

The mind is always running towards music. That's why, when you are very tired, let's say when you return from work, you put on very soft music, sit and relax. Wherever there is sound, the mind will run towards it. For those who know about *Atma Kriya*, there is a part in it, which deals with the sounds. *Atma Kriya*, actually, is a form of *Kriya Yoga* that Mahavatar Babaji has given, which is a very simple way to help to awaken and come into contact with your True Self. So, one part of *Atma Kriya* is the *Nada Kriya*, which deals with sounds: how the mind runs towards sounds, how the mind runs towards beautiful sounds and how the sounds affect the body and the mind. By chanting the Name of God continuously, what happens? You lose your identity, your ego, your pride and you become completely Divine.

Very often we forget about the main aim of our life. We think that we are here in this world just to comb our hair nicely, to put on some makeup to make ourselves beautiful or just to work and have a big house, have a big car, have a boyfriend or a girlfriend. But life is not only about that. Life is about realising why we are here and who we are. We have an identity in this outside world, but we don't know who this identity in Reality is.

Once there was a Guru who said to one of his disciples "My dear, you have lived in the world, now. You have lived very happily, but, now, it is time for you to dedicate yourself and to realise your Self." Then the disciple said "But Master, I have a beautiful wife who loves me so much and I, also, love her very much." The Master didn't argue with the disciple. He just told him "Listen, I will give you a secret technique of *yoga* practice. Practise it and you will see the result."

A few weeks later, the man was practising his new *yoga* technique, where he was locked in a certain *asana,* so that his heart stopped beating. Then the wife came and saw him in the middle of the living room. She said "My dear husband, what has happened to you?" She tried to wake him up, but she saw that he was cold like he was dead. She started yelling and crying very loudly "Oh you have left me!" Hearing that, all the neighbours ran to the house to see what was happening and they saw that the man was dead. They tried to comfort the lady saying "You know this is God's Will." But the lady was crying very dramatically "Why have you left me? Why? We still have a lot of dreams and you promised to make this and that!"

Then, one of the neighbours came with an axe and started to break the doorframe, because the man was in such a yogic position that it was difficult to take him out of the door. Seeing that, the wife stopped crying, went directly to the neighbour and said "What are you doing? Why are you cutting my door?" The neighbour said "Well, you see in which position your husband is, so it will be difficult to take him out of the house." Then the lady said "My goodness! Why are you breaking this door? Look, this ill fate has happened and he has left us early. Now I am a widow. I have nobody to sustain or help me, so, because he is already dead, you should chop off his hands and feet instead of cutting the door." Hearing that the man came back to himself and said "Wife, is that what you meant when you said that you loved me, that after I died you would cut me into pieces?" He realised that his Master was right and he left everything: it was time for him to go.

We always say this is ours or this is mine. We always say that we possess things. But I am asking you "What have you come here with?" In the *Gita* Krishna said: You have come with nothing; you came empty-handed. Everything that you took, you took it from here and when you go, you will leave everything here."

So, what is this *I*? What is this "This belongs to me" and "This is myself"? There is an *I*, but what is this *I*? We say that this is my hand, these are my eyes or those are Paul's eyes. Who is this Paul? We can know Paul from the outside, but deep inside there is another Paul. Maybe he doesn't know it yet, but inside each one of us there is our true Self. And we are here to realise this Self, so that our body, our mind and our soul become one. And as long as you don't realise that and think there is a difference between the Divine and you, without trying to make them one, there will be always a barrier. And, in that way, you will have to come again and again and again to work only on this unity between the human and the Divine.

Very often people try to compromise with God; people try to bribe God. It is not possible or, actually, it is very easy to bribe him. Do you know how? You can bribe Him by loving Him, by letting Him steal your heart. You see, often we approach the Divine with such pride and in an egoistic way. We think that we can give Him everything, forgetting that everything belongs to Him already and that the only thing that we can give to Him is our heart. And that's the only thing He wants: this heart full of love and humility. But often in religion, we offer our heart with lots of guilt, pride and ego. Of course, these, also, have to be offered; they are also part of us.

> Very often people try to compromise with God; people try to bribe God. It is not possible or, actually, it is very easy to bribe him. Do you know how?

This reminds me of a story of a very rich merchant. In India there is a place called Puri and there is a temple for Lord Krishna in the form of Jagannath. He is an aspect of Krishna, a funny one. Every year there is a big festival where they bring the Deities out and carry them in the street. Millions of people gather there. All the people, even the King, would go and help to clean the street where they would be bringing the chariot of the Lord.

It happened that one day a very rich merchant came to Jagannath and seeing the Lord together with his brother Balaram and sister Subhadra he said to himself "This is just a mere wooden statue with big eyes and a big smile. It's just a black statue." Then he said, very proudly, "I will show how wealthy I am and I will give one hundred thousand rupees." So he went to the priest and said "I will donate one hundred thousand rupees to the temple to feed the Lord, but I have one condition: you have to use all this money for the food." The priest thought "How will I use one hundred thousand rupees only for the food? Even if I use the best *ghee* and all the best ingredients to make the *prasad* for the Lord, still the money will not be finished." So, all the priests gathered together and started discussing "How can we use up one hundred thousand rupees for the *prasad* of the Lord?" Finally the high priest came to a conclusion: he said "OK, it seems that we can't take any decision, so let Lord Jagannath , let Krishna Himself take the decision." They went to the merchant and said "Listen, we haven't come to a conclusion, but we will let the Lord Himself decide which kind of *prasad* He would like to have. Meanwhile, please stay with us until the Lord Himself tells us what kind of *prasad* He wants."

Three days went by and then the high priest had a dream. In this dream Lord Jagannath appeared to him and told him what to say to the merchant. Of course, the Lord knew the pride which was inside the merchant and in what way he was offering the *prasad* to Him. So, finally, the priest went to the merchant and said to him "The Lord has come in my dream and said what kind of *prasad* He would like to have." The merchant said very proudly "Yes, tell me!" The priest said "The Lord has demanded some *betel* leaves with some paste inside." Then the merchant said "What? He wants only these leaves? But this is nothing." So the priest said "Wait, I am not finished. The Lord has asked that inside these *betel* leaves there should be pearl powder. They should be smeared with the finest ground pearl powder." And the merchant said "Still, this is nothing for me." But the priest said, "Yes, but the Lord said another thing, also. These pearls that you will use should not be just ordinary pearls. They have to be pearls that come from under the skin of the forehead of an elephant."

Then the arrogant merchant started to think "Yes, but how many elephants will I have to buy to be able to get just one pearl? I am offering one hundred thousand, but it will cost more than that." He realised that he could not offer to Lord Jagannath what He was asking. At that moment he threw his very expensive turban at the feet of Jagannath, kneeled down and said to the Lord "Please, forgive me. Out of pride I tried to bribe you. I know I can't give you anything which is on the outside, but I offer you my heart." And he changed completely. A few days later the Lord appeared to him in his dream and said "I am very pleased with your heart and this is the only thing that I want: a heart which is full of love and devotion." And it's very simple and easy to offer your heart to God. So, whenever you think that you have to offer something to the Lord, first, inside of you, offer your heart to Him saying "Lord, I offer You my heart. It is not mine anymore, it is Yours. Make me love the way that You love. Make me Realise this Divine Love." Spirituality is just about a relationship to God, and this Love relationship to the Divine will make you Realised.

"Lord, I offer You my heart. It is not mine anymore, it is Yours. Make me love the way that You love. Make me realise this Divine Love."

When you love somebody, you are not scared of anything. In the same way, when you Love God you should not be scared of anything. When you love somebody, you will do anything to please that person. In the same way, when you Love God, try your best always to please Him. When He sees that you are trying your best to please Him, He will run to you and He will give you liberation, He will give you Self-Realisation. Work always towards Self-Realisation, towards God-Realisation, and make this the aim of your life.

He will provide you with everything. Whatever you need He will give you. In the Bible, Christ said, "If the Lord is giving the birds their food, and clothes the grass of the field, are you not much better than they?" Your Heavenly Father knows what needs you have, God is ever looking after everybody. You have just to trust that He is looking after you, to trust that He is with you all the time. Whatever you do–good or bad–He is there. His Love pervades everything. If one-percent of your heart opens up to this Divine Love, it's enough.

Work towards this opening of your heart. Work towards Self-Realisation. Work towards knowing the Oneness of God beyond all limitations that human beings create. We create limitations, we say "God is only this; God is only that." But when we place our limitations on God, then is He really God? This is not God. He becomes only the limited concept that we have of Him.

Limitation is ignorance in Man and knowledge is what removes ignorance. I mean the knowledge of the Divine, the inner knowledge, this knowledge that you have inside of you. But when you have some knowledge, one day you will have to let go even of that, because you don't Realise God either with ignorance or with knowledge. Knowledge will bring you only to a certain point of realising the Divine, but to Realise God, to truly know the Divine, you have to cross over everything, to go beyond all limitations.

It's like if you are walking and a thorn goes in your foot. You need another thorn to remove it. And then, what will you do? Will you keep both of the thorns in your pocket or will you throw them away? You will throw them away! So, it's the same thing to Realise God, to know about the Divine you have to cross over all limitations that you put in your mind.

Maybe you have heard of Ramakrishna, an Indian Saint. During His time, one day a beggar came in front of the Kali Temple and, while standing in front of the temple, he just chanted one *mantra* and the whole temple started to move. Another man was looking and, when he saw that the beggar had such power, he started running after him. When the beggar saw that this man was running after him, he started to run even faster.

After a while, when the beggar saw that this man was still behind him, he stopped and said "What do you want?" The man replied "I saw that just by standing and praying in front of the temple, you made the whole temple move. So, for sure, you are a great person and I would like to learn from you and to become your disciple." The beggar said "No, I don't want you. Go away," but the man kept bugging him and saying "Hey, I want, I want, I want!" Then the beggar finally told him "OK, do you want to be my disciple? Fine! Do you see this river here and do you see that river over there?" One river was dirty and the other river was clean and the Saint said to the man "Come to me when both of these two rivers seem alike to you!"

So, to Realise God you have to cross over all the barriers that the mind creates. And, as I said before, the easiest way to do that is to chant the Name of God so that the mind will merge completely into the Divine Name and become Divine.

RADHE, RADHE!

Darshan, Steffenshof, Germany, 23 May, 2008

Radhe Radhe. You know in Vrindavan, actually, they don't say *"Hare Krishna"* or they don't even mention the name of Krishna to greet somebody. They always use the name of Radha. Do you know why? It's because Krishna left Vrindavan and they are still angry with him. Well, there is something to be angry about. The *Gopis* had such Love for Krishna, which is not comparable to any kind of love. That's why when he left they were angry. Also, the descendants are still angry with him. It's amazing the love relationship that *still* today the people there have for Krishna. It's really a one to one [relationship]. It's like He is the dearest one. They will tell Him anything. They will scold Him even. When something goes wrong, they scold Him.

They know that He is God, but yet the Love that they feel inside their hearts is even stronger. When do you really feel that you are free to tell somebody something? When you are close with that person, isn't it? When you are not close, you don't bother about it, but, when you are close with someone, you will feel free to express whatever, even if it is anger, but this closeness, this relationship, this love is what the most important thing is.

This is the kind of Love our soul has for the *Paramatma* and if we awaken this relationship, He will come. It is said that the *Queen Gopi*, which is Radharani, she will do anything for Krishna. Name it; She will do it. Even giving Her life, she will do it. It so happened that once the Gopis were all singing "Krishna, Krishna, we love you so much" and everybody was saying "Oh, Krishna, we will do that for you." You know that very well. You know, when you are in love, you have big, big promises, but sometimes, when it comes to practice – nil, zero. Well, the *Gopis,* also, were saying "Krishna, we love you so much", but, yet, Krishna wanted to test them. He is the Lord, who is seated in each one's heart so of course He knows; He knows better than what somebody's mind perceives.

So, one day He pretended to have a terrible headache and He was screaming "Ah, I have terrible pain." Everybody was shocked, you know, and said "Oh, my Lord, what can we do for you?" All those who had said they would do *anything,* said "Lord, we will do anything for you; tell us." Even Narad Muni came, who sings always, *Narayan, Narayan,* said "I will do anything, my Lord, to cure your headache." Krishna looked at them all and said "OK, fine. To cure my headache I need the dust off your feet; I need that you press my head with your feet." They all got shocked. He, the Lord of Universe, is asking that His head be pressed by their feet. None of them considered themselves worthy for that. They were very scared, because to press God's head with their feet is so disrespectful, firstly, and secondly, for sure they would go to hell!

So everybody was a bit aghast. Everybody was discussing, talking with each other how they would do that. At that moment Radha came and she saw Krishna in such a state that she went to Him and said "My Lord, tell me what can I do?" and Krishna said the same thing that He had said to the Gopis. Then, when she heard what she had to do, without thinking, without considering herself, she said "Yes." and she started pressing with her foot the head of Krishna who was lying in pain and it disappeared. Everybody was shocked and very angry with Radha and started cursing Radha saying "Oh, you are so bad, you are mean. How come you have put your feet on the head of our Lord? Then for sure you will go to hell." Radharani answered "Well, even the deepest of hell will be a blessing for me for it has cured my Lord's pain."

You see, in the relationship to the Divine you forget about yourself completely. You forget about your own realisation, you forget about what will make *you* happy. Like it is said in the Bible – the greatest happiness is when you can give your life for your friend, isn't it? A true relationship is when one can give oneself completely. When you are in love you always forget about yourself. Look, you all have been in love and when you are in love, do you think of yourself or do you think of the other person? You think about the other person. So, the soul can always be in love with the Divine, no? And you can always think of God.

So, if we love God in that way, then we will be detached, also, from whatever is attaching us to this world. We will be detached from whatever is stopping us from our advancement. We want Self-Realisation, we want God-Realisation, but yet, we don't want to let go of everything. That doesn't mean that you should renounce everything and become *sannyas*, no, be in the world but know that everything comes from Him. Everything *is* Him. It's only Him who gives and everything will go back to Him. As long as we stay in the circle of birth and death we will enjoy this play, meaning not only the enjoyment of being happy, but also the pain, which you always complain about.

So, if one wants to always stay in the circle, one will always be in the circle. But if one wants really to go out of the circle, one should develop this Unconditional Love for the Divine, unconditional love for everybody, unconditional love for all His creation, because the unconditional Love of God knows no limit, knows no "I love this one; I hate this one" and there is no judgment. It's like a mother's love.

When a mother loves a child, does that mother have conditions? When a mother has a child in her arms, there are no conditions. She doesn't think 'Oh, I am looking after you; when you grow up you should look after me.' There is no such thought. Afterwards, maybe it happens, but when a mother is holding her child, there are no conditions. Such love is the Love of God, also.

Whatever you have done, good or bad, when you turn to Him, Him who has the Love of a million mothers inside of Him, He will happily forgive. If a child makes a mistake and goes to the mother, the mother forgives and wishes that the child will be good and change. Whereas the father, he will forgive, but with time. The discipline part and the loving part, both are important.

So, when we turn to the Divine with our good and with our not good qualities, He will accept us because He loves us. He is calling all of us to Love

> Whatever you have done, good or bad, when you turn to Him, Him who has the Love of a million mothers inside of Him, He will happily forgive.

the same way He Loves, but yet our mind is a big barrier. All Holy Scriptures, all the Scriptures talk about the Love of God. Many discuss about how it has to be, but yet, in the simplest form, when you go inside your heart, you know what Love is. It's not about me to say with words what Love is, because Love can't be expressed as words. You can only feel Love.

Yet, you see in the world how many wars have been happening for people expressing their views of how God Loves people. One says "My God Loves better." The other one says "No, no, no, you are wrong. *Mine* is the best. Yet all are talking about only *One* God, you know? So try to find this Love. It's like the Greeks said "First, find yourself, then you will find your path." First find what you are looking for, what is your aim in life, what *really* your heart is asking. Your mind will ask for many things and when it gets whatever it asks, it will ask for something else. But, if you dig deep inside of you and take time for yourself everyday when you introvert and find the Divine, find this Love, you will see that it was never far away from you. It's just here all the time. It's just that *we* don't want it to flow, we don't want to let it go and as long as our mind comes in the way, chant *Haribol, Hari Nam, Kevalam.* The only name is Sri Hari. The two syllables of Hari can even give liberation, it can even get rid of all the karmic things in one's life. It's simple: 'Hari'. We like to have big, big, *sadhana*, but yet we don't understand anything! We like to chant big, big *mantras*, but yet we don't understand anything. What will please Him is to chant *simple* things, but with Love!

„*Sabse Oonchi Prema Sagai*" we say, [meaning] "Love is the greatest worship" and the only thing that He accepts is this Love and out of Love He does everything. Whatever one asks for, whether it is material, whether it is spiritual, whether it will bring joy or pain to that person, out of Love He will give it.

So *awaken* this Love. "Heart of Man let this love awaken and see that each one becomes a messenger of peace and love! Each one will spread this love, without words, because with this Love, you don't need to say "I love you," you just need to radiate it, you just need to know, that you carry the love of God; the rest He, will look after. It's simple."

JUST LOVE

DIVINE NAMES

The Name of Rama is even
stronger than Rama Himself.

Hanuman

CHANT HIS NAMES

Darshan in Kiel, Germany, 11 July 2008

It's lovely to see all of you clapping your hands. You see, God has given you this instrument, which are the hands. He has also given other instruments which are the ears and the tongue. Of course also the legs and the body are all instruments of the Divine, but there are certain instruments that are given to us humans for a greater purpose in life – like our ears. Imagine if you couldn't hear, how uncomfortable it would be? Very, isn't it? It would be very uncomfortable.

Imagine you can't talk. It is very difficult, but *yet* we misuse this instrument. If we go deeper into the Scriptures it is said how to use this instrument. How can we make a better use of this instrument for our spiritual advancement? By reciting the Names of God. Our tongue is not given to gossip. It's not only given to discuss about other people's stuff behind their back, which very often human beings like to do very much. If you tell some people "Let's talk about somebody", everybody stands up straight. But if you tell them to sing the name of God, they will say "Oh I feel tired."

Greater use of this instrument will bring you closer to the Divine. Sometimes we hear things and we are happy about it. Other times we hear things and we make ourselves sad. What we are hearing affects our mood; but there is a greater sound that will make us ever blissful, which is present inside of us, which is present all around us, but yet we don't hear this sound, because our hearing range is too low.

You know very well that sound goes as waves and human beings can hear sound waves from 1,000 to 20,000 sound cycles per second. Animals, like dogs and cats, they can hear from 20,000 to 60,000. Other animals, like dolphins, mice, elephants and so on, they can hear from 60,000 to 100,000 sound waves per second.

So, imagine the hearing of men, how limited it is, how little it is, but we can develop it. We develop it by our spiritual practice. This quality gets developed by spiritual practice. It doesn't matter which practice you follow, but as long as you practise it, as long as you are happy in it, as long as you are sincere towards yourself and you are sincere in your practice, the Divine will come to you.

So, as I said, the easiest spiritual practice is to chant the Names of God, to recite the Divine Names. You see, when we call somebody - let's say I call a Mataji - what will happen? She will look at me and say "What does he want from me?" It's the same thing when you call Him inside of you, He will also ask "What do you want from me?" Then you can tell Him your request "Lord I want Self-Realisation. I want God-Realisation."

But this relationship that develops between you and the Divine is not only now, it's eternal, because this relationship, you brought it with you through lives and lives. That you are all sitting here is not just a coincidence. That you are all spiritual is not just a coincidence. Things that you have already worked on from previous lives, you continue working on now, until you achieve the Divine, until you achieve the Love of God completely.

Whether you believe in God or you don't believe in God, deep inside of you, your spirit knows that there is a greater Self, knows that there is a greater Consciousness that pervades everything. For example, if something bad in your life happens, whom do you call first? What do you say? You say "Oh, my God." You don't say "Oh my husband, oh my wife, oh my father, oh my mother." Why? They are also very dear to you. But no, there is the higher consciousness, there is God, which is even closer than everything to you. That's why, whether you believe or not, the first thing that will come out from your mouth is "Oh, my God."

You see, the secret in the Name of the Divine, in the Name of God is that it's God Himself, whereas the name of a person is not *the* person.

If I call someone who is not here, if I chant his name, he will not come to me, whereas, if I chant the name of Mahavatar Babaji, if I chant the Names of Krishna and Jesus, chant the Name of Allah, for sure They will come, because the Name of the Divine is the fullness of the Divine Himself.

So in that way you will go into the fineness of the sound. The more you chant, the more you will go into the fineness of the sound within yourself and the more you will know the secret and you will enjoy the beauty that you have inside of you because after some time of chanting in the outside, the chanting becomes silence within you. Even while you are sleeping, inside of you the chanting always goes on.

There was a saint called Chaitanya Das Maharaj in the 17th century. He was always chanting the Name of Chaitanya Mahaprabhu, but he would not say Chaitanya Mahaprabhu. He would say *Gauranga, Gauranga* all the time. Even while he was sleeping, people would just hear *Gauranga, Gauranga, Gauranga* vibrating from him. Each breath of his changed to *Gauranga* and he rose to such a divine spiritual advancement that even when he died, when he took Samadhi, his whole body was vibrating "*Gauranga, Gauranga*". Gauranga is another aspect of Krishna, which appeared in 1500.

So just by chanting, reciting the name of God you are making good use of these two instruments which are the tongue and the ears. Your hearing will become finer until you realise the vibration within yourself (there is also one exercise in Atma Kriya that can help you with hearing). So this will lead you to Self-Realisation or

God-Realisation or to attain the Love of God completely.

Love is not just to say "I love you", because, you see, when two people meet and when they like each other, what do they say? They say "I love you." Let's say, two people meet and the guy says to the girl "I love you." The girl looks at the guy and says "Do you love me? But we just met only a few hours ago, how can you love me? You don't know me. I don't know you. How can you love me?" We feel something in the heart when we recognise the other, when we recognise: "Yes I know that person, there is something here." But *real* Love develops only when you start to know that person. The more you know the person, the more you love that person.

> The more you start knowing God, the more your Love for God will become greater and greater.

It's the same thing with the Divine, the more you start knowing God, the more your Love for God will become greater and greater. When you look at the lives of the Saints, they realise the Divine completely and for them the ultimate is to Love Him only. Until they find this True Love within themselves, until they find their Self, until they realise their Self, they just love. So knowing it is very important. To know the Divine, the easiest way, like I just told you, is to sing, to chant His Name. And He has given so many Names. He is like a mother who loves all her children the same and knows what each child needs, so she gives according to each child what the child needs.

And there is no special time or place to chant the name of God. Whatever you are doing you can always chant, you can always recite the Divine Names and know that He is with you. The moment you chant His Name, He is there. Like Babaji said, just by merely chanting His name three times He will be there. Whether you see Him or you feel Him or not, He *is* there! With all the Divine aspects, all the Divine Names that you chant, the Divine in that form is present next to you.

So keep chanting. Start that way on the spiritual path. You will see that even your meditation will be perfect, because when you chant and when you meditate, afterwards you will *hear* this vibration going through you, not just quietness. You see, in this vibration, the action of the mind gets busy, because your mind will run after this vibration. So, when your mind runs after the vibration, it will lead you to the cosmic vibration within you. So chant; you will be happy, always.

About the Divine Names in the Scriptures, let's take the *Psalms* 113. King David said, "From sunrise to sunset, I should praise the name of God." Take the Bible, Saint Paul said "Whoever finds refuge in Your Name, shall be saved." Buddha said "Whoever chants my name at the end of their life, they shall reach me and I will lead them to paradise." In the *Veda* it's said "In this time chant, chant, chant because only the name of Sri Hari will save humanity. Mahavatar Himself, has said "Chant *OM Namo Narayanaya*. If you want peace in the world, recite the name of Narayana, it will bring joy and peace."

So like that, almost every saint has said to chant the Divine Name. Shirdi Sai was always telling his disciples to chant *OM Namo Narayanaya*. Lahiri Mahasaya also said to his disciples "Read the *Srimad Bhagavatam* and chant the Name of God, always, so that on your lips there are always the Divine Names". When the Divine Names are always on your lips, there will be no time for you to think of negative things, unless you like to think of negative things, because you see, the more you think of negative things, what happens? The more you become negative, the more you become depressed, the more you become aggressive and all this makes you, makes the world itself not good. Spiritual people are here to change the world, no? Change yourself first, so that the world can change.

THE SWEETNESS OF THE NAME OF RAM

Ram Navami, Shree Peetha Nilaya
Springen, Germany, 24 March 2010

Today is the last day of *Ram Navami*, the last day of the nine days in which Lord Ram has been praised and the day where the Lord came to manifest Himself. You see, Sri Ram manifested Himself to kill the demon Ravana. Ravana symbolises the great pride, the great ego. And Sri Ram – as you probably have read about – He is the manifestation of Maha Vishnu. Sita Devi is the incarnation of Maha Lakshmi. So I will not go into detail about the Ramayana here because if you don't know the story of Rama, it would be nice if you could read it and find out.

In short, Rama manifested himself to kill this great demon. And, also, He's a manifestation of *compassion,* because He was always compassionate with everybody. From early childhood you will see how He always was towards the people – different from Krishna, actually – He's the opposite. He's the same incarnation, but showing two different aspects of the Lord, making Him full in itself. When you study the Name Rama, you see that it's a very powerful Name. All the Divine Names are very powerful, but the Name of Rama is very special because it is said that if one at the end of life chants this Divine Name, one gets liberated from the cycle of birth and death. That's why this Name is called *Taraka Mantra,* which is a mantra that can liberate someone. That's why you see in Hindu tradition, when somebody dies, they always chant the Name of Ram: *Sri Ram, Sri Ram, Sri Ram.*

The word *Rama* in itself is the fullness of two Divine names: *Ra,* which is taken from *OM Namo Narayanaya* and *Ma*, which comes from *OM Namah Shivaya*. So with the combination of *OM Namo Narayanaya* and *OM Namah Shivaya* comes the name *Rama*.

So this *mantra* is not that easy to chant, actually. Even if you just say "OK, we will chant it like this: *Rama, Rama, Rama, Rama, Rama, Rama*", it will not be easy at the end of life if you have not learned to *practice* the chanting. Because you see, at the time of death, very often, you are so attached to the world, you are so attached to things or to people, that to free yourself, even if you are well aware that you would not have to take another birth, it's difficult. Because of the power that is generated at this time, if you don't use the Divine Names, you will incarnate as the last image that is in your mind. That's why, you see very often, when people are dying, they have the image of their children, or people that they like so much and the attachment is so strong in the mind that the next life, when they come, they come again as a human being, but to finish certain karmic things with that family.

Some people very often ask if you can incarnate as an animal. Well, in some cases, yes, you can, because, you see, you are the master. The soul that is inside of you is God and He can create any aspect. Let's say somebody is attached to a dog, which is better than being attached to human beings, actually, because they are more loyal, more faithful. But it creates a problem. You see, if you are attached to an animal, at the end of life when you die what will be the image in your mind? You will think of the animal, how much you will miss the animal, how much you will miss for example your dog. Imagine at that moment your soul already creates your next life. So, what will it be? It can't be a human being. You will degrade yourself to an animal state. You will degrade yourself to a lower sphere. That doesn't mean that whatever you have worked on as a human being has disappeared. It is still there, but it becomes dormant. The same thing when animals look at a human being, they think "Wow! How lucky is this human being", but human beings when they look at animals they think "How lucky are the animals!"

This is when Divine Names come in, where the Names can liberate one's Self. Without the power of the Divine Names, without the infusion of the Sacred Names inside of you, you are always empty; it is always only the Divine names that fill you and give energy to you. It doesn't matter if you believe or you don't believe in the Divine Name because actually, it's the Name of God that is giving you this energy. So the Name of *Rama*, like I said, is a *Taraka Mantra*, which helps one. Even if somebody has attachments to the world outside, it helps to dissolve these attachments, but you have to chant it regularly. So that's why I said "The name of Rama is even stronger than Rama Himself".

An incident happened during the life of Rama, when they were building the bridge to cross over to Lanka, which is Sri Lanka nowadays, or Ceylon. They needed to build the bridge to cross over, but they didn't know how to do it. Every stone that they threw would sink. So Hanuman had a great idea, because Hanuman, you see, He was really a great devotee, actually, one of the greatest devotees because there are not many *great* devotees in this world. There's *Prahlad*, there is *Meerabai* and some others but one of the main, main, main devotees is Hanuman. He came up with the great idea to write the Name of Rama on each stone and throw it in the sea. So when they threw the stone, the stone would float. Ram was looking from a distance and wondering, He approached Hanuman and said "Hanuman, I've been looking at you. You are writing my name on a stone, throwing it in the sea, and it floats, but when I throw a stone, it sinks." Then Hanuman said "My Lord, it is like that. Look, when Your Name is inscribed on it, it is saved, but without Your name on it, of course it will sink, and in the same way, when *You* let go of somebody, of course, he will sink."

It reminds me very much of Peter. When Jesus walked on the

water, he rushed to the Lord, he was big-mouthed so he said "Lord, I shall walk on the water." But what happened? He started sinking, because he had doubt inside himself. Then, Jesus held him. It's the same thing with the Divine Names. Of course, nowadays human beings can't see the Divine, can't get hold of the Divine so easily, but through the Name, actually they can. And also, the name of Rama, like any of the Divine Names, is very sweet. It's different from Krishna, actually. Krishna is sweet, yes, but there is a sharp sweetness inside. It is like sweetness with a spice, you know? Krishna was very spicy, you know. Rama will give you a chance, but Krishna will not give you a chance! But both of them will liberate you. So the Name of Rama is wonderful. Really learn to chant it, to remember Ram every time and He will be a close companion to you. So that's why when somebody is dead [in India], they always chant *Ram Naam Sathya He, Ram Naam Sathya He*, which means: the only Name which is truth is Rama; Rama is only one; Rama is the beginning and Rama is the end.

So today we are celebrating the birthday of Rama and, actually, Ram was born at twelve o'clock noon. Krishna was born at twelve midnight. It's the opposite. So in these two incarnations, Rama and Krishna, the Lord shows that He's full in all His qualities, whether in the incarnation of Krishna or the incarnation of Rama, which is soft. In any of His incarnations and aspects, He shows that you will never be able to understand Him with your mind. When Rama was on Earth, everybody knew Him as *Raja Rama*, as the King or Prince Rama. Of course, for some people He was just a normal person, a normal human being, but for some, like the great *rishis*, they knew that He was an incarnation or manifestation of the Divine Himself. The great Vishwamitra, who created the *Gayatri Mantra*, Himself, He initiated Lord Rama into many mysteries, so he knew that Rama was very special and that His Divine Names could save somebody. Hanuman, when He was small, heard the Name Rama from Vayu

[His father]. Vayu told Him that Rama would be His *Guru*, that Rama would wait for Him. He didn't know about Rama but He always chanted the Name *Ram, Sri Ram, Sri Ram, Sri Ram*. He was chanting and meditating on the Name of Rama with intensity and He didn't have ten *mantras* like nowadays where everybody likes to have hundreds of *mantras* and hundreds of Divine Names to chant – no, He had only one Name, the Name of Rama, and Rama was fully inside of Him. Each part of His body, each cell of Him was Rama. Each hair when plucked out from Him would vibrate the *Rama Naam*, the Name of Rama. Such was the intensity of the Divine Name inside of Him.

It so happened that after Rama killed Ravana, they returned to the palace and Rama was installed in the kingdom as King of Ayodhya. He removed one of His pearl necklaces and gave it to Hanuman and, of course, everybody sitting in the kingdom was very happy to see Hanuman receive a gift from Lord Rama. It was a great blessing. So what did He start to do? He started breaking each pearl with his mouth, looking inside and throwing it away. Of course, this gesture was an offence. In the court all the sages who were sitting there, they were a bit aghast and they said to Hanuman "What are You doing?" The sages then said to Him "You don't have much faith in your Lord. You know that your Lord resides inside You." Then Hanuman said, "I'm looking for Rama and Sita inside these pearls, but I don't see them." So why was Hanuman doing that? They said "Rama has given You a gift and You are destroying it? You're offending Rama!" Of course, Rama was smiling and I suppose Sita also could not understand. Hanuman said "Rama is not inside so what is the use of them? I throw them away."

That's what everybody is doing! You're looking for the Divine in the world, you know that you will not find Him in the world outside, but that you will find Him inside of yourself, but you keep looking for Him outside. You think "Yes, I will find Him, not now, but later on I will find Him", but you will never find Him unless you find Him, firstly, inside of you. Once you have found Him inside of you, then you will find Him everywhere. So the same thing they said to Hanuman "Don't you know that He's inside your heart? For sure, you have little faith because you don't know that the Lord is sitting in your heart." Then Hanuman said "No, no, no. I know He's in my heart!" So with His nails He tore His heart open in front of everybody and sitting inside it were Ram and Sita. This is the *Virat Swarupa* of Hanuman actually, the great form of Hanuman showing the intensity of *bhakti,* where the Lord consumes you completely.

It was the same thing when Saint Theresa of Avila said, "The Lord has pierced my heart. My heart has been pierced by the Lord's arrows". It is this intensity of Love, a Love that transcends happiness and transcends pain itself; not what everybody understands as love where they say "Yes, I'm feeling very happy." No, it is not like that. When Theresa of Avila died, they removed her heart - this was the culture in the 16th century - and when they removed the heart, they saw that her heart was pierced. It was the same when Jesus showed his heart, it was pierced.

So this intensity, like I have explained many times before, is a burning sensation for the Lord. But sadly, nowadays, people don't know about this intense longing for God. They know only a little bit about how to long for God, but then the next moment what passes through their mind, is "Oh, I need this thing." They forget about the Lord and they run after the world. It's so easy to run after the world, because the world itself is running after you, but *you* have to run after the Lord.

I know, I'm talking and what I am saying doesn't make much sense, but anyway, it's good to remind oneself about that, it's good to remind everybody that we are not here to run after the world. The world can run after you, but you have to run after the Lord. The world will always be there for you, but *you* have, firstly, to gain Realisation, which is why you have incarnated. Once you have gotten this, you can run after the world as much as you want.

That's what a great philosopher said, "First find yourself, then look for the world, no?" So once you have found yourself, then you become a *jivan mukti,* you become free from the bondage of karmic things. Then you can do whatever you want, as much as you want. Nothing will bind you. But as long as you have not found your Self, keep trying. Keep looking and the Divine Name of Rama will help you, the Divine Name of Krishna, the Divine Name of Jesus, all the Divine Names will help you to find that. That's why they say that the *bhakti* path is one of the easiest paths, but you have to dedicate yourself. It's not that whenever you see you can divert your mind from the Lord, you then divert your mind from your path or when a little wind blows, you let yourself fall from left to right.

So hold tight to the Divine Names, any Divine Names that you feel close to. You don't need to have ten Divine Names. You just need one Divine Name. If you have a *guru mantra*, just chant your *guru mantra*. If you have one Divine Name, one form of the Divine that you feel close with, just concentrate on that one. It will be more intensified than concentrating on ten Divine Names. In the minds of Men, they think that if they have ten they will advance faster but they will not advance faster. Actually, they will advance more slowly, because one Divine Name is like digging one hole and getting the water. Ten Divine Names is like digging ten holes to try to get water.

You will not get it. So if you want, just chant one Name.

DRINKING THE CUP OF DIVINE LOVE

Darshan at Shree Peetha Nilaya,
Springen, Germany, 3 July 2010

The Name of the Lord can be understood by everyone in any language, can't it? So, even the baby in the crowd was dancing while we were singing. The saints always say that an unborn child, when he is inside the mother's womb, goes through agony. Because it is in the darkness, it is in water and blood, the spirit of the child calls to the Lord and says to Him "Dear Lord, by letting me come into this world, You will reveal Your glory to me. I surrender to Thy Divine Name. May this life that I will be taking on be a service to You and a surrender to You."

"Dear Lord, by letting me come into this world, You will reveal Your glory to me. I surrender to Thy Divine Name. May this life that I will be taking on be a service to You and a surrender to You."

But what happens? The moment the child is born this link to God, this link the child has been asking for, is forgotten. And it is not me who tells you that, this is actually written in the *Vedas*. And it's true that the moment one goes out into this world, the moment one becomes engrossed in this material world, the mind becomes active. And once the mind becomes active, one forgets what one has asked for.

Love is the most important thing in life but when we come into the world, we get so engrossed in it that we forget our duty, we forget our task, we forget why we incarnated, why we came into this world. There is one thing that reminds us always of this Love of God, and this is spirituality. What is spirituality? Spirituality is surrender. And I know that many people do not like the word surrender; they do not like to hear this word because they think that surrendering means that one has to give up everything. Yes, it is true. You *do* have to give up everything, because you have not come with anything. So what would you take and what would you give that is not already here? You just take it from one place and put it in another place.

In spirituality, the word surrender means the surrendering of one's *mind* to the Lotus Feet of the Lord. That is, in fact, what one has to surrender. The Lord has everything else, but your mind, when it is surrendered to the Lotus Feet of the Lord, gains peace, gains happiness, gains joy, gains freedom but as long as one does not surrender the mind, one is a slave of the mind.

Our mind is bound by the five attachments: greed, lust, anger, ego and jealousy. These are the five gross qualities that make up the mind and above all, the ego is the strongest one. In place of surrendering the mind to the Lord, pride and ego make one surrender to all other things except the Lord. That is why people become restless, because the mind is not at the right place.

The soul inside of us is jumping and telling us "Hey, mind, surrender yourself!", but the mind says "No! I am better off with my own worries, because that is how I can drag you down completely." The soul says "But this is just an illusion", because deep inside you know that reality is only to surrender to the Divine Feet, to realise the mystery of your incarnation, to realise your *dharma*, your duty here and achieve that. Deep inside, each one of you does know about it. It is not about me saying it but it is about you, yourself, knowing that, but the mind makes it impossible, because whenever we say "Don't do something, detach yourself from it", what does the mind do? The mind gets more active and says "No, no, no. Do it!", but the moment you do it, you get entangled in it. And then, one will lead to the other. It will never end.

Then when you look back, you say "Oops, if I could have changed it from the beginning, I would have changed it!" How many times in your life did you take certain decisions and then, afterwards, you said, "I should have done it differently!" It happens, doesn't it? Then, you wish to go back into the past and change it, but it is too late! What is done is done! You have to bear the consequences. But if you listen to your intuition from the beginning, when your heart tells you to not do something, and you listen to this intuition - call it the Voice of God - and don't do it - this will give you freedom.

So learning to listen to one's intuition is very important. It's very easy, too, because whenever one hears their intuition, there is no doubt in it and the voice of intuition is strong and direct. Very often the mind will rebel against it, but if you take the decision to listen to this intuitive voice inside of you, you will be away from the mind and the mind will surrender itself. Because, the more you listen to the mind, the more your mind will drag you, but the less you listen to your mind, the further you will be away from it and the easier it will be to realise your Self.

So surrender is about surrendering the mind to the Lotus Feet, surrendering the mind to the Divine Names because the Names of God have the power to calm the mind, have the power to bring the mind to the right path. That's why in all religions it is said to chant the Name of God. Like I have said before, chanting the Name of God is like being in love with the Divine. The more you chant the Divine Names, the more the Love of God will reveal itself inside of you - not on the outside, but inside of you, the more you start to resonate the Divine Names, the more you start to have the Qualities of the Divine. It's all in the Divine Names. It could be so simple.

Take just the Name of Ram. We were singing before *Jai Raghunandana Jai Siya Ram, Janaki Vallabha Sita Ram.* We were just chanting the Name of Ram, no? It is said that through the mere chanting of *Ram Naam,* one can attain *Moksha,* one gets liberated, one is free from all karma. Such is the power of *Ram Naam,* such is the power of the Name of the Lord that it can instantly liberate you, *but* there is one thing: to get the full benefit of chanting the Divine Name, one has to chant it really sincerely. One has to chant it really wholeheartedly. At first, the chanting is just mechanical, but when one goes deeper into it, one loses oneself into the Divine Name and drinks the cup of Divine Love. Once you drink the cup of Divine Love, one sees the world completely differently, because this Love has nothing to do with how we understand love with our minds. This Love is pure nectar and to understand it, one has to drink it.

> Once you drink the cup of Divine Love, you will see the world completely differently. This Love is pure nectar, and to understand it, one has to drink it.

So, chant the Divine Names! All the thousands of Names of the Lord have equal power to release you from this karmic bond that you have created through many lives. And it's only through His grace that today you have been given a human body, so that you can achieve Him. This is the *dharma* of life. The *dharma* of your soul is to attain who you really are. Until you have reached that point of drinking the Cup of Love, don't renounce. No matter how beautiful and how tempting the outside could be, drink the Cup of Love. And see that there is another reality than this world – a reality that these physical eyes will never permit you to see. Krishna said in the *Gita* that a true *yogi* is *the one who sees Me everywhere - in the animals, in the trees, everywhere*, but you can't just see it like that. Even if you know it in your mind and say "Yes, the Lord is present everywhere", do you see it? No, not many people see it. To come to the point of seeing that, first, the base is to chant the Divine Names. Whatever Name you feel close to, chant it, chant until you become the Divine Name yourself.

And it is possible, I tell you. It is not something that is not possible. You just have to try it! If you try it, you will succeed in chanting the Divine Name with every breath you take during the day. You breathe 21,600 times in 24 hours and if you practice *consciously* during the day, chanting the Divine Names all the time with your breathing, you will be chanting even while you are sleeping. It will become an *Ajapa Mantra,* meaning, a mantra that is chanting by itself, it is not you chanting it, but it is chanting automatically inside of you. With each breath that you take in and out you will recite the Divine Name and you will transform yourself.

Firstly, you will transform inside. You will feel the joy, you will feel the freedom, the happiness inside of you and, of course, this will not just stay inside of you, but it will reflect also on the outside. You will become an instrument of this Divine Love, you will become an instrument of the Divine, so that you may become Divine yourself. You will realise this unity between you, which is the *Atma,* and God, which is the *Paramatma.*

But the *you* which is gross, on the outside, which is just made up of the *Pancha Tattva* – the five elements - will dissolve itself. This identity, which has been given to you when you were born, is that really you? To a certain degree of reality, yes, because whatever is created from the Lord is also real because He infuses Himself into everything, but this is not the Ultimate Reality. Only when this minimum reality - what you call reality and what the world itself looks at and says "that's real" - dissolves itself, the Ultimate Reality can reveal Itself inside of you.

So, practice! In simple words: chant the Name of God all the time and remember the Divine. Whatever you do, wherever you are, the Divine is with you.

FLOATING INTO DIVINE JOY

Darshan in Helsinki, Finland, 23 August 2010

I'm very happy to be here with all of you. It's true that when we sing some *bhajans*, not all of you understand, not all of you can sing because of the language, but one thing that everybody can do, is to clap their hands. To clap the hands, you don't need to sing, it's easy. What happens when you clap your hands? You know, on your hands there are lots of meridians. All these meridians are connected to certain inner organs, such as the heart, the liver, the kidneys... So, while clapping you are sending certain energy there and if one of these organs is sick, it releases it, so that this inner organ may function in a better way. That's why when you're happy you are always clapping the hands. Why when you are happy do you clap hands? It's because it generates, also, happiness and joy.

Everybody wants to be happy and everybody wants to be joyful, but there are two kinds of happiness and two kinds of joy. There is a certain joy that lasts only for a short while, a short-term happiness, but are you looking for that or are you looking for a longer happiness or a longer joyfulness? While chanting, when singing, you are expressing yourself also, by certain movements, which creates this inner joy and this inner joy is connected with Love.

So, you can find the simple joy everywhere, even on the corner of the street, because simple joy comes just from the limitation of things you find in the world. The easier you get it, the easier you lose it. Whereas the Eternal Joy is within you and you have to dig deeper inside of you. You have to unite your mind with your heart to find this Eternal Joy, to receive the grace of this Eternal Joy. The easiest way to find it is to sing, sing the Name of God, because while singing the Name of God you're happy and this happiness will awaken this Love.

You can talk about Love, but as long as you don't experience it or you don't feel it, it's difficult to understand. But if you really want to feel it, it's easy to feel it. You have to quiet this mind and awaken your heart and, when your heart is awakened, Love will flow. And in Love there is no difference, you know. It crosses all the barriers of difference. That's how God Loves and how human beings have to Love, but very often it's *very* difficult. We try our best to Love like that, but it's quite difficult, because there are so many things on the

> If you write the name of God inside your heart, what will happen? You will also float, but you will float in Divine Love, you will float in Divine Ecstasy, Divine Joy.

outside that disturb the mind, so many things that stop one from loving. But one should not to lose hope, one has to keep trying and trying and while you chant the Divine Names, this awakens this Love and makes you also strong.

There is a story in the life of Rama. Rama is the seventh incarnation of Vishnu. Once there was a demon, called Ravana, who kidnapped his wife, Sita. To rescue Her, Ram had to go to Lanka, which is Sri Lanka nowadays. So He had to make a bridge. All His companions brought stones and tried to build the bridge. Each stone, thrown in the sea sank. But Hanuman, the closest devotee of Rama, said "Why not write the Name of Sri Ram on the stones before putting them in the sea?" When they wrote the Name of Sri Ram on the stones and threw them in the sea, they didn't sink but started to float. This is how they built the bridge.

If a stone floats just by writing the Name of Ram, the Name of God, imagine if you write the Name of God inside your heart, what will happen? You will also float, but you will float in Divine Love, you will float in Divine Ecstasy, Divine Joy.

This Joy is the Eternal Joy, which everybody is looking for – it's not a joy or happiness that lasts only for a short while. The mind is always focused upon the outside, but we have to learn to turn the mind and gaze inside ourselves, see the Lord there and let Him reveal Himself. When you chant His Name, when you recite His Name, when you sing His Name, you're calling Him. You're calling to Him "Please, reveal yourself." Like Krishna said in the *Gita*: "I don't reside anywhere on the outside. I don't reside even in the heart of the people, but I reside where my glory is being sung."

The same thing is written in the Bible, "If two or three are gathered in my name, I shall be near to them." That means that when you sing the Name of God, you are calling, you're asking Him to awaken within you. You are asking Him to come to you and to reveal Himself to you. The more you do that, the more He will reveal Himself as this Love you will feel for Him. The more you long for Him, the more you will love to do your *sadhana*, the more your mind will be controlled and when your mind is controlled, when you have peace of mind, you are peaceful. So you will feel peace in your body and in your surroundings, you will be an instrument of this Divine Love, but you have to take this first step. Don't only contemplate on the outside, but contemplate within yourself and find God.

This reminds me that very often people are scared about the outside, they always look at what the outside thinks of them. This is the weakness of Man actually; always looking at others and forgetting about how they can change things.

That reminds me of a story where there was *a sannyasin, a sadhu*. He used to live just opposite a house where a prostitute lady lived. Every day the *sannyasin* looked at how many men visited this prostitute and he counted them. So one day he decided to go to the lady and said "Lady, you don't know how much you are sinning. For sure, you will go to hell for all the sin you are committing. You have to really repent and change your life." This poor lady, when she heard that, she was very alarmed and shocked. She was crying very bitterly, crying and repenting inside and feeling so bad when she heard how much sin she had committed. So she prayed to Maha Vishnu and said "Lord, forgive me, I didn't know how much sin I had committed." So she cried and cried, but as prostitution was her only means of living, she could not really change her life.

Seeing that even after talking to her she didn't change, the *sannyasin* was thinking and he said "For each person who visits her, I will put one stone in front of her house, just to show her how much she sins." After some time there was a big heap of stones, so he went to the lady and said "You see this big heap of stones; it's all your sin." Again, the lady was crying; every day she was crying and asked God sincerely for forgiveness.

It so happened that after this incident the prostitute lady died and, coincidentally, the *sannyasin* who was a *brahmin* also died. While he was waiting for who would come to get him, he was thinking that since he was a *brahmin*, the angels of God would come and take him. As he was waiting, he saw that the angels of God, of Maha Vishnu came and took the soul of the prostitute lady to *Vaikunta*, to Heaven and as for him, the God of the Dead came to get him and brought him to hell. So, out of protest, he started to scream, saying how unfair it was "I am a *sannyasin*, I am a *brahmin*, I spent my life praying to God, but the prostitute is going to heaven and I'm going to hell." At that, the servants of Maha Vishnu said "Well, whenever you accused her, she repented sincerely and asked God for forgiveness and she was chanting the Divine Names continuously in her heart whereas you, you were not contemplating the Divine, even if you were sitting and praying on the outside, inside your heart you were contemplating the sin that this lady was committing, so that's why you are going to hell.

In the same way, where you put your heart, there it shall be. That's what is said in the Bible. So if your heart is focused on the Divine, the Divine will always reside inside of you, in each part of you and you will start to radiate this Divine Love, give it to everybody and you become this instrument that I was talking of before. But if you concentrate on the negativity that you always see, because your eyes always perceive things that are not good, you will get trapped into this illusion. The only way you can really un-trap yourself is to surrender to the feet of God, and really say "Lord, take me."

Know that God is compassionate. He will hold you, He will carry you and He will always send help for you. That's how His Love is. So concentrate, not on the negative, but on the Divine and call Him within you. Don't be shy to chant the Name of God, don't be shy, because it is not about the others, it is about you and God.

GOD'S TUNE

Krishna Janmashtami at Shree Peetha Nilaya,
Springen, Germany, 2 September 2010

We are celebrating the Lord's birthday. You know the life of Sri Krishna, no? Yes. What does He show us actually? What happened five thousand years ago is still valid today, though, of course, we have to see it according to *this* time. In the life of Sri Krishna, you see that from early childhood He killed lots of demons, but actually, at that time, these demons were outside, whereas nowadays the demons have entered mankind and are inside. In the same way that He resides within the core of the heart, these demons reside in the core of the mind. These are different qualities that awaken in the mind.

That's why it is said that in this time it is easy to attain the Lord only through devotion, only through pure devotion, *suddha bhakti*. But if your devotion is fifty-fifty, He will not come out for that, you know. He hides Himself, because He knows that, if you're giving only half to Him that means later on, you will get caught up again on the outside. That's what I said last *darshan*: you start the spiritual way very excited, then later on, you gradually start getting less and less excited, but nonetheless you don't lose it completely. When you realise that you are going down, you do everything possible to rise again. In the same way, when a child falls down, he cries for some time, but then he tries his best to get up or the parents come and lift the child. It's the same with the Lord: He can't see any one of His children suffering, so even if you are falling down, He will

125

always be there to help you get up.

By calling Him, by chanting His Divine Name, you get more and more accustomed to Him. What is the Divine Name? It's the Name of God. So the more you chant God's Name, what happens? All this negativity that is in your mind gets dissolved. Of course, it doesn't happen just like that! It happens through practice, through years and years of practice. Some people, after practicing a year or two, say "OK, I don't see any results" and then they let go. Well, these people will not get anywhere; because they will move from one [practice] to the other, from this other to yet another one. This is how their life will carry on. It's like digging many holes, trying to look for water. If instead of digging just one hole and attaining the water, you dig ten holes, you will never get the water.

So, in the same way, when you start chanting the Divine Names, for the Lord to reveal Himself to you, you also have to prove yourself. Of course, everything happens through His Grace, nothing happens through your grace. Even moving, even for me to talk, it is possible only through His grace. But, as you have a mind, you have to prove that you *really* want to let go of this mind. So, by chanting His Divine Names, you start to call Him and the more you call Him, the more you are tuning yourself into *His* tune and the old you becomes less and less, until only His Grace starts to shine through. It's very simple. For example, when you start chanting Krishna's Name, at the beginning, you will feel tired about it, you will wonder what is happening and why is He not listening?" But actually, these are all different qualities that awaken, you see, even to be angry with Him, because you wish for Him. In the same way that you wish for Him, He wishes for you, much more. Let's say you get depressed or you think "Ok, I'm praying and all this, but He's not listening," but actually, this is His *Maya*, His game. When He doesn't show Himself, it is for you to long for Him even *more*. Of course, we can talk about it like this, but when you are in it, it is completely different. For you, it's as if the world is going upside down.

I was talking with somebody yesterday and this person said to me "Swamiji, I would love to see Krishna!" And then he reminded me of something that happened about twelve years ago, when he had the wish to see Krishna and He showed Himself to him, but because at that time he was not ready, I took this grace away from him. So yesterday he was telling me "Look, what happened twelve years ago, you took it away. I would love to see Krishna again I want it back!" And I said "What would you do to get this?" He said "Anything!" And I said to him "Are you *sure*?"

You see, it's easy to talk about, but when it comes to the act, when it comes to practise, it's difficult. Many people say "Yes, we love God", but how many really do everything so that this love may grow? Very few. Like the Lord said, "I can count them on my hand." Well, His hands are not like human hands, He doesn't have only one; He has many. So in the

> The more you chant the Divine Names, the more you tune yourself into this Divine Name, the more He starts to shine through you and the more He starts to act through you.

same way, the more you chant the Divine Names, the more you *tune* yourself into these Divines Names, the more the Divine starts to shine through you and the more He starts to act through you, of course, I am talking now about His qualities, not Him.

To get Him fully, you have to go deeper and deeper. It's the same as when you dig the hole: first you get a little bit of water, which is muddy, but the more you dig, the more you get water which is clearer. It's the same when people reach a certain degree of spirituality, they develop certain qualities. He gives them certain qualities, but the sad thing is that people get stuck to these qualities. They think they have already reached a very high level of spirituality, and they think of themselves as being everything. Then, of course, nothing [further] happens.

But whereas, when you forget about these qualities and don't give them too much importance but you go for Him, He will not be able to deny you His presence, He will even not be able to deny you Himself. The way you give yourself to Him, He will give Himself to you. It's so easy, actually, but yet, difficult for the mind to understand, no? You see, it's because everybody wants to understand how to do it. When I just say to chant the Divine Names, recite His Name, think of Him continuously, you say, yes, you will do it, but then what happens? If you analyse your day, very often you forget about Him. You actually forget about Him more than you think about Him. That's why it doesn't happen.

And, also, when you tell somebody to chant the Divine Names, they just chant mechanically. "Because Swamiji said to chant, let me chant it, chant it, chant it". No, it's not like this, because when you chant His Name, your mind has to have His vision also, you have to have His image in the mind. Of course, just to chant His Name, it's very good, it's better than nothing, but if you *really* want to achieve Him, chant His Name and visualise Him. Like He, Himself, said in the *Gita*, visualise Him in your third eye, visualise Him in your heart, visualise Him in each breath that you are taking in and out. Let's say you are chanting the *Maha Mantra*: *Hare Ram Hare Ram, Ram Ram Hare Hare, Hare Krishna Hare Krishna, Krishna Krishna Hare Hare.* You don't need to rush; you have all the time. When you have a party, you have all the time for that. It's the same thing when you take time to chant the Divine Names, you have to really take your time. Sit, chant and visualise Him sitting in your forehead, in your heart, in each breath that you take in and out, it's only Him. So the more you chant like this, the more you are aware that He is not outside of you, but He's inside of you. You will not just know it, you will start to *Realise* it. Then this identity that you always give to yourself, this I, I, I, will start to dissolve. It will become You, You, You. So it dissolves this ego identity and what is left is only Him.

THE JOY OF DANCING FOR GOD

Satsang in Bern, Switzerland, 23 May 2007

Often we think that we know God and we can always think that "God is like this and like that", but it's wrong. Each one has their own perspective of God and each one has their own way to achieve God. Some can just sing the Name of God and they will be in bliss and Realise God completely, but for some, they have to really strive, strive very deeply to achieve, to Realise God. So, each one is in his own level and that's why very often I say to people "Make your own experience about the Love of God." I can talk about the Love of God and you can read about the Love of God, but it's each one's own experience. When you make your own experience, even a small experience, you will feel great joy and great bliss and you will enjoy it!

(Note: Swami is singing with everybody but then stops and starts to explain the following)

When you sing for God and lift your hand up it means "Lord, we are drowning in this illusion; we are drowning in this *Maya*. We are lifting our hands up to You, so that You pull us out of *Maya*; so that You pull us out of this illusion and make us Realise ourselves and Realise that we are part of You, that we are Your children, that we are Your Divine Love." So I would like that all of you lift your hands up and cry to the Lord.

It's the same, you see, when somebody is drowning in the sea, he always lifts his hand out. Even if he is committing suicide, the hand is always up, expecting that somebody will pull him or her out.

Here in this *Maya,* we are all drowning and we are pulled deeper and deeper every day by this illusion, by this great illusion of Maya Devi. So call upon the Lord to pull you out of this illusion!

You will see when you dance, when you are moving, you keep your body fit. You are doing dancing *yoga,* and at the same time, you are doing *nama smarana,* you are singing the Name of God. God is so addictive. When you start singing and dancing His glory, you will always Love and dance, you will always want to sing His Name and dance continuously. You will not even get tired. You will forget about thirst. You will forget about hunger. You will forget about everything.

It's not the same dancing as when you go to the discotheque. In a discotheque you dance, dance, dance, and after sometime, you say "I have to go and eat; I'm hungry and I'm thirsty". Or you go home after dancing in the discotheque, what do you do? You throw yourself on the bed and you sleep, feeling very tired. Whereas with the Name of God, you can sing It all the time, you will not get tired and you can dance, you will not get tired.

> God is so addictive. When you start singing and dancing His glory, you will always Love and dance.

This reminds me that two weeks ago I was in Croatia and for seven days, every day, we sang and danced from morning, till late the next morning, until four o'clock or five o'clock in the morning. It was like this every day and it was so addictive, so beautiful.

On the last day of my visit, for *darshan,* there were six or seven hundred people. After *darshan,* we came back to the place where we were staying and there were about seventy people in the living room and we were sitting and singing all the time, we just had food and then we were again singing and dancing. We were singing the

Names of Krishna and Jesus, all the Names of God.

Then, before going to sleep, I was on a balcony, talking with someone and when I looked down, there was a lady who was trying to go to bed but she was going left and right and she was still singing the last bhajan that we had been singing. It was like she was drunk on the Divine Names. So I said to this person next to me "Look, what God's Love is doing, everybody becomes crazy in His Love." So I looked at him and I looked up in the sky – it was getting light, already – and I said "I am sure God is very happy seeing all of his children crazy like that!" And at that moment, the moment I said that, there was a big ball of light, blue light, which appeared, it split into two and went back again together and flashed everywhere. It was really amazing, you know. He was giving, in his own way, His approval "Yes, I am happy that all of you are drunk on this Divine Nectar."

(Note: Swami asks some people to show how to dance, then he talks again)

You see, it's very simple, you are doing a kind of yoga and at the same time you are doing namasmarana and at the same time the mind becomes less powerful. So it's really good.

You know, Christ was Love and this form [love] of Christ, we don't picture in Christianity anymore. When you look at icons or statues of Christ they look so miserable, but Christ was joy and that's how people follow His message of Love. Once I asked Him whether He was dancing, also. He said "Of course, I was dancing." In the Jewish tradition, of course, dance is one of the very important things and He gave me a vision of Him dancing. There is this song, *Lai Lai, Lai Lai, lai lai Lai Lai Lai* and I had a vision of Him and His disciples with arms over one another's shoulders and all of them were dancing in the same way you were dancing. Of course, you know, this part we don't see, it's not expressed. You have probably noticed that when you dance, you can't think about anything.

That's why when you look at the discotheques everybody goes crazy, because they can't think. But what is going on inside of them is different. When you're singing the Name of God, positivity goes inside of you, but when you sing something negative, of course, negativity will go inside of you because when you sing, all the *chakras* are opened up. Especially the heart *chakra* is open and only the Name of God can leave it open. Other things can't leave the heart open. That's why when somebody comes out of the discotheque, of course, they are very aggressive because there is the imprint of this negativity.

Whereas when you come from a *satsang* or when you come from *kirtans*, when you have just sung the Names of God, you want to be peaceful, you want to enjoy this Divine Love inside of you and when you dance and sing, you will feel more strength. After dancing, if I tell you to meditate, you will see that your concentration is much better than when you just sit and meditate. Try it at home.

So, it was lovely to be with all of you. I have emptied my heart, which was only about the Love of God, which is the most important thing in life.

THE POWER OF THE NAME OF RAMA

Satsang Retreat, Flüeli Ranft, Switzerland, 26 May 2007

We were just singing, *Sri Ram, Jai Ram, Jai Jai Ram, Vastu amolika, di mere Satguru,* meaning *I have received the secret of the Name of Rama. My Guru has explained to me the power of the Name of Rama, so I treasure it.* It is said that Rama Himself didn't know the power of His own Name.

Once Rama was with Hanuman and all the monkeys and they tried to build a bridge between India and Sri Lanka. They did their best. They would go near the lake carrying big, big stones and they would throw them into the sea thinking that it would fill up and they could walk across. Every time that they did that, the stone would, of course, sink. Then Ram decided "Let me, also, go and put a stone." So He went, took a stone and put it in the sea. He thought that if He put it in, it would float, but the moment the stone left His hand, it sank deep into the water.

So He called to Hanuman: Hanuman, come here for one minute. You know, I don't understand one thing. It is said that by singing my name the people will get liberation, but here, look, I can't even make a stone float, because at the moment I put the stone on the water it sinks. You know, Hanuman is considered as the Ocean of Wisdom, so He said to Rama: My Lord, with all my respect to You, I don't want to offend You, but I will tell you something. It is not Your fault, because the point is, as long as the stone is in Your hand, the stone will float, it is in safety; but the moment the stone leaves

Your hand, it sinks, of course! That's why, as a solution, Hanuman wrote on each stone the Name of Rama and they would float.

There is another story that shows again the power of the name of Rama. There was once a king who sinned a lot in his life. He knew that he would die soon, so he went to see a guru in one *ashram*, but when he went there, the guru was in deep meditation. So he waited and waited and waited, but the guru didn't come out of his *samadhi*. The king saw that the son of the guru was there, so he called him "Please, your father is in deep *samadhi* and I can't tell him to come out of it, so you tell me what to do. Look, I have spent my whole life hurting people and doing bad things, but now I realise that I have to change certain things in my life. Tell me how would I forgive myself for all this?"

The son thought for a while and said "Chant three times the Name of Rama and all your sins will be forgiven, but, of course, you have to chant it with faith. You can't just chant it with the mere mouth." The king was very happy. When the guru came back to himself, the son was very excited and said "Father, father, you know, the king came here" and he explained everything about why the king had been there. Then the father asked him "What did you tell him?" The son said "I told him to chant three times the Name of Rama with faith and that all his sins would be forgiven." The father got *very* angry at that moment and said "My son I curse you, because you don't even know how powerful the Name of Rama is. You didn't need to tell him to chant it three times, even *one* time would have been enough!"

CALLING GOD: SING WITH YOUR HEART

Darshan, Poland, May 2007

(Note: Everyone is singing and suddenly Swami stops and starts talking)

When you need something, especially when you are in an emergency, you have the courage and the strength to call "Hey you, Tom, bring me this! I need that!" Here you are singing the Name of God. You desperately want Self-Realisation, you desperately want liberation and you are calling to God. So let the strength from deep within come out and sing loudly. You'll see the more you sing loudly, the less there will be thoughts in your mind. The more you sing loudly, the more your heart will be open.

So don't be scared of singing and be happy. Don't be depressed. When you call God, you don't say, in a low voice, "OK, God, I'm calling you, come." He'll look at your face and get so scared, that instead of coming, He'll run away. As He is sitting in the middle of your heart, deep inside your heart, when you're calling Him to come, if you say "Come" like this, in a low voice, He'll say, "Oh, my goodness, he says 'Come', but he doesn't really want me." Instead of opening the door to your heart, He will close it. So sing!

THE GLORY OF PRAYER

Darshan at Cudrefin, Switzerland, 20 August 2010

I am really happy to be here with all of you. We'll be singing the glory of God. Some people may feel shy and be thinking "Oh, my voice is not good." But, it doesn't matter how you sing the Name of God. Even if your voice is not beautiful, for Him it is probably the most beautiful and it will not pain His ears. Actually, it's like a melody for Him. As it is said in the *Srimad Bhagavatam:* It doesn't matter how you chant My Name, how you recite the Name of the Divine. Some have a beautiful voice and some don't, but it's equal to Him. The main thing is that you chant, that you pray.

> **The main thing is to pray. Thats what transform you, what gives you inner glow!**

Prayer: that's what transforms people. Some people pray to find solace through prayer, some to attain the Lotus Feet of the Lord, some to achieve whatever they desire in life; but the main thing is to pray. That's what transforms you, what gives you this inner glow, so that you can call yourself spiritual. Humans are always on a search, they are always searching for something. Some people search in the outside world and some people search in the inside world, but only few really know the importance of prayer. In the *Ramcharitmanas*, Tulsidas said that the value of a stone is known only to somebody who knows about gems. Then they can value how precious the stone is. It's the same thing when somebody knows the glory of prayer, the glory of chanting the Divine Names, they know the value of it.

Once there was a *Guru*, who gave a stone to a disciple and said to the disciple "Go to the market and have it valued at different stalls, but don't sell it to anyone. Then, return the stone to me."

So, first he went to a potato seller and showed him the stone. The potato seller said "OK, I will give you two bags full of potatoes for that stone." The disciple answered "OK, but first I have to ask my Guruji because he told me not to sell it."

So he went onto the next stall. The stall was for clothing. There he asked again "How much would you give for this stone?" So the man said "That's a beautiful stone. I can make beautiful jewellery for my daughter. So I will give you 100 meters of cloth for this stone."

Then he went to a jeweller who was looking at the stone and he said "Well, I will give you twenty kilos of gold for that stone." Again the disciple said "But my Guru said not to sell it." As he said that he would not sell it to him, the jeweller asked him "Do you know what this stone is?" "No", replied the disciple. Then the jeweller said "It's a very precious stone, where did you get it? A simple man like you with such a stone! For sure you have stolen it from somewhere." So, he brought it to the king and the king said "For that stone I will give you my whole kingdom."

Of course, he was a bit shocked. Just for a stone, first someone would give only a bag of potatoes, then some cloth, then some gold, and now, the king would give the whole kingdom. Then he said to the king "But I can't give you the stone, because my Guruji has said not to sell it to anyone and to bring it back." And, then he said, "What is your Guruji's name?" He said the name of his Guru. They called the Guru. He was well known in this place and everybody respected him. Then, when he got the stone back, he explained to his disciple "Well, whoever knows which stone this is, they know the value of it."

The king recognised that the stone was not a normal stone, it was the philosopher's stone, the touchstone, which can turn everything into gold. So it is the same with prayer, which can turn all your life into gold, it can turn all your negativity into purity. That's why it is said: Whoever recites my Name at the time of death, all their sins are forgiven. But it is not that easy to recite the Divine Names if you don't practice it. It's only by regularly practicing chanting the Divine Names that you can really remember the Divine Names at the time of passing to the other side.

> Prayer can turn all your life into gold. It can turn all your negativity into purity.

Like I said before, through prayer, you can distinguish spiritual people from people who are not so spiritual. There is spirituality everywhere, but in different ways. In spirituality you radiate, you glow and the more you chant the Divine Name, the more you start to reflect the qualities of the Divine, the qualities of love, compassion, joy, happiness, calmness. You start to reflect all these Divine qualities, through prayer, through the chanting of this Divine Name. So you start to become like the Divine and you don't need to say this joy to somebody, you don't need to express to somebody that you are happy. This joy that you will have inside of you will reflect itself.

It's the same when you take the lives of Saints. Take the lives of Meerabai, Bhakta Prahlad or any Saints who have attained the Divine, they glow with this light of the Divine. The Love of the Divine reflects through them. So, they don't need to talk about God, but they just need to be around. It's the same with all of you: The more you chant the Divine Names, the more the Divine will start to reflect on you. Then, you can call yourself spiritual, because when you become spiritual, all the negative qualities are removed from you, all the negative *karma* that you have created through many lives before gets removed. And the joy takes place – the joy of serving, the joy of really being here, the joy of trying to attain the Lord. When this joy starts to appear in you, the more you attune yourself to the Divine, but *you* have to take the first step, because the Divine is already there, He's waiting for you and the moment when you take the first step, He will just shine through you.

So, when we were singing earlier, maybe some thought "I feel shy to chant. What will people think? What will my neighbour think?" It's not about what your neighbour is thinking, you know. It's how *you* think. You know what I noticed: that many people think about what other people think of them. That way, you will never be free. If you always think 'What is he thinking about me or what is she thinking about me?' how can you be free? Your mind is always busy thinking about what others are thinking! But your mind always has to be busy with the Lord, with God. This is how you will find peace. In this world, nowadays, you see that not many people have this peace, because their mind is not on the right way. People may have everything in this world, but yet, if they don't find peace, if they don't find happiness inside of them, nothing else on the outside can make them really happy, because whatever happiness comes from outside lasts only for a short time. After that, again there is the same drama.

So, try to find this inner happiness, this inner freedom. It's not far away, you know, it's here inside of you. When you take your first step through prayer, through chanting, the Divine will run to you. And, it is possible to attain Him. Open up the mind, surrender it to Him and let the Love which you have inside of you flow. If you have not yet attained this Love, do everything to attain it, because that's who you are and that's why you are here.

DIVINE NAMES

JUST LOVE

HUMILITY

Be humble like a Child,
and then you shall enter the
Kingdom of God.

Jesus Christ

MAKING THE BIG BEAST HUMBLE

Darshan in Steffenshof, Germany, 30 January 2008

Today is the *Samadhi* of Gandhiji. Many people take him as an example. Many great people take him as an example for what he did for the world, but above all, when you go deeper into his life, you see that he was a model of *bhakti*. He was a model of devotion. Whatever he was doing, he forgot about himself. He was devoted to the people, to his country.

It's not just that he wanted to make his country free, but he showed a way to free the country through non-violence. The basis of non-violence is Love and that's the greatest thing. Without Love there is no non-violence, there is no peace. Of course, his life was not only joyful. He had lots of tribulations; there were lots of tests on the way that he had to go through. We know how he died, but yet, even at the time of death, he forgave [his killer]. He said "Let him be free. He did it out of ignorance, let him be free."

We have to take such a life as an example. Of course, we can't do what Gandhi came here to do. But however little, each one of us can participate. Each one can become a model of devotion and peace. And for that, you have to cultivate humility. Of course, he had fame, names, everything, so that he could have put himself very high up, but yet, he put himself the lowest of all. He had a great simplicity. Such is the life of masters.

Like I said on *Guru Purnima*, very often we see Masters high up and people say "Oh, they are very high. We are here to serve them!" It's not *you* who are serving the Master, but the Master who is serving you, all the time. Whether you know it or you don't know it, it's the Master that is serving you. The Masters don't come here for themselves. They come to lift you all up. So by taking the example of the life of saints, taking the example of the life of great ones, we learn a lot. We learn how to develop selfless Love, unconditional Love and humility.

People will say "Swamiji, you talk about humility, but how do we cultivate it?" I tell you, it's really so simple, it's the simplest thing that you can do. Love is there in the heart, but humility is in the mind. How to make this mind, which is so ferocious - this big beast - how to make this mind be humble? We always say that it's our mind, but we don't say we *are* the mind, do we? The truth is that the mind is something apart from man. Man is the master of the mind. Man is the master of all the negative qualities that emerge from the mind, but the illusion from the mind is so great that it seems that they are the master. So to remind the mind continuously who is the master and to build up humility, I am not telling you to flagellate yourself every time you have a thought, no, but flagellate the mind with the Divine Names and always remind the mind that it's God that does everything, He's the cause of everything, every thought is Him. Whenever the mind becomes negative, remind it continuously "Mind, it's not you, it's only the Lord himself. It's only God. If God didn't allow you to think, where would you get the power to think?!"

> How will we make this mind, which is so ferocious - this big beast - how will we make this mind humble?

In the *Gita*, Krishna said, "If the Lord doesn't allow the leaves to move, the leaves will not move." Even if there was a great wind blowing, the leaves would not move. Such is the power [of the Lord.] So if He who governs everything is inside of each one of you,

He's seated in each one's heart equally, how come we forget about Him?

Train the mind to remember that it is not this pride, it is not this big I, which is the ego, the *me, myself* [who is acting]. Transcend this pride and say "God, it's You" and continuously talk to Him whether you have an answer or not. Whether you hear from Him or not, it doesn't matter. Deep inside know that He's listening. From time to time He will give you a hint. From time to time He will give you a sign in the outside that he's listening. And rejoice in this sign; look at this sign and say, "Yes, He's with me."

But, don't let pride rise inside of you. If you are on the spiritual path and you want to Realise God, let go of pride because pride will attack everybody whether it's a Saint or not but the saint knows how to have pride under control. I always gave an example of the huge elephant roaming in the market place. If the mahout doesn't control the elephant with his feet and the stick, what will happen? The elephant will take everything from left to right; he will break everything on his path.

And such is this huge pride that if we let it control us, it will take left and right. Then there's no control, but when you have the control over it and say "God is the Master", Love will generate. Love will grow. And you will see that the love with pride that you know will become a different kind of love and you will experience Unconditional Love, you will love the same way the Divine loves.

You will experience this Love because you are part of the Divine. The Divine is seated in each one of you. So if He can love like that, you also can love the same way. If He can be humble, you also can be humble. Christ was so humble that He even accepted the Cross. Krishna was so humble that he accepted to be the charioteer of Arjun. If these Divine Incarnations, these Avatars, great *Mahavatars*, are so humble, who are we not to be humble? We have to be more humble than them! It's true that they have everything, yet they're humble.

It reminds me of what Ramakrishna once said about a lady. This lady used to clean the roads and she was very humble and quiet. One day she got a few gold pieces of jewellery as presents. I tell you, she became so arrogant! She was speaking to people in this way "Hey, you! Move away from here! What are you going to do?" If such a little piece of gold can make somebody become like that, imagine the pride when people know a little bit about the Divine. Very often such pride arises when people read and they think they know God. They read one or two books and they think they know everything.

> To realise the Love of God you have to live it; you can't read it.

I tell you something: to realise the Love of God, you have to live it; you can't read it. To realise devotion, *bhakti,* you have to live *bhakti.* Then you can have just a glimpse of this Love. I tell you something more: Even a glimpse of this Love is a lot for this body. Try your best always to achieve this Love, because this is the only reality. All we think, as real, all these things are just an illusion and will fade with time. The body is an illusion; with time it will grow old and disappear but yet, the reality of the *Atma* will stay.

How many people really arrive in a lifetime to the point of realising the *Atma Swarupa* - the real form of the *Atma*? We know, because we have read in books, about the *Atma*, about the soul, but how many really realise it? Do you want to Realise God? Be truthful towards yourself, you don't need to answer me, I don't need to know, I don't need to judge anybody. It is not by saying "Yes" to me that it will happen. I will help a little bit, yes, but the major part I leave it up to you to do, also.

AT THE FEET OF THE FATHER

Good Friday, Chapel Shree Peetha Nilaya
Springen, Germany, 10 April 2009

(Note: After reading some parts of the Gospel, Swami starts his talk).

So, in this reading of the Gospel you see the Crucifixion of Jesus, but before the crucifixion, He had given many commandments to His Disciples. Above all, the commandment that He gave to the Disciples was to love. How many times in this small piece [of the Gospel] has He been talking about Love? Many, many times He spoke about Love in it. And He also shows the non-duality, the non-duality of the Self, of being One with the Father. Because we are bound by the dualistic aspect of the body, we are limited. He even said it: Whoever loves me, they are with me and I am with them; they are with the Father and the Father is with them. So if they are with the Father, the Father is with them, there is no duality. That means that whoever loves, is One with God. But this word 'Love', very often we take it for granted.

We are like little Judases who love God for His gifts, who love God always *for* something. Ask yourself how many times do you *really* love God for the sake of loving Him and not for asking anything? Always we ask God for something, but He is not bound by anything. He is not saying not to ask. He says ask, yes, until you really ask what you are here for. And you are here to realise this Love. And when you realise this Love that you have inside, you transcend everything and all becomes One, there is no duality that separates you from the Father.

All the practices that you are doing, your meditation, your *Kriya*, all you are doing is for what? It's to realise your Self, no? But many people think they are Realised and become very arrogant and they are the ones who judge everybody, they are the ones who say "Oh, this is right; this is wrong." In this part of the Gospel, Jesus said: The Father is present everywhere, in everything. It is not up to me to say it, but you will know about it. If you just take this part of the Gospel and meditate only on that, you will have the whole truth in it – especially about Love. I also always talk about Love, Love, Love. It is true that the world doesn't yet know about it, but yet, all of you who are spiritual, all of you who are searching for the truth, you are working for that,. It is not outside, it is here inside of you, but *you* have to want to change. You have to really say "Yes, I want to change." Like He said, "Even if you want to change, the world will be against you."

How many times do you *really* love God for the sake of loving Him and not asking anything?

It's perfectly true! Look at your life, when you took the spiritual path, how many people became against you – firstly, in your own family? So, it is normal. The more you advance towards the light, the more the others will be jealous, because inside everybody wants that.

Everybody wants to be with the Father. Everybody wants to be close to the Divine, but yet, they don't want to make any effort. They don't want to make any change to their life. They want to get everything happily and for free. So if you want this really and sincerely, then be sincere towards yourself and ask the Father, ask God and you will have it. It's simple.

If you are sincere towards yourself, you are more free and you will enjoy it. Whenever you pray, whenever you sit for meditation, whenever you chant, you'll be more free, because you are not bound by any guilt. The guilt is symbolised in the Holy Gospel as Peter. He was very guilty for so many things. Actually, we constantly see our own mistakes and with the guilt that we amass on ourselves, we limit ourselves.

We speak very big, big words, because it is so beautiful for the mind. We have read in the books these beautiful experiences, yes we know it through books but experience it! It's for everybody to experience and it is not limited. If you *really* want it, you will experience it.

You will see that in this small piece we read right now there is so much similarity to Hinduism. The washing of the feet, actually, is not a Jewish tradition, this is a very Hindu tradition and it's to show humbleness. Jesus said, it is not about washing the body outside, but it's the inside that you have to wash. But the washing of the feet is symbolic. As you know very well, everything is present in the feet. All the organs that are inside the body are connected in the feet. So, by washing the feet, He washes the inside, also.

You see how important the feet are. When you go to the Hindu Temple, the first things you see are the feet of the Deity. The first thing that you do is to bow down to the feet. When you go to the Master, you bow down to the feet. So you bow down to the greatness, you bow down to the Divine inside, you bow down to the Father within the Teacher. And that is what Christ said. He said it word for word. I don't even need to say anything about it. I don't even need to comment on it, it's very clear! This non-duality of God within yourself is so clear on the way to God Realisation, Self Realisation, but you will not reach God-Realisation, Self-Realisation, with pride. You will not reach it being very arrogant. You will reach it only when you are humble, and He said, "People will be against you. You know where you are going and you know why." So meditate on that.

Glory be to the Father, the Son and the Holy Spirit, now and to the ages of ages. Amen.

VENERATION OF THE DEAD

Good Friday, Chapel Shree Peetha Nilaya
Springen, Germany, 10 April 2009

So, today is the day where the dead are venerated. The veneration of the dead is not only found in Christianity where in the West family members go to the tomb of the deceased, but also you will see that many religions, also ancient religions have a lot of respect for the dead. In Hinduism actually, the dead are well respected and also their memory is well respected. Krishna said in the Gita, "It's only through them that all of you are here."
When you are born into a family, you are bound by certain karma towards that family, as well as towards the descendants. So you keep the memory of the dead in honour of them, to show also your respect, to show how much they mean to you and so that they help you. Of course, they are dead and they are maybe born again but you see, the eternal souls that were inside of them, even if they are born again, *still* can bless you, can help you in your spiritual advancement. And also, they can share their knowledge with you. That is why the dead are very important. So Christ has shown that we should not be scared of death, but many people think it is a terrible thing and that we have to fear it. Actually, it's not to be feared. Realise that you are eternal, realising that the Light, which you have inside, your Soul, your Spirit, is part of God Himself, so it is eternal.
Christ said, "I am the Way, the Truth and the Light. There is no one who goes to the Father without passing by me." This means that

we have to become like Christ. We have to become the children of God. We have to become the sons and daughters of God, so that we can rise from this just human nature to the Divine state. When we become the Truth, when we become the Light Itself, we can attain the Father. We can raise the inside, which is the pureness of the Father, so it can be exalted, it can be radiated through us. And in *this* glory, in the Divine aspect of your true Self, there is no judgment. There is just pure Love.

By His death and resurrection, Christ, like all the great Saints and like all the *Devas,* also, who have shown that, to reach that state one has, above all, to be humble. One has not to be bound by pride and ego. And only when one is humble, can one attain the Father. Only when one loves the way Christ has shown us to love, like all the Saints have shown us, one can really attain God.

> Actually, it's not to be feared realising that you are eternal, realising that the Light, which you have inside, your Soul, your Spirit, is part of God Himself, so it is eternal.

So many people do things always with pride and judgement and they will never reach God. Very often you will see that many of these people who always judge, think of themselves as being very spiritual and think highly of themselves. And this is how pride makes us think that we are very important and that we are very special. *Everybody* is special. We all carry the same Light, so all are special, but some can shine it and some can't, though they have it, they have the same Light. So, the death [and resurrection by Christ] of Lazarus is showing us that we all carry this Light and that we all can make things happen.

It is not only about us, but also about helping other people, but we have to will it, we have to really want it. And all of you will say one thing "Yes, we want it, but it is not happening." It will not happen, because your want has so much pride inside, so much ego "only for me, only me", then you will say "But if I have it, then I can give it". I'll tell you one thing: if you have it, you will never give it, because you think that when you have it, then you will give it, but the moment you have it, you will disappear! So we think that we ourselves know best, but only God knows best. He knows when to give and He knows what to give and to whom to give.

What we can do is to just purify ourselves, always. If we have not purified ourselves, it's very difficult. If we have not purified, firstly, our mind, it is very difficult. Like Swami Shivananda said "One of the main steps on the spiritual way is self-purification, is purification of the mind, and when the mind is pure, you can go slowly, step by step. You don't need to run. Let everything come to you, because if you run, you will fall, you will hit yourself, your feet will hurt, and you will badly fall down. But if you go slowly, God will help you, the Divine Mother will help you."

The Gospel is showing how important death is. It is showing how important it is to have reverence for all the people who have died: your mother, your father, your grandfather, your grandmother, etc. They can help you because they are probably on the other side, they have risen to the other level, if they were good. So they can intercede next to Him and say "Help them down there."

Why do we pray to the Saints? Of course, they are dead and we go to the *Relic* Chapel with all the dead and all the bones there and we are thinking 'Why are all these bones here?', but the bones carry the spirit of the Saints, they carry the Holy Spirit. Like Saint Augustine said "the Saints, they are the movable temples of the Spirit." Remember in the Bible, Christ said "you can say something against me, you can say something against the Father and you will be forgiven, but if you say something against the [Holy] Spirit", you will never be forgiven. So, the bodies of the Saints carry this vibration of the [Holy] Spirit.

In the Orthodox Church they really have great veneration for the Saints and they know how important it is to venerate them. That's why when you go to the Orthodox Church, if you go to Egypt, to Greece, or to Russia, you will see that the veneration of the Saints is very, very important and that they have great respect, really great veneration for the dead. But if you go to certain churches, especially in the West, you can remove a lot of dust from them, because they don't care.

(Note: Swami asks one of the residents to relate an experience and she says: "Last week, in the antique market, a man was throwing away all the bones and he said that he just cared about the artistic point of view of the object, and the relic was not important.")

So you see, they just throw them away without any respect, without any veneration. Why are these things in the antique shops? It's because the Church has thrown them away, you know. The Saints will help, when you ask them for help. You see, all the Saints are still doing lots of healing and lots of miracles when people go to visit their tombs, because they are present, even if they have been dead for a long time. For sure, the Saints have incarnated again, many more times and the Spirit of God which is inside of them, the Spirit that has risen to Christ Consciousness is *still* present. You can't kill it, nothing can burn it and not even time can destroy it.

Glory be to the Father and the Son and the Holy Spirit, now and to the ages of ages. Amen.

LOVE AND HUMILITY

Darshan in Springen, Germany, 25 April 2009

Someone suggested that I talk about Love and death – interesting themes actually, because what does always come together with Love? It is humility. Love and humility go together. When there is Love, there is humility and something dies at that moment. What is it? It is the pride, the egoism. In the presence of Love there is no egoism, there is no pride.

So the questions arise, "How can I be humble? How can I awake this Love? How can I awake this humility inside?" Because we are hanging so much onto this big ego or pride, we always say *I, mine* and *me*. Have you ever counted how many times in a day you use these words? If you were to count them, you would scare yourself. It's a lot of times! It's true that we have different *I's*. There is the *I* of the ego and there is the *I* of the Self, but most often, what our mind first understands is the *I* of egoism. And with this *I*, it's very difficult to awaken Love. Even if Love awakens, it gets diluted with the power of the mind. The ego is *so* strong.

And with this "I", it's very difficult to awaken Love. Even if Love awakens, it gets diluted with the power of the mind. The ego is so strong.

It's true that to achieve realisation, to achieve God, we have to be humble, but there is one problem. Very often, when someone thinks of himself as being humble, he starts to say "I am very humble." These people are very proud people. What is this called? This is the ego of humility and the pride of humility. Actually, it's very difficult to be humble, but it's not impossible.

Have you heard about a great Persian Sufi poet called Saadi? You should read about him. His poems are very beautiful. There is an incident in his life, which marked him very much and which made him completely humble throughout his whole life. One day he went to the mosque with his father for an all-night vigil. It's when you pray the whole night. So they were all sitting in the mosque with the *Mullah* and they were praying and praying.

In the middle of the night everybody dozed off, everybody was falling asleep; even the *Mullah* was falling asleep. Then Saadi went near to his dad's ears and whispered "Dad, only me and you are keeping vigil. All of them are sleeping." At that moment his father became annoyed and angry with him and told him off, saying "It's better to sleep and not to keep the vigil all the night than to judge others and consider oneself more superior than anybody else." At that moment, Saadi realised that one has to always be humble and he took the decision that nothing should ever come between him and his humility. So he became very, very humble.

It's easy to talk about humility, but sometimes difficult to practice, because we are so bound by our pride that makes us perceive ourselves to be above everybody else. If we really want to change something, if we really want to let go of this pride, it will happen, but first we have to want it. We have to say "Yes, I want it!" and not superficially. Many people say "Yes, I want it, Swamiji. I try my best to get rid of it, but it's not leaving me!" But it's not that it is not leaving you, but *you* are not leaving it. This is the difference, you know?

When one is humble, one will not even care about putting oneself completely down and regarding everybody else higher. This is the beginning of how to learn to be humble, to learn to put yourself down and say that everybody else knows better than you. Keep repeating to yourself, keep reminding yourself of that and you will learn from everything and from everyone. That's true humility.

Have you heard about the *Baha'i* faith and the prophet Baha'u'llah? He used to say to his disciples "If you find in a person nine bad vices and one good thing, forget about the nine bad ones and think about the good one." But what do you always do? You judge. You have to cultivate Love for all. Then you can really be humble and you will see: it's very easy to get rid of it; it's easy to put it away. But it all depends on your sincerity when you say "Yes, I want to change; yes, I want to be humble." Don't just say superficially that you want to be humble because you have read about it and, when you meet someone who offends you, you fire this person. No, learn. Learning will never finish. Like the great saints say, from day one until the end you will learn, because there are so many things in this world to learn about. And there are so many beautiful things. There is so much beauty around and inside of you, but you have to take time and see it. If your mind is always running forward and your body is running backward, you are missing a lot. So calm the mind. It is only in the stillness that you will find relief.

That's why you meditate, no? Why do you think you meditate? Why do you think you practise your Sadhana? Is it to get a note saying: I have practised *Kriya*. I have practised this meditation or that meditation? No, it's not about that. It's about Realising your Self, about becoming this true Self, and to become that true Self, the easiest way is to be humble and be loving to all.

LEARNING HUMILITY AND UNITY

Holy Thursday in the Chapel of Shree Peetha Nilaya
Springen, Germany, 1st April 2010

In the bad times you have nobody, because even your good friends they don't want to partake of the suffering. But in good times they all sit with you and gather with you, singing, dancing joyfully. We all know that very well, isn't it? Well, this is life actually. Each one is very egoistic, looking out for herself or himself.

Even if they are among a teacher, they don't know the glory of it; they don't know the blessing of it. And then afterwards when they read in the books they will say, "Oh, how great it was, to be among this teacher." But this is in everyday life, we see it everywhere. When people are near a teacher, they always judge the teacher. Actually they are not judging the teacher, they are judging their own Self. The teacher is a mirror to yourself, so that you can learn something. But, if you are stupid, you will never learn it, because even if the teacher gives you the lesson a hundred times, the stupidity in your mind will blind you completely.

Christ did *so many* wonders but yet the disciples were all blind with pride, were all blind with fear, to the point to deny Him, to the point to betray Him. Even when they came to get Him, He didn't react. He knew that the Will of God is the most important thing. He surrendered to the Will of God. The Master surrendered to the Will of God and did what God told him to do. Even in death, he accepted it happily. And he said, "As I, the shepherd is being led for the sacrifice, the sheep will be scattered." He already predicted it, but indirectly. He already said everything to them, but they were *so* blind to themselves that they couldn't hear it.

Know one thing, a Master will never say directly, "You are stupid. You stupid man, do it like this, like this, like this." Sometimes they do, but most often, they give hints only. If you are clever enough you will get it, if you are not clever enough you will not get it. Like that, he has given many hints to them. He has said to them so many times that the son of men will be betrayed and will be lead to crucifixion, but yet they didn't understand anything.

In this Gospel, we see also the beauty of Christ, how he humbled himself down. He humbled himself by washing the feet of the disciples and when Peter said, "No, Lord, I don't want that you wash my feet." Christ said, "If I don't do it, you will not have your place with me in Heaven." Then Peter said, "Then, wash my head and wash my hands also." Then Christ said, "No need for that, because when I wash your feet, I wash the whole body."

This is very symbolic, because in the Hindu Tradition the feet are considered the most blessed of all. That's why, whenever you go to a Temple, whenever you bow down to the Deity, to the Master, whatever, what do you do? You bow down and touch the feet, because the feet are the source of all the powers that the Master has. That's why just by touching the feet of the Master one receives the blessing and also shows reverence and humility. He said, "What I have done to you, all of you have to do it also. All of you have to humble yourselves. All of you have to be ready to *lower* yourselves. In the Gita, Krishna said, "If you want to realise me, you have to be *more* humble than a dry grass." If we look at a dry grass, we see that it is always bent downwards. So if you want to be humble, you have to be even more bent down than that. And Christ has shown it by washing the feet of the disciples, he has shown humility. He is one with God, he has realised the Unity with the Father, the Father sent him, but yet he showed this humility to all the people. To be able to understand, to be able to realise God one has to be humble. Without being humble you can forget about it.

Very often spiritual people *think* they are humble. Actually, they have spiritual pride of humility. They *think* they're humble, but when they really have to act in a humble way, it is completely the opposite. It is not about judging anybody, but it is about each oneself-analysing *where* one can change, *what* one can change, how one can serve one's brothers and sisters. How one can reach the point to say, "Okay, let's forget a little bit about I, I, I, but let's think about 'us', 'we'."

Imagine if your right hand starts to do something that is not in communion with your whole body. What will happen? It will be chaotic, no? Imagine if my hand starts moving left, right, now. What would happen? I would not be able to be here, to talk with you to do my work properly. Imagine if one of my eyes would be up and the other eye wanted to do something else, nothing would work. It's only when every part of your body works together in unity, when each one is doing its own function, each one is doing its own duty, own *dharma*, that there is perfect unity.

To be able to understand, to be able to realise God, one has to be humble.

The same in one family, all work together to make one family. In a community, it's the same thing, but at the same time each one has to do one's own duty. That doesn't mean that people in the community cannot come together. They can come together, make the community one family, that's what unity is, coming together. But if one starts working against each other, then it will be chaotic and problems will arise. And this is the weakness.

I have given many examples. Last year, also, I told a story about a teacher who knew that his time to leave his body was coming near. But looking at his disciples, he saw that they were all fighting against each other, because each one wanted to take the place of the teacher. So seeing that, the teacher thought for a while and said, "Okay, all of you go in the forest and bring a sixty centimetre stick." So all of them went, and all the twelve disciples came back and said, "Here Master, we brought the wood." So the teacher took the sticks and started to break them one by one. Then, he called one of his disciples, gave him a stick and asked him to break it. So the disciple took the stick and of course it broke. Then the teacher tied all the remaining sticks into a bundle, called his disciples and said, "Now break it." Because they were all tied together, no one could break it! The same thing, if everyone is together one can do anything, but if one is against each other, then nothing will work.

> It's only when every part of your body works together in unity, when each one is doing its own function, each one is doing its own duty, own *dharma*, that there is perfect unity.

So in this Gospel, Christ also showed the humbleness that we all have to have towards each other, the understanding towards each other, the Love towards each other. Love *is* there, but very often understanding is not there. Christ also showed his all-knowing Self, He showed that He knew everything, He knew what was happening and what will be happening in advance, but He had also to fulfil what was written in the scriptures, what God said to the prophets. Among the disciples, many of them were expecting that Jesus would raze everything and build up something new. And as it didn't happen according to their expectations, they felt bad. That's why Judas went and betrayed Christ. The disciples expected that He would do this and He would do that, but yet Jesus knew what His work was. He knew His duty. He knew why He had incarnated and He did his job accordingly. But yet the disciples didn't know what their duty was. They thought they knew, but when they realised their mistake, it was too late.

Actually, it happens very often to everybody, it is not only to the disciples of Jesus. Whenever you go to a Master, to a teacher, you go there and in your mind you already expect certain things. You already create in your mind, "Oh, the teacher will do this and this and that for me, he will tell me this and this and that to flatter me." So, you already create it in your mind, but if in your mind you already have something created, you already expect something, even if the Master talks to you ten times, you won't hear anything. Easy example: Last week, while I was travelling, somebody called me and asked me something. For half an hour I explained to that person: "Please don't do this." But the person would not listen. What can you do? You can't do anything, no? So, I said, "Look, I can't do anything. I can just pray for you." And the person did, what I told her not to do. Of course, the result was not what the person expected. But this is how it is, you know? People always think that they know better. But, if you know better, then why you ask? If you don't know, then you can ask and you can receive, Ask if you can take the answer, accept it and change, but if you can't, don't ask! If you are not ready to change, don't ask. What is the use of asking?

Even 2000 years later, it's the same thing with disciples, *nothing* has changed! The same betrayal, the same procedure. When I read this part of the Gospel and let's say, I look at my own life, it's so similar. That's why while reading it, I was laughing about it. Every year, when I read that, I laugh, because it is exactly like that. And people will not change, like I said, as long as they don't *really*, *sincerely* want to change. Only when you say to yourself "I *really* want to change," not to the Master, not to God, not to anyone, but to *yourself*, "*I* want to change!", then you will change. Then you will develop this energy, this power inside of you, where *really* you will change.

Know one thing, the world now is different from the world 20 years ago. 2000 years ago and now *is* also different and the next few years coming will be different again. When we look at nature, Mother Nature is reacting in such a way that it's not pleasant to see. But when we look at humans, the way they are reacting is even *worse* than unpleasant to see. So it's time to change our mind, to change the way we see things, it's time to look at ourselves and ask, "What can I change. What am I willing to change?"

You have to *really* want the Love of God. Why I said 'really want the Love of God', is because many people put on the tag 'I love God', but really, they don't. They just want the quality of God. They want only to get and get and get from God, but they don't want to really receive the manifestation of the Lord, of the Divine within themselves.

And I tell you, if people don't want to change, Mother Nature will make them change. Sometimes, if they don't want to change in a certain way, nature reacts in another way, that can be painful sometimes, but that creates change.

So, with this Gospel, let us learn to become humble like Christ, let us learn *sincerely* to *love* one another. Let us learn to be in unity with each other. Let us build one family. Like we said in Hinduism, *Vasudeva Kutumbakam*, which means, *the whole world is one whole family*. And peace can come firstly within you and then, through you to everybody but only when you are in unity together. When you work with each other together, you will be stronger. But if you work against each other, you will be the weak one while all the others will work together.

HUMILITY

JUST LOVE

DEVOTION

O God,
Grace me with Love of You,
and to love those who love you,
and to love whatever brings me
nearer to You.

Prophet Muhammad

THE STORY OF AHILIA

Darshan in Fatima, Portugal, 7 February 2010

Right now we are in the time of preparing for Shivaratri, which is the Great Night of Lord Shiva, so we will just sing one *bhajan* and then we will start the *darshan*. So, like I always say, please, participate together, even if you don't know the words, because sound and light, these are two things that our mind runs towards. And if you want peace of mind, let it run behind the Name of God. You see, the Name of God is a mystery. Even to great saints, the Name of God is a mystery. Like it is said in the *Gita*: 'Not even the greatest of saints can understand My Name', so imagine the power that the Name has.

Why do we see saints emphasise meditating? What does one see in meditation? In meditation, when the mind is calm, you have a contact, personal contact with the Divine, not outside, but within you. And this inner contact is the most wonderful and the most powerful contact that you can ever have. Through many generations in life men have been searching, but being born as humans, we are bound by *runanubandhana*, which is, in short, *karma*. We are bound by certain things that we have done, deeds that we have done in previous lives that don't let us be free. Of course, you can run to many places, but if you don't take the time to run within yourself, all the places that you run to outside will be of no use.

It is said: "If you take a bath in the Ganges or other Holy Rivers, you get purified of one birth." But when you are bathed in the Divine Name, whatever Name, whatever Deity you feel close with – the

Name of Jesus, Muhammad, Rama, Krishna, Devi – if you get bathed in that Divine Name, you are released from many births. Misery is removed just by chanting the Divine Name. Liberation is granted just by realising the connection that you have with the Divine within you. This is where *Kriya* comes from. When you do *Kriya*, what you experience is sound within your body, which later on, gradually, will reveal itself as light, also. Very often when we talk about the spirit, when we talk about the *atma*, we have an image of a light. Where does this light reside? It resides within ourselves. So, all our spiritual practice will lead us to attain the Lotus Feet of the Lord, even if it takes many lives.

When praying, what do we pray for? We pray, we ask, and the Divine is not deaf. The Divine always hears the prayer of everybody. If He can hear even the small anklets on the feet of an ant, of course, He can hear our prayer, also. But very often we expect, if we pray, that we have to have it very quickly. We are not patient. But the Lord has created us. He knows what is best for us, no? So, why don't we trust Him? Why don't we trust in His Will? Christ has said, "Let Thy Will be done, not my will be done." This is a great statement that He Himself, being part of the Divine, teaches us to be patient and trust in the Will of God. Of the whole of our search, the basis, actually, is trust. To trust what? To trust in whom? – To trust in God. But yet, some will say "I don't know Him", but it doesn't matter. Even if we don't know Him, know that He knows us. When we start trusting in ourselves, trusting in the inner voice, trusting in the light within us, trusting in the inner sound inside of us, then He will start to reveal Himself.

Actually, I wanted to say, I'm really very happy to be here, in this place, for the second time. The first *darshan* that I gave in Portugal was in this monastery and also here in Fatima where the Divine Mother resides, it's really a blessed place. That doesn't mean She doesn't reside in other places. She resides everywhere. She resides within the core of your heart itself. But being in a place where She has left an imprint of Her manifestation is special. So She will be with all of us.

(After singing a bhajan about Rama, Swami starts to talk again).

You know the word, the name Ram. Three letters: R, A, M. This word sounds so simple, but has such great power. When you see Shiva, He is always sitting in deep meditation and in the Shiva Purana, He said to Parvati, "When I sit in meditation, the only name which is in my mind, in my consciousness, is the name of Rama", because this simple Name can liberate everyone. It can grant instant liberation. Even all your *karma* from the past can be erased just by chanting the Name of Rama. If one really pierces the mystery of these three letters: R, A, M, one attains liberation.

There is, in the *Ramacharitamanasa*, the story when Rama was crossing to Lanka to liberate Sita. Rama was a great King, a manifestation of the Lord Vishnu, and Sita was a manifestation of Lakshmi, who was abducted by the evil king Ravana. Rama had to go and liberate Sita – just to cut a big volume of *Ramacharitamanasa* short – so He had to go. Rama's father had three wives. One of the wives said to the father "You have said to me that whatever I ask you, you will not refuse me." Ram was to be the King, but the wife wanted her son, Bharat, to be the King, though Bharat was younger. In the tradition it is like that: older sons take upon themselves the rule of the kingdom. So she said to the King "Grant me the wish that you promised me. I want your son, Rama to go into the forest for fourteen years."

So He went into the forest. There, in this forest, there was a great Saint called Ahilya. Ahilya was cursed to become a stone, because Indra tested her, taking the appearance of her husband, but she didn't know about it. When her husband found out, he cursed her to become a stone, saying that "Only the Lord will liberate you." So Ahilya was a big stone. As Rama was passing by the forest, He came to that spot where the stone was lying and He touched the stone with His feet and instantly the curse was removed. Ahilya turned back into her real form. In that moment Rama said "Ahilya, I would like to grant you a boon, a blessing. Ask me for whatever you want. I will give it to you." Ahilya said "My Lord, I have been waiting for many lives here. For many centuries I have been waiting for this moment to attain this, that just the dust of Your feet could touch me and liberate me. I don't ask for any boon. The only thing that I ask is that I'll never forget about Your Name. Even if I take a birth as a pig, may I always chant Your Name, because only Your Name can grant liberation."

Such is the power of the Divine Name. Why do you think in all religions, they say to chant the Name of God, to recite the Name of God? Even here, in Fatima, you just go outside and you see, they are selling rosaries everywhere. And for what? It is not just to wear it and make you beautiful. No, you use it to pray, to chant the Name of the Lord, so that you realise the unity between the *Atma* and the *Paramatma*. When you realise this unity between the *Atma* and the *Paramatma*, what will stay? Only the *Paramatma* will stay, because the only reality of the *Atma* is the *Paramatma*, the only reality of the soul is God. Your soul wants to merge back again and become One with God. It wants to attain His Lotus Feet. The one who has realised this will join [with God]. Just with the simple Name, Ram, it can be granted.

LORD HANUMAN,
THE STRENGTH OF DEEP DEVOTION

Hanuman Jayanti, Shree Peetha Nilaya
Springen, Germany, 30 March 2010

I don't need to explain much about Hanuman because last year I already explained. Actually, if we could ask something to Hanuman today, it would be to ask Him that He infuses in us just a little bit of the way that He loves God, of the way that He dedicated His life to Rama, because just a little bit of His devotion would be great. Hanuman is considered to be the model of *bhakti*. He represents how one has to be in one's spiritual path and how devotional one has to be. So, in this aspect of Hanuman, He is bestowing wisdom and also showing that one doesn't need to fear anything when He is around. So today, accordingly to the *Shastras*, is His birthday, the day that He manifested Himself on Earth. As you know, Hanuman is an incarnation of Lord Shiva. When Rama came down, all the Deities manifested themselves in the form of Monkeys –

In this aspect of Hanuman, He is bestowing wisdom and also showing that one doesn't need to fear anything when He is around.

Vanara Sena. And Hanuman is Shiva Himself, actually. That's why it is said: when you pray to Hanuman, you receive the Grace of Gauri Shankar. And as I explained during Ram Navami, the Name Rama is a mixture of *OM Namo Narayanaya* and *OM Namah Shivaya.* The first syllable of Rama is in: *OM Namo Na**ra**yanaya*, which is *Ra*, and the second is in *OM Na**mah** Shivaya*, which is *Ma*.

So, the Name of Rama is infused in Hanuman through His devotion. He was initiated into the Name of Rama from childhood and His devotion had no limit. Even till now it is said: wherever the Name of Rama is being read, He is the first one to come and the last one to leave. Hanuman is immortal and He travelled around the world, protecting, giving His blessing to Rama devotees, to whoever prays to Lord Rama.

Tulsidas knew that he would not be able to attain Ram by himself. He knew that his devotion was weak and that he had to strengthen his devotion. The only way to strengthen His devotion to Lord Rama was to take *Rama Bhakta*, become a devotee of Lord Rama. That's what Krishna said in the *Gita*, "Whoever wants to come to me, be devoted to my servants. The devotee of my servants is dearer to me."

So, Tulsidas took what is written also in *Rama Charitra Manas*. He surrendered to Hanuman and asked Hanumanji for His help and, of course, he didn't know who Hanuman was. So, through his penance of roaming around for days and days, he reached a spot where he heard a voice saying "Go to Varanasi. Go to the temple where the *Rama Charitra Manas* is being read and there, you will find Hanuman" Then he asked "But how will I know Him?" and the voice said "You will recognise Him, because He is an old man who will come. He will be the first one to come and the last one to leave." So he went to the temple and it was filled with people, but he saw only one old man sitting. When everybody left, He was the only one remaining and the last one to leave. So, he knew that He was Hanuman.

He went and held the feet of the old man and said "Please, *Prabhu*, you are such a great devotee of the Lord, please guide me to Him and bless me with a little bit of your devotion that you have to

Lord Rama." Hanuman at this moment, because He was in disguise, said "No, no, no, what are you doing?" He wanted to test him. He rebuked him, pushed him away, but Tulsidas would not let go of His feet. And Hanuman was pleased with his devotion and said "I bless you that Lord Rama will come, but you will have to recognise Him".

So when a few days later Tulsidas was on the bank of the Ganges preparing pure sandal paste, two young men came to him and said "We see that you are preparing some nice sandal paste. Can we have some?" Then Tulsidas said "This sandal paste is for the King, for royalty and as I see that you are royalty, you can have the sandal paste." Of course, he could not recognise who was in front of him. Then Hanuman who was up on the tree where Tulsidas was sitting, called to him and said "Tulsidas, this is your Lord in front of you." When he realised that the Lord was front of him, Tulsidas put the *chandan* on [Rama's forehead] and held His feet. This is how Hanuman helped the devotees of the Lord to find Him. So He is a model of devotion and you can pray that you can change and become a little bit like Him.

THE BURNING HEART

Gaura Purnima at Shree Peetha Nilaya
Springen, Germany, 2 March 2010

Today, actually, is a preparation for tomorrow, where we celebrate *Gaura Purnima*, when Lord Chaitanya Mahaprabhu manifested Himself and then, Holi the day after. It's known as the colour festival. There are many stories about why the Hindus play with the colours.

Of course, this is a time of joy. It's different from other festivals. In India they play it for a month and in Mauritius they play it for two days, three days. But the main day is the day after tomorrow (Monday) and tomorrow is *Holika Dahan*. Holika was the sister of Hiranyakashipu (the demon king who was killed by Narasimha), and she was blessed because of so many years of penance, with a shawl. Whenever she wore this shawl, fire couldn't burn her.

You probably know the story of Prahlad whose father, Hiranyakashipu, wanted to convert him, wanted to make him a little demon. He sent him to this demon school, but instead of changing into a demon, he changed the others into devotees of the Lord by chanting the Lord's Names, by making them chant the Lord's Names and showing the power of the Divine Names. So they tried all things to change him and it was of no use. At the end his father was very angry and said "By any means, kill my son!"

You know that before Christianity was legalised, Christians were persecuted for their faith, so at that time this also happened. The father tried to kill his son by all means, but could not, because the

Lord was always there to protect him. So finally, the sister said "As I'm blessed by Brahma with this beautiful shawl, I can't get burned. If I take your son and sit in the fire, he will get burned and I will not." So, thinking of that, she sat in the fire but, to her great misfortune, the shawl overturned, covered Prahlad and instead of Prahlad getting burned, she was burned to ash.

Then she blamed Brahma and said "Brahma, your blessing was in vain, you said it would protect me, but look, I burnt." Then Brahma reminded her "This was given for your protection, for helping, not to destroy another's life." So that's why this shawl turned over and protected Prahlad. Tomorrow, in Mauritius they will make an effigy of Holika, like a scarecrow, to represent her and they will burn it and sing the glory of Lord Krishna, Nrsingadev and Ram.

This story reminds me very much of us humans and our tendency, where if we advance a little bit, pride can take over, how our arrogance can take over and then we think we are the best, we are the only ones, nobody else. We think "I deserve everything." We forget that if the mind could fathom God, we would not be slaves of the mind, but yet, we let ourselves be ruled by this mind. We don't have it under control. We are never free, but yet, we create the illusion of being free. We think about ourselves being the best, but how will we find God? How will we find the Lotus Feet of the Lord if we are so filled with this pride inside? Only with humbleness will one find Him, but not in the mind. You say to yourself "Yes, I'm humble, I'm humble," but it has to be here, within yourself, inside of you. When you think to yourself "Yes, everybody is greater than me" you can learn things. There are so many things that you can learn, but how many like to learn? Not so many.

It is said that in this world there are four kinds of people: the one who is attached to the world, the one who is looking for freedom, the one who is ever free and the one who is liberated—well, actually, liberated, then ever free. These four kinds of people make this world and where is each one situated in it? Are we trying to be liberated? Are we liberated? We can't be ever free, because the ever free is only the Lord Himself. And, of course, whenever He manifests Himself, He's ever free. He's not bound by any law of *karma* like people are, but yet, you see how humble He is, like when He killed Hiranyakashipu for Prahlad.

The Lord manifested Himself into a form, here, in this level and limited Himself for his devotee, to show the greatness of devotion, how important the devotion of His *bhakta* is. So the Lord is ever free to take whatever form, wherever He wills it, but yet we fight and say "Ours is the best; yours is not!" Forgetting that He's the Lord, He has created everything and He's not bound in the way people are bound with the mind.

There's this beautiful story that shows these four categories of humans. When a fisherman throws his net in the sea, the ever free will never get caught in the net. The fisherman can try as much as he wants, they are too wise for that. When the net of *Maya* is cast, the rest of them, the other three, get caught in it - the one who is attached, the one who is liberated and the one who is on the way to liberation, who is searching for liberation. They are like these fish that are caught in the net.

The ones who are trying their best to be liberated see the net and they try their best to jump out of the net, but yet, they don't succeed. They try and try and try and they can't, but the liberated ones, they will jump out of the net and then they will go! So, the fisherman says "Look at this big fish, it's going away." And the ones who are caught in the net are like the fish that don't even try their best to come out. They don't do anything. They think that "Yes, I will be saved; let me go down deep in the mud and hide myself", but yet, forgetting that they are caught in the net. They will go and hide, forgetting that when the fisherman pulls the net, they will be also caught.

So, such are the men who are caught in the world outside, who don't even try their best to realise why they are here. They don't even try and do something. They don't even want to think about it, because they think "Life is beautiful; let's enjoy it!" Enjoy for how long – ten years, twenty years? They're getting old; time is running! And we don't realise that, you know. We don't realise that one day there will come a time where we will look at life and say "What have I done?" We have danced in the routine all the time, every day. We have danced in the routine, which has made us a slave to this world. The merciful Lord has given a chance to change, but yet, we have not taken it.

Then when you look at life behind you, you realise what a waste of life, what a waste of time it has been. Then you will say to yourself (probably some among you, have even said it already), "Oh, I should have changed that time." You realise that there were times for you to change, but you didn't take the opportunity. Then you fall into the category of the fish that has been caught in the net and when the fisherman pulls it out you say, "Oops! Too late!"

But it's never too late when you have practiced to surrender to God. When you have the Grace, take the chance and change! It's not up to me to tell you to change, but it's up to you to tell yourself to change. When you try, of course, it's not in one go you will get the Divine. Of course, for some it's easy, because of the past *karmas*. They can try and very quickly they receive the result. But for some it takes time, but one should not lose hope. When the Divine sees that you are trying, He will send help. If you accept the help, He will lead you to liberation, but it's up to you. This is the freedom that He gives to mankind: to choose the way we want.

That's why you see the world in this state. We have forgotten why we are here. We forget that our soul wants to be one with the Divine; our soul wants to reach the Lotus Feet of the Lord. A great example is Lord Chaitanya Himself, who was for some years living normally. Even though He was a manifestation of the Lord, He lived a normal life until the Lord called Him; when He received the Grace, realising that "I'm not here just for this. I'm not here just to teach. I'm not here just to be in this world. There is something greater to be realised: "That is who I am."

I was just reading, before, the prayer of Saint Augustine. He always said this prayer "Lord, make me Realise Who You are and make me Realise who I am." This was his prayer that he was saying and his heart was burning with this Divine Love. You see, when we talk about a heart burning for the Divine, some of you may understand, some of you may not understand, because we look at things with our mind.

"Lord, make me realise who You are, and make me realise who I am".

Like I was saying at the beginning of the talk, if our mind could fathom the Divine, we would not be here, we would be with Him. That's why He has given us so many aspects of Himself, so that our mind can be focused on until we Realise our Self. I will not say just until we Realise God in ourselves, but until we realise that we are part of Him.

So, Lord Chaitanya reached a point where He showed that only through *bhakti*, only through devotion, can this Love be awakened. But this devotion has to be really from your heart, because if you just try with the mind and say "Yes, I have devotion", you will be stuck only to the outside and the burning of the heart will not happen inside of you. You don't need to be scared, because when the heart burns, it is not like in medicine when you say there is heartburn, you have an acidic problem! It's not like that. It's burning with Love and that is what the saints really experience!

It's the same in all religions, because they are all searching for the Lotus Feet of the Lord. Name Him by whatever Name you want, call Him by whatever Name, picture Him by whatever form, but it's the same Lord. That's why each one of you has your *Ishta Dev*. So that it makes it easy for you concentrating on your *Ishta Dev*, so that this longing for the Divine in that form, may appear inside of you.

So, may Lord Chaitanya make your heart aflame and help you to love the Lord the way He loved the Lord, until at the end they became One. He could not live in this world, He could not bear the separation. It's the same thing when our soul looks at the Lord, it has the same longing, "When will I be One with you, again. When will I go back to this state where I realise that I am One with You and You are One with me, all the time."

> The moment you close your eyes and call for the Lord in any of His forms, He is there and He hears each prayer. Whether you see Him or not, He is there. This reminds me of what Christ said: "Blessed is the one who believes without seeing."

That's what your *sadhana* is here for. That's why you are praying and you are meditating, which is very good, but try to do it in a selfless way, without expectation, because whenever you expect, it will take a longer time.

Whenever you pray and you expect, saying "OK, I will pray to the Lord, now. Probably He will be happy with me and He will come to me." But He is happy with you, you know. Whether you see Him or whether you don't see Him, whether you see Him or not, He is there! The moment you close your eyes and call for the Lord in any of His forms, He is there and He hears each prayer. Whether you see Him or not, He is there. This reminds me of what Christ said:

"Blessed is the one who believes without seeing."
So know that whenever you pray, He hears everything and, above all, He knows when to give you what. When you are ready, when you are able to handle it, He will give it; but as long as you are not ready, make yourself ready. Long for Him, call for Him night and day, so that you have just a glimpse of this longing of the heart. And just a glimpse can make you wait very patiently throughout your life.

THE LORD WITHIN ONE'S HEART

Darshan in Kenya, September 2010

It's lovely to be here with all of you. Last time somebody asked me a question: "Does whatever we do in this life, whether it is in our *sadhana* or in our daily life, depend on this life or our previous lifetime?" Well it depends on both, actually. The majority of whatever you do in this life depends on what you have done in your past lives.

Sometimes when you have a great plan and it doesn't turn out the way you planned, it's because in this life your mind functions in a certain way to create what you perceive for you to be happy, but still, there is *karma* from the past that you have to burn. So that's why, very often when you have a plan, it doesn't turn out the way you wanted, because of these past *karmas*. What is permanent in this world? Nothing! With time, everything changes, with time, everything gets destroyed, but yet,

Only when you are wholly directed towards Him, He will turn wholly towards you.

one hangs onto these perishable things, forgetting the Eternal. So as long as one hangs onto perishable things, there will be suffering, because what will give you real joy is hanging onto the Eternal Lord. Only when you are wholly directed towards Him, He will turn wholly towards you. And how to do that? It's through your *sadhana*, by doing *japam*, chanting the Name of the Lord, doing your spiritual practices and serving. Through service, you realise that you are serving not out of ego, not out of pride, but you're serving through your heart. Of course, when you start to serve, there's always the pride in it. You are proud of how much you are doing. You say "Look how much I am doing." I, the big I, is always there and you are forgetting that it's only Him who is doing through you. When you serve, with time, it comes to a point where [the idea that it's you who is doing], is transcended. Then you start to realise that whoever you are serving, you are serving only Him and that it's only Him who is serving. Then you have peace, because if you look for peace in this world, if you look for joy, you will not find it. Everybody is looking for peace. Who doesn't want to be peaceful? Is there someone who doesn't want to be peaceful? Everybody is just looking for one thing: to be peaceful.

In Sanskrit we call the world *Jagad a*nd when you translate *Jagad*, it means ceaseless motion. It's always on the move. Whenever we look at the world, it is always on the move. When we take time and calmly look at ourselves, when we look at human beings, we see they are constantly on the move. Even when sitting here, their mind is far away, somewhere else. They are sitting here, listening, but the mind is somewhere else, doing something else. So how can there be peace when one is not in peace with oneself, when one can't take five minutes to sit down in one place and bring the body, mind and spirit here, in the same spot? And yet, human beings are looking for peace.

So, to have this peace, one has to learn to calm oneself. You see, it's the same with everything else. When you have a child and you want him to study, what do you do? You make the child sit and then you make him study, no? First you have to make the child sit down, then study. In the same way, without effort from you, without self-discipline, sitting down and practising your *sadhana*, it's difficult to find real peace, because today you have something, but you don't know tomorrow if you will have it or not. But if you have attained real peace, once you have it, you will have it always. It's the same thing with Love, I am talking about real Love, pure Love. Once you have Realised it, you will always have it with you.

You see, in this world people like to hang onto their problems and onto their worries. Why? You see, whenever a problem arises, the solution is also there, but Man focuses easily on the problem but not on the solution. Do you like problems? If you don't like problems, why do you let yourself be drawn toward your worries? It doesn't give you peace, no? So the more you hang onto the problems, the more problems you will have; the more you hang onto the worry, the more you will not see the solution. But if you take a little bit of time to sit in your prayer room and sincerely surrender to the Divine, the problems will get solved. That's why, whenever there is a problem, what do you do? You run to the temple, no? Then you pray "Oh, God, I have this problem" or "I have that problem", because you know deep inside of you that He's the only one that can solve your problem, nobody else. You can tell your problem to hundreds of people but what will they do? They will say "Oh, poor you, you have a problem." Very often they say "Poor you" outside, but inside they are saying "Good for you." So who is your best friend? Who is the real one looking after you? Who is the one really listening to you? It's only Him. It's only the Lord Himself.

As long as there is happiness in life, people give very little importance to their spiritual practice. They say "When I become very old, then I will have time to do that." That's why often, there are problems on your path, there are problems in your life, so that you can remember God continuously. It's like what Gandhari said in the *Mahabharat* when the war was finished. Gandhari was the Mother of the *Kauravas* and Krishna's auntie. So, during this war, all the Kauravas had been killed, and she was very angry with Krishna because, you see, he could have stopped the war completly but he didn't. After the war, Krishna went to see his aunty, Gandhari, to get her blessing and He asked her "What can I do for you?" She answered "You are the Lord of the world but yet, you didn't stop the war, so what more can I ask of You? The only thing that I can ask of You is to give me as many problems as possible, so that I will never forget You". This was how much Love she had for the Lord! She had so much Love that she asked the Lord "Give me many problems, so that I can always remember you."

This is how it is also in our life. Things happen in life so that we can always remember God. But we don't like to continuously remember God; we like to continuously remember the problem. We like to focus our mind, all our attention, all our energy, on the problem, thinking that we will get the solution. But you will not, because you have limitations. You are limited with your mind. Your mind is limited to matter, only. So, if you concentrate on God, no matter what comes into your lives, you will accept it, you will take it in a positive way. You will not let the mind become negative, because when the mind becomes negative, you start to think negatively and out of this negativity whatever you do in life will be negative. But if your mind is positive, then whatever you do in life, the fruit of your labour will be positive. When your mind is focused on the Divine, it will get better and better all the time.

You have to be happy when you are chanting, when you are doing your prayer to the Lord, because He's always with you. Your parents, your mum and dad, will be with you for some time, but He will *always* be with you. He was with you from the beginning and He will always be with you until the end, until you realise your Self and until you attain Him. He's your best friend, He's the *only* one that you can *really* trust and He's the only one that gives you solutions for everything, not human beings. Any human being that gives you a solution, any friends of yours that give you a solution, will always have expectation behind it. They will say: "I you give this, but you will have do that for me!" You know about it, no?

Yes, because each human being does this, you know. It's a human reaction. So don't forget that within this human self, you are also Divine – you have part of God inside of you. I said *part*, remember this word *part*. You are not fully God, because you hang so much onto your humanness that the Divine part gets covered. That's why the *karma* of the past can affect you. But when you realise your Self, that the Lord is within you and you realise that your *Atma* is part of the *Paramatma*, you will transcend this human quality.

It's the same thing when you do *japam*. Why do you do *japam*? You do *japam* to realise the Divine. You do *japam* so that your mind continuously thinks of and chants the Name of God. The more you chant the Divine Names, the more His qualities will reflect on you. The qualities of goodness, Love, compassion, joy, all these qualities will start reflecting on you, but this is when you chant sincerely.

Humans are hanging onto the outside and not much onto the inside, because they don't know about the inside. They know only what is in the outside, what they can see and what they can touch. With these two things, you think you will be happy, but you have one thing, which is not seen, and that is your *Atma*. You can talk about the *Atma*, you can say "Yes, we have the spirit inside of us, we have the soul inside of us", but how many *really* know about the *Atma*?

Whenever you talk about death, people get scared. They don't want to mention death. Well, you were born and you will die! This is not something that you will escape. You will have to go through that, but *you*, not your body, but your True Self is permanent. So by realising the *Atma*, letting the *Atma* reveal itself to you, you will have the greatest joy, you will *always* be happy. Even when problems come, you will be happy, because you will have attained the purpose of life, of lives! Not only of one life, but of lives.

So, try your best to do your *sadhana*. Try your best to remember God in whatever you do, even if you don't consider it as *seva*, but try to think of God in whatever action you do in life. If you have five minutes during the day, try to sit down quietly and during these five minutes forget about husband, wife, children, everybody. When you sit in your prayer room, just sit – you and God. If you don't have five minutes, then even two minutes are fine. Whenever you have problems you say "Oh, my God!" No? So, you look for God, but when you are happy, well, you don't say "Oh, my God, I'm happy!"

So why do you have to wait for a problem to come to remember God? You can remember Him every day. I will not say all day, because you will not, but *at least* morning and evening, for one minute in the morning and one minute in the evening. He has a multitude of forms that He appears in. Each one feels close to certain Divinities, though they are only One, it's only Him. It's like when you look at a tree: there are many leaves, many branches, but all of them came from one seed only. Imagine from a small seed, a huge tree can come out with thousands of leaves, hundreds of branches, but yet, the seed is one.

So try to Realise this Unity and build up this relationship with the Divine. The more your relationship with the Divine becomes intense, the more He will reveal Himself to you. It's like when you're in love. At the beginning you say "Yes, I have a feeling for that person", but yet, you don't know that person. How do you know the person? By being close to that person, by being near to that person, you will start to know the person, no? So the more you become close to that person, the more you know the person, the more the love grows.

It's the same thing with *Bhagavan*, you know. The more you remember Him, the more you chant His Name, the more He will reveal Himself to you. So little by little you will start to feel Him. Little by little you will start to Realise that He's next to you.

Sometimes you will see Him in dreams and sometimes you will see Him manifested in front of you. Then, as time goes on, the objects wherein He manifested start to disappear. Only *He* stays. So wherever you go, you will see only Him. As your Love grows, you will see Him inside of you, you will see Him outside of you till you will realise that it's just Him. We're just doing a big play. He's just playing with all of us. He's acting through all of us. He's doing what He has to do through each one of us.

TULSIDAS AND THE BEAUTY OF BHAKTI

Darshan in Steffenshof, Germany, 8 August 2007

It is said that to Realise God, one has to have complete trust, one has to have complete dedication to what one really wants, because if we give ourselves halfway, God will also give Himself halfway. But if we give ourselves fully to Him and call sincerely from our heart to Him, He will respond back to us. Such was the Love of Tulsidas. Tulsidas was a saint from India, who lived in the 16th century and his Love for Lord Rama was so great that, wherever he looked, he would see only Rama. He was an orphan and was from a very low caste. At that time in India, and even till now - people followed the caste system. There are the *Brahmins*, the highest caste and the *Sudras*, the lowest caste. But Tulsidas´s Love for Rama was so great that he always carried a small statue of Lord Rama with him. When his parents died, nobody looked after him and wherever he would go the people went away from him because he was from a low caste. One day his Guru took him to his *ashram* and said to the people "You people who always think that you know God, you know Him only through scriptures; only through what is said in the books, nothing else. But the Lord Sri Hari is above all this. He loves everybody and everybody is equal to Him. He is with anybody who calls Him with sincere heart." So the Guru took Tulsidas under his care and looked after him. Tulsidas grew up and he became well versed in Sanskrit and his main aim was to give the *Ramcharitmanas,* which means *The story of Lord Rama*, to the people in their own language.

So, he started to compose poems and he was also singing the

Ramcharitmanas in Marathi, his own native language. The *Brahmins* didn't like this at all, because they said that Sanskrit is the language of the *Devas*, of the Gods. Well, that's what they said. Similarly, some people think that God speaks only Latin. So, Tulsidas´s main aim was to translate the *Ramcharitmanas* and give it to the people, to everybody, equally; because of that, he had many enemies.

When time came for Tulsidas to get married, one of his brothers was against him and said "No, I have to get married to that girl! Not you!" But it was the girl´s father who wanted Tulsidas to get married to his daughter, Ratnavali, and finally he got married to her and they were very happy. They went to get the blessing of the Guru, and the Guru gave him back the small statue of Rama, that Tulsidas had bought in the *ashram* when he was very small and told him "I don't have anything to give you on this special day, but take this statue of Rama and never forget about Him!" Tulsidas replied "Guruji, how could I forget about Rama?" He took the statue of Rama home, put it on the altar and at that moment he completely forgot about Rama, because his mind was focused only on his wife. He got so obsessed with his wife that she became everything to him. Every moment, day and night, he wanted just to be next to his wife. They had a shop, because when they got married his father-in-law gave him a shop.

One day he had to go to another town to get some clothes for the shop. So in the morning, he said goodbye to his wife and went to the other shops to buy his stuff. At the same time, his wife got a message that her father was not well and he would like to see her for the last time before he died. So she rushed quickly to the father's place and when Tulsidas came home and didn't find his wife, he became mad. He found a note on the bed saying, "I have gone to my father's place. I need some time for myself, because I have seen how obsessed you are about me and also because my father is ill."

Tulsidas could not bear this and he went to his father-in-law's place. On the way, there was a big storm and he had to swim across the river. When he finally arrived, he saw that the door was locked and he was wondering what to do and how to go inside. So he started climbing over the wall of the house and some people who saw it thought that he was a thief. They started running around and called everybody, saying "There is a thief come, let's catch him!" But Tulsidas managed to get inside the house and when the people who tried to catch him went inside and saw that it was him, they asked him "Why did you climb over the wall like this? It's your own father-in-law's house. You can use the door." They understood that he was madly in love so they went to the wife and said "Do you know what kind of husband you have? He is so much in love with you that he cannot let you go like that."

The wife became *very* angry. She went to Tulsidas and said to him "Listen, I do appreciate whatever you're doing for me, but I will tell you one thing: if you would have this kind of Love for Rama, for sure you would get liberation, He would liberate you. If you would have such a Love for Him, He would always be with you. Instead, you are just looking at me for your own pleasure with your lustful eyes. You desire only my body, which is just a bag of bones and it can give you satisfaction only for some time. So have such Love for Rama and he will liberate you from this!" Then she left but her words stayed in Tulsidas's mind, he was thinking and thinking and again this urge for Rama awoke in his heart. He left everything and said "How could I forget about You, Rama? I have forgotten about You, because of this illusion of this world. I forgot about You for a *bag of bones*, but as this *bag of bones* has become my guru, I look for You, again. Rama, reveal Yourself to me!" For days and days he kept walking around, just repeating the Name of Ram. Finally, he could not walk anymore and he fell down in a forest, but still he kept singing the name of Rama: *Ram Ram Ram Ram Ram Ram.* He was singing and singing and singing *Rama*.

After some time he heard a voice say "Tulsidas, you are such a great soul. I know why you are chanting the Name of Rama and I will tell you how to find Him." Tulsidas lifted his head up and looked around, but couldn't see anybody. So he asked "Who are you? I can't see you." The voice answered "I am a ghost who lives in this tree. I became a ghost because of my own wish. I had a desire to have some Ganges water on the last day of my life, but I didn't have any. Now I consider myself very lucky, because I could hear you chanting for nine days continuously the Name of Rama next to me. I will reveal Him to you, but for that you will have to bring some Ganges water for me."

Tulsidas agreed and went to collect a pot of water from the Ganges. He brought the pot to the tree and the ghost from the tree said "I am blessed and I got liberated, firstly, because you fulfilled my wish by bringing the Ganges water to me and, secondly, because I have heard the Holy Name of Rama continuously for nine days, so I will reveal Him to you. Go to Kashi, there you will find a priest who will be chanting the story of Rama. There will be an old man who will come first and he will also leave the last. He is Hanuman, the servant of Rama, and He will direct you to Rama." Saying this, the ghost which was on the tree got liberated.

Tulsidas went to this town. There, he went to this place where the ghost had told him to go. As he was sitting there, the priest was reading the *Ramcharitmanas* in Sanskrit. It was *so* boring that one by one the people fell asleep and one by one they all went away. When everybody was gone, only Tulsidas was left so, he went to the priest and said "Why do you do like that? Why are you singing the *Ramcharitmanas* in Sanskrit? Why don't you sing it in the native language of people from here, in Hindi?" Then the priest, who was jealous, said "Oh, you can't sing the *Ramcharitmanas* in any other language, because it would be blasphemy. You can sing it only in

Sanskrit!" Then Tulsidas said to the priest "If it were in Hindi, it would be more interesting, people would not go away and they would listen to you." The priest became very angry with Tulsidas and pushed him away, but as he was going away he saw an old man sitting there.

He went to this old man who said "Oh, you were right. It's good that you said to him that it would be better to chant the *Ramcharitmanas* in the native language of the local people." Tulsidas knew that this old man with white beard was Hanuman in disguise and he fell down at His feet and said *"Please,* reveal Rama to me!" The old man said "Me? How will I reveal Rama to you?" Tulsidas answered "You are Hanuman." The old man said "Hah, Me Hanuman? No, no, no." But Tulsidas insisted *"Please,* remove your disguise, show really Yourself! I know it´s You, the servant of Rama." He was asking with so much faith and devotion that Hanuman appeared in His real form. He blessed Tulsidas and said to him "You will see Rama. Go to the Ganges tomorrow and you will see Rama there. Rama will come to you."

The next day Tulsidas was sitting on the banks of the Ganges, where he was preparing some *chandan* paste. Two young princes came to him and said, "Holy man, give us some *chandan.*" Without even looking, Tulsidas just took a little bit of it, put it on betel leaves and gave it to them. Of course, these men were in disguise. Poor Tulsidas, he could not know who was in front of him. His desire was to see Rama, but still, when Rama was in front of him he was too blind to recognise Him. At the same time, Hanuman appeared on the tree just above and said "How blessed is Tulsidas to have the *darshan* of Lord Rama and Lakshmana who have come from Heaven to Him." Hearing that, Tulsidas recognised that it was Rama and Lakshmana who were standing in front of him. He bowed down to their feet and Rama blessed him without saying anything. Just the smile of Rama was enough for him.

Later, Tulsidas translated the *Ramcharitmanas* into Hindi and many, many people followed him. Many of the *Brahmin* priests changed and started to sing it in Hindi, but one of them was jealous and tried everything to stop Tulsidas. He knew that Tulsidas had only one copy of the *Ramcharitmanas*, so he decided to steal it. He sent one man to steal it, but as the man was approaching the hut of Tulsidas, he saw Rama and Lakshmana guarding the gate of the place. When this man took one more step, Hanuman pulled him with His tail and started to beat him up with the tail. So the man rushed quickly back to the wicked priest and said to him "It is impossible. I got beaten. There are guards guarding the hut." Later they tried to burn the hut, but all the fire merged into the *Ramcharitmanas*, into the book. It went inside the book and disappeared. In this way, they offended Tulsidas many times.

Once, the son-in-law of the King of Kashi died and, during the funeral procession, the King's daughter was walking by the side of her dead husband. She was ready to be burned, as well, because at that time, when a husband died the wife also had to be burned alive. It is called *sati*. Actually, they carried on with this tradition until the English occupied India. Also, Gandhi was one of the main opponents of this *sati* tradition in which the wife is burned on the pyre of her husband.

So during this procession, they met Tulsidas and when the wife was passing by him, he blessed her and told her "May you always be happy in your family." When the wicked *Brahmin* priest heard this, he said angrily to Tulsidas "How can you bless her to always be happy in the family, when her husband has just died?" Tulsidas answered to him "I don't know, I just blessed her, because Lord Rama told me to bless her." Then the *Brahmin* priest said "If your faith is really strong, it is said that through the Name of Rama, one can be brought back to life, so bring him back to life!"

Tulsidas started to pray to Rama and said "Rama, if I am truthful to You, give back life to this man. You give the life back to many people, so You can also give life back to this dead man." His Love and faith in Rama was so strong, his prayer was *so* strong that when he was chanting *Sri Ram, Jai Ram, Jai Jai Ram,* suddenly the man just started to breathe again, awoke (after being dead for a few days) and started to sing the Name of Rama. But even this miracle didn't change the mind of the wicked priest. So he tried again to burn Tulsidas´s house, while Tulsidas was inside. When he did that, everybody tried to put out the fire from Tulsidas's hut, but they could not. But by the Grace of God, by the Love that Tulsidas had for Rama, the fire ceased by itself. It became a ball of fire, which started to follow the wicked priest who ran to his wife and said "Save me!" Then the wife said to the ball of fire "Out of ignorance, my husband has offended your devotee, Lord. Please, have mercy on him." Then she said to her husband "Go, and ask Tulsidas´s forgiveness. He will surely forgive you." The priest went to ask Tulsidas´s forgiveness and became one of his devotees and started also to chant the *Ramcharitmanas* in Hindi.

Things carried on like that and one day the wife of Tulsidas came to Him and said "Out of anger, I sent you away, but now I'm calling you back. Please come back." Tulsidas replied "No, I can't come back, but because you sent me away, I have got Rama seated completely in my heart. So you are my Guru and whatever you say, I will do." So the wife said "I will follow you, wherever you are, whatever you do. I will also do that. You want to live for Rama, I will live to serve you." So, whenever the *Ramcharitmanas* is being read, the *bhakti,* the devotion of Tulsidas is always mentioned. The first thing, before even reading the *Ramcharitmanas,* before even saying the Name of Rama, is to bow down to Tulsidas, who gave the Name of Rama to the whole world, and to Ratnavali, who let Tulsidas free, so that the Name of Rama could be spread out.

This story shows how one has to have complete surrender to God, complete surrender to one's path, complete surrender to the Deity which one feels inside his heart. One should also know that God is beyond everything and that He loves everybody equally. It's not upon anybody to go and try to change somebody's mind, saying "My way is right; your way is wrong." Thinking like this is completely wrong. We say we have only one God, but we adore Him in His many forms until we reach a point to see this Oneness everywhere. The life story of Tulsidas or any Self-Realised saint is beyond the comprehension of the mind, because they live completely in God and they are calling everybody to live completely in God, to live in the Love of God and to know that God is everywhere, that God is present in everybody.

First we see the duality, the separation, and through that separation, God unites us and makes us One with Him. He makes us Realise His Divinity, then we stop talking about Him and we become completely quiet. As long as you have not found God, as long as you have not come to the point of God-Realisation, Self-Realisation, you should *never* lose hope, you should *never* let go of God's Name. You should *never* let go of whatever you are doing.

Once there was a farmer who was living in a small town and in this town there was a big drought; there was no rain. So the farmer decided to make a canal from the river to his field, so that he could water his field, and the cows could have water to drink. He said to himself "I will make this canal and I will not take any rest or eat any food or drink anything until I have finished it"

During the day, his daughter came with food saying "Father, come

> We say we have only one God, but we adore Him in His many forms until we reach a point to see this Oneness everywhere.

and eat; it is already lunchtime", but he said to the daughter "No, go away. I have to finish this canal first. Then I will eat." The daughter went back home and told this to the mother. So the mother went to see him and told him "My dear Lord, you have been working the whole day, surely you can take 5 minutes rest and have your lunch." Again, the man said "No", but the wife kept insisting. Finally he stopped digging the canal and ran after his wife, shouting to her "Leave me alone! I told you that until I finish the canal, I will not leave this place! Go away!" The wife saw that her husband was really very angry and that he would not change his mind, so she stayed quiet and went home.

The man carried on digging. Late in the evening, he finished the canal and as he finished it, the water from the river started to flow towards his field. Then he sat down with appreciation, hearing the beautiful sound of the water, looking at the water flowing to his field, he felt great satisfaction. Then he went home and called his wife "Come here and give me tobacco. I will smoke now." Very happily he smoked his tobacco. Then he took a shower, had his dinner and slept very peacefully.

His neighbour also tried to build a canal from the river, but when his wife came and called him for his lunch, he also said no, but when the wife insisted, saying "Come, my dearest Lord, five minutes will not cost you anything", he left his work, saying "As you have said it so sweetly, I'll come!" So he went and sat and had his lunch and after the lunch he would, of course, have a small siesta. He had his siesta, but at the end of the evening he hadn't done anything else than eating and sleeping. So he never succeeded in making the canal to his field.

What lies behind this story is that one has to *completely* surrender to one's path and whatever obstructions or obstacles come on the way, one has to always say "No" to them. Your aim is to have God-Realisation, Self-Realisation. Until you have reached your aim, until you have come to the point of complete trust and complete faith in yourself and in God, keep trying. Don't let anything come on the way.

Many times the mind will come in the way and say "No, no, no, no, no, no, you should not do like that, you should do like this!", but if you listen to the mind, you will stop and you will become lazy. Only when you *really, sincerely* dedicate yourself and surrender to your path, surrender to what you really want, you will achieve your aim. The aim is to realise this Love that you have inside and to become completely this Love, to become this Love, so that *every* atom in your body will radiate this Love of God. And this Love, you will always spread it around. This Love is beyond everything: beyond the mind, beyond the body, even beyond the spirit itself and it is this Love that we have to attain.

YOGA OF DEVOTION

Darshan in Munich, Germany, 19 September 2007

It's lovely to be here with you after a long time. What I have to say is all about Love and devotion. Whatever we do in our daily life, in our work, in our spiritual path, it's all to attain one thing: to attain the purity of Love, to become Self-Realised, but you cannot attain this purity, you cannot Realise the Self without devotion. It's possible only through *bhakti*, through devotion. Without *bhakti*, it's difficult. Like Sri Krishna said in the *Gita*, "Cast away all dogma. Cast away all what is from the mind and surrender to me. Only then true Love can be realised."

Otherwise, with *jnana*, you stick only to the mind. I don't say that *jnana* is not good. It is good, but it will lead you only to a certain level. It is very good to do *karma yoga*, to help, but if you are not helping with the right attitude, it will also bring you only to a certain level. Whereas with *bhakti*, like Sri Krishna said to Uddhava, "Above all the yogas, I prefer *bhakti yoga*. I prefer the yoga of devotion where the devotee and the Lord become One, where there is no difference left, whereas in all the other yogas, the difference stays."

> Above all the yogas, I prefer *bhakti* yoga. I prefer the yoga of devotion where the devotee and the Lord become One

When I am talking about devotion, I don't mean the kind of devotion that will fade after one month, but pure devotion that lasts forever.

There are lots of people who have devotion in the beginning. When they start their spiritual path they are very excited, but after some time their devotion fades. But *real* devotion is like the Lord said, "If you surrender to me, open your heart and say 'Lord, take complete possession of my heart. It's only you that I'm looking for!'"

In reality, all the happiness that you are looking for - whatever you are doing in the outside - is to achieve *Satcitananda*. Wherever you look, whoever you look at, they are all running towards this. The priest is praying, why do you think he is praying? He is praying for real happiness. People on their spiritual path are also looking for real happiness. Even people who are taking drugs, why do you think they do that? They are looking for real happiness, too. Of course, our mind doesn't see it in the same way, but at the end, they are looking for real happiness. And this real happiness lies deep inside of you.

Through devotion, through singing the glory of God, all the Dogma will be removed and you will feel that He is continuously present with you, you will feel His Love continuously with you. The more you feel Him, the more you become part of Him. Like it is said in the *Gita*; "When one chants the Name of God, the Lord takes full possession of that person". The more you lose yourself, the more you lose your ego and pride, the more you will Realise the Divine, but the more you hang onto pride, the more you hang onto identity, the less you will find real happiness. So the easiest way that the Lord has given to you is to sing His glory. Just sing any Divine Name and, when you sing, let yourself be drawn into it and don't try to think with the mind.

I know that, especially in the West, we like to use the mind a lot. We like to understand things with our mind, but our mind has a limit. Does the mind understand the heart? It will never understand it. The mind will understand things only when there is a limit to them, when there is a wall where you can bang yourself against. And then, of course, you will complain about it, because it hurts. Whereas, when you centre yourself in your heart and awake this Divine Consciousness, this Higher Consciousness inside, you will always flow. No matter what, you will enter into Divine Ecstasy and you will feel different energies flowing through you. The mind will not understand and then it will cry and say "I want to understand it, but I can't!" When the power of the mind decreases, the power of the heart increases. It is so simple and the Lord has sent you here to Realise this, to develop *bhakti* and get Self-Realised.

When the power of the mind decreases, the power of the heart increases.

Whenever we sing *Radhe Shyam*, of course we have in our mind the image of Radha and Krishna, but who are these Radha and Krishna? Krishna is *Pure Love* and Radha is *Bhakti* so one cannot exist without the other. That's why we always see them together and we always mention their names together. *Radhe Shyam*, which means *prema bhakti* - Love and Devotion. If this True Love, if this true devotion arises inside of you, it will lead you to Self-Realisation. We have to put in our minds what is our aim. Life is like entering into a boat on the Ocean of *Samsaras*. The boatman is the *Satguru*, but into which boat do you want to enter? You have to know the destination, you have to know where the boat will lead you. Don't just enter any boat without knowing its destination! So, let devotion arise, it will lead you on your spiritual path. Let pure Love guide you because when you Realise the Purity of Love, there will be no difference in your mind. The mind will see the Lord everywhere.

There is a saint called Annamacharya from Andhra Pradesh, South India. His Love for Narayana was so great that he started walking towards Tirupati, where it is said that Narayana resided when He incarnated as Venkateshwara. The saint wanted so much to see

Him, but he had one attachment: the shoes that he was wearing. And when he wanted to climb towards the temple, he fell down. He was wondering why this happened and prayed so much to Narayana that Narayana said "I'm hearing him, but let the Mother, let Lakshmi go to see him on Earth." So Lakshmi came on Earth, but She changed her appearance and transformed Herself into on old lady. She went to the saint and said "You want to see the Lord, but you are still attached to your shoes. Remove them and you will see Him. He is present everywhere. He is residing in each plant and each stone of this place." The saint thought for a while, then he removed his shoes and, in the moment he removed these shoes, he saw light everywhere. Everything was transformed into light.

If we really have this urge of seeing the Lord, if we have this urge of Realising Him, feeling Him, He will come to us, but if He sees, when He comes, that we are still hanging onto things at the same time, He will not do anything.

It's like the story of Draupadi. Draupadi had five husbands, the Pandavas, and when the Pandavas were playing dice with the Kauravas, they lost everything. At the end the Kauravas said "Put also your wife into the game." The Pandavas said "OK." They thought "She is a Goddess and maybe with her *shakti*, she can change the things for us." But they lost the game and lost Draupadi. So to humiliate the Pandavas, the Kauravas dragged Draupadi into the court where they tried to undress her. But Draupadi was holding her clothes while they were trying to pull them off. She called Krishna and said "Govinda, Govinda, Govinda!" She was calling Him with so much faith and strength, but nothing happened. Govinda didn't come to her rescue. Finally she lifted her hands up and shouted "Govinda!" The moment she lifted her hands up and called Him, they were still pulling her sari, but meters and meters of cloth kept coming, it was never ending. They could not undress her of her sari. After that, they were sent into exile in the forest and one day while they were in the forest, Draupadi said to Krishna "My Lord, it's not that I doubt you, but there is a question in my mind that I would like to ask You. You remember when they were trying to remove my clothes. I called You several times, but why didn't You come instantly?" Krishna looked at her and said "My dear sister, the moment you said Govinda, when I heard *Go*, I left my palace and when you said *Vinda*, I was already there, but when I arrived there, I saw that you were hanging so much onto your clothes. How could I help you, then? If you are calling me for help, you have to surrender to me, but if you are calling me for help and don't really trust me, I cannot help you."

That's how it is nowadays. We say that we want Self-Realisation, but we don't want to take any responsibility. We don't want to let go of certain things in our life. We want to have the whole thing. We want everything. But know that when you come to a point of Self-Realisation, your life will automatically change. There will be new things in your life and you have to be ready for that. It is only then that He can say "Yes, this one is ready. I can give Myself completely to him, he can handle me." Otherwise, if God just gives you Self-Realisation like that and you could not handle it, you would mess up everything.

JUST LOVE

SURRENDER

Surrender mind and body
to the Lord your Friend.
This is the most
excellent pleasure.

Guru Nanak Dev

BY THE GRACE OF GOD

Darshan in Kiel, Germany, end of December 2006

It gives me great pleasure to be with all of you. We are all very happy in this period of great festivities: Christmas just passed and New Year is coming. Everybody is joyful and well prepared for new things, but joy should not be only during this period. New years are coming all the time. Ask yourself if you are changing, in which way you are changing, you always have to change. Outside there are lots of changes, there are always new things inside also there are always new things. There are always ups and downs. It's a time when you have to really say "Yes I want to move forward. I want to move up in my spirituality." And you will realise this great change within yourself, this great change that you will bring to the world.

It's not a change outside, but a change inside, because, like I said, with changes on the outside, new things always come and new things always go. So as long as we hang on to the outside, very often we find that it's very painful. The outside brings expectation and expectation brings misery and pain. All kinds of expectation bring pain, because the real expectation, the real thing that our soul wants, is the true Love of God. And this true Love of God, we can only find through devotion within our heart.

You can go to a Master and the Master can show you the way, but it's up to each one of you to really desire God, to really yearn for God, because as long as you don't yearn for God, as long as you don't *really* want God, you will always be searching, you will always be putting one foot in one place and the other foot in another. To find this real Love and really realise this deep connection to God within oneself, it's only through *bhakti*, through devotion.

When you surrender yourself full-heartedly, with full love from your heart and say "God I want you. Reveal Yourself to me!" God will reveal Himself. God can't say "No" to you, because your Self can't hide from yourself. This higher consciousness which you have deep inside you, can reveal itself when your mind is centred on God. So, yearn for God. Call from deep within your heart, "God reveal yourself to me. I know you are deep inside somewhere. From time to time I do feel you. I know you are here, but I would like to feel you constantly, all the time."

Isn't it what each one of you wants? To feel the Love of God all the time, so why is it so difficult? Why is it so difficult to love unconditionally? Is the mind too busy with the world outside? How long will you look for love in the world outside? As long as you look in this world outside you will get trapped in it; because you have to realise true Love here [in your heart] and feel it first here. If you Realise God first and then step in the world, how joyful and peaceful it will be.

But people choose the opposite. They like to step in the world first, *then* they want to Realise God. Once you step in the world, you get trapped in the grip of Maya and it's quite difficult to get out of Her grip. Her grip is so strong once She grabs you, it's only by chanting the Name of God that you can release yourself. It's only by saying, truly from your heart "God I want you. I surrender completely to you. Do what you have to do with me.", that She will let go of you. Don't think that Maya only acts on normal people. She acts on spiritual people, also. I think there are more attacks on them than on anybody else, but if the spiritual people are aware of it, they know whenever She is playing Her game and they know how to go out of it. And each one of you does know.

This reminds me of a small story. Once in a town there was a shoemaker. He would make his shoes while chanting God's Name all the time. Whenever he went to sell the shoes in the town market, he was very sincere. He would tell the people "Look, I bought the leather for 1€ by God's Grace. I bought the nails for a few cents and I made a profit of 2€ on it and altogether it cost 5€, by God's Grace." He was so sincere. In everything that he was doing, his mind was centred on God and he was accepting everything as God's Grace. People saw this innocence and this Love that he had for God so, without any bargaining, they would buy the shoes.

It happened one night that he could not sleep and while he was sitting in his courtyard, some robbers came and kidnapped him. Then, they went with him to another house to rob it. When the owner of the house heard noises, the thieves left the man in the middle, with all the jewellery that they had stolen and they ran away. When the owner saw this innocent man there with lots of things from his house in his hands, he said "It's impossible," but as he saw that the man had all the jewellery with him, he doubted and he said "Let me call the police." He called the police. The police put the shoemaker in prison and the next day he was brought in front of the judge. And in front of the judge he said "By the Grace of God yesterday night I could not sleep. By the Grace of God I went outside of the house and, while I was sitting there, by the Grace of God some robbers came and kidnapped me. And by the Grace of God this man found me. And by the Grace of God he thought that I came to steal in his house. And by the Grace of God I am here." But seeing also his innocence the judge said "This man is not the one

> Behind all our actions, behind all that is happening, there is God's Grace. And if we start seeing it in this way, we will be very happy.

who has stolen. He has spoken the truth." While coming out of the court, the shoemaker said to his friend "It is by the Grace of God that I came out."

This shows that, very often, when we do things, we take everything for granted. We forget that behind all our actions, behind all that is happening, there is God's Grace. And if we start seeing it in this way, we will be very happy, we will find peace in everything. Even when the worst thing that comes into our lives we will look at it in a different way. So, like I said, as a new year is coming, build up devotion, make the foundation of *bhakti* within your heart, within your mind and grow on it. And trust, firstly, you're feeling, trust your intuition and follow it. With that, I wish all of you Happy New Year. May God guide you on your spiritual path and whatever path you follow may you grow in it and flourish.

OPEN YOUR HEART AND SURRENDER

Darshan, Vienna, Austria, 2 August 2006

It gives me great joy to be among all of you. Some of you are here out of curiosity, some for spiritual search and some just to see who Swami Vishwananda is. But actually, all of you – knowingly and unknowingly – you are here to open the heart, to know who you really are, not here in this room, but here in this world. Often people come and ask me "How can we open our hearts?" For me to answer this question is very easy because I know how to open the heart. It just depends on whether the person will accept it or not. The first question that I will ask is "Do you love?" and the answer will be, "Yes, I love." But do you love yourself? This is the main important thing. We love towards the outside, but the same way we love the outside, the same way we also judge the outside. As easy as it is to love, as easy it is to judge.

You see, Mankind is made in such a way that the attention is always turned towards the outside. Very rarely does it turn towards the inside. And this is the search: to go inside. The moment you stop judging, the moment you stop looking for fault in others, you will start truly loving everybody. And for that, you have to start looking within yourself, looking for what you have to change in your life. I'm not saying to judge yourself, but to look at the negative parts of you and face them. By looking at the negativity, you will see that *you* create this negativity.

To understand Love, it's simple. It is just absence of fear. You can't understand Unconditional Love out of fear. If people really want to understand Love, really want to understand who they are, they will; but often the fear is so great that it makes a barrier and then you ask the question "If I realise Who I am, what then?" The fear of the unknown stops the desire for realisation. But if you accept whatever as the Will of God and say "God, Thy Will be done" Christ has shown it by saying: Thy Will be done, God's Will, then you will realise that the Will of God is also your will without egoism. The Will of God is one's own will, it is the will of the soul, the will of the true identity, which is without any egoism. The purity is inside and it's one's Self.

> The will of God is one's own will; it is the will of the soul, the will of the true identity, which is without any egoism.

The *yogis* knew that it would be difficult in this age for man to really open up the heart, because of how the world is. Today I put the TV on just for a short while, looking at the war, it never finishes. So I was thinking mankind is looking for security, but looking at the world, what security will the world give? Each one has to be secure with oneself. And this security is only in the trust of God. Trust in yourself. Even if one person is positive and really achieves that state, it's really great.

So, I will give you one *mudra*. It is very simple. It will help you on your spiritual path, any path, whatever path you are on. You can practice it anywhere, because this *mudra* will generate Love for everything. It will help you to open your heart and be positive in your mind. The *mudra* is called the heart *mudra*, *Hridaya mudra*. The *mudras* are simple. Normally you do them with the hands, but there are some *mudras* that you also do with the body. Because there is no space here to do the *mudra* with the body, we will do it with the hands. But, like I was saying before, the *yogis* knew how the world would be, they knew that the heart of man would be difficult to open up, so they created with their yogic power certain exercises that would be very good for the heart, for the body and for the soul. Are you ready to open your heart? You see, to open the heart, you really need to want it. You are saying "yes" because I asked you, which is lovely, but carry on saying "yes." In whatever situation you are, know that God is *always* with you. Even if you are not thinking of the Divine, the Divine is with you all the time.

(Sri Swami Vishwananda demonstrated the Hridaya mudra)

Editorial note: For further information about the Hridaya mudra and other mudras, please contact the Atma Kriya Institute www.atmakriya. org.

FREE YOURSELF

Darshan in Steffenshof, Germany, 12 January 2008

Often, we reach a point in our life where we pray, we sing God's Name, but yet, we don't have peace of mind. Whatever we do, we still feel this pressure on us and we ask ourselves why, why we don't feel free? It's just because we hang onto our expectations too much. That's why we never feel free. In whatever we do, there are always some expectations, either indirectly or directly, whether you are conscious of it or not conscious of it. Any expectation will never let you be free. If you are on the spiritual path, only when you let go completely, when you surrender to God, you will feel this peace of mind, you will feel that you are free.

> Only when you let go completely, when you surrender to God, you will feel this peace of mind, you will feel that you are free.

But, sad to say, even spiritual people hang on too much. They say "Yes, I trust Narayana. I trust God", but *yet*, they don't trust fully. Yet, there is still this doubt inside. When you trust that God will look after you, when you say, "God, I surrender to You", you don't keep thinking about things, you don't keep troubling yourself. But here, we do trouble ourselves, we do question ourselves, we do question our feelings, we do question everything so, where is the trust? Like I said, we hold onto everything. We hold onto expectation.

It's like once there was a kite - it's a bird - which flew down on a lake and caught a big fish. Then he flew up again and, as he was flying up, there was a group of crows. When they saw the kite carrying this fish, they all - a big group, thousands of them - started chasing this kite. When the kite flew north, all of them followed, with a lot of noise. When he went south, they all went south. When he went east, all of them still followed. When he went west, the same thing. So the kite was wondering why this group of crows was following him. Then, all of a sudden, he opened his mouth and the fish fell down. As the fish started to fall down, all the crows let go of the kite and started going toward the fish. The kite flew onto a branch and, looking down, said "Oh my goodness, it was just for this fish that they were after me like that and stressed me so much!"

It's the same thing in human life, also. When we let go of things, we will feel free of them, free of everything. You have to do your duty but don't expect great things. Expect only Him. The only real expectation that one has to have, the only real expectation is the Love of God. Even the saints will tell you that even that they don't expect, they are not worthy of expecting that. This is the humility of saints: to consider themselves not even worthy to be able to handle the Love of God.

But, if you really want something, cut down your expectation and free yourself, let go of things that are troubling you. If you analyse yourself, if you have anything that is troubling you or stopping you, analyse and see that this thing that is troubling you is inside of you. Yet, you have to let go of this, also. Like the kite had to let go of the fish, let go of this problem and when you let go, surrender to Him. Know that He's with you all the time, but as long as you don't let go, it's difficult.

There's this beautiful story of Draupadi, the wife of the Pandavas. She was involved in the *Chaturam game*. It's like a dice game. So in this game, the Pandavas lost everything; even their wife. At that time it was common. Even now, if you look at people gambling, they can lose everything. So they lost their wife and, in order to disgrace her, she was brought to the court of the Kauravas - their opponents. The Kauravas tried to remove her clothes. There Draupadi was standing with all the men around her but nobody could say anything, not even the Queen or the other people who were around her, because this was the law of the kingdom.

The Kauravas, who were the bad ones, tried to pull off the clothes of Draupadi, but she was resisting. Of course, she would not say: "Here, remove my clothes!" So she was hanging onto her clothes and at the same time she was calling for Krishna, saying "Govinda, Govinda, come and help me!" but she got no response. Then she let go of her clothes by putting her hands up and deep inside of her she was chanting Krishna's Name. At that moment they were still pulling all her clothes but metres and metres of cloth kept coming! They tried to pull her clothes off for hours and hours, but there were bundles of cloth coming out from her and they could not remove her clothes.

Later on, Draupadi asked Krishna "You are my brother, tell me something. When I was in the court and they were removing my clothes, why did you take so long to come to my rescue?" Krishna said, "It was not long at all. The moment you closed your eyes and called to me, saying "Govinda", when you said "Go," I left my palace and when you said "Vinda", I was already there! When I was there, I saw they were trying to pull off your clothes, but you were holding on too much to your clothes, so I could not help you! But when you let go of them, I helped you."

People come to me and say "Swamiji, I have this problem." So, I give you the solution for it, but you also have to do your part: let go of the problem! Otherwise you can go everywhere, but it will never get solved. It is like that with everything, you know, as long as you hang onto them, you will suffer. The earlier you let go, the quicker you will be free.

DON'T BE SHY TO SAY "I LOVE YOU"

Darshan in the Algarve, Portugal, 10 April 2008

(Note: Swami is singing with people and some people are not singing)

I see that some people are not singing. Maybe the song was new to you or different because of the language, but there is one language that everybody understands and this is the language of the hand, the clapping of the hands. You see, if you go under a tree, there are birds on it and if you start to clap your hands, what will happen? The birds will fly away. Here, this tree is your body and the leaves are your head, which is filled with so much negativity, which is represented by the birds. When you clap your hands, you are telling all this negativity from the mind to fly away. So the birds of negativity will fly away the moment you start clapping your hands. Also, clapping of the hands will generate happiness. When you are happy, what do you do? You clap your hands, no?
(Note: All the people clap happily at this moment)
That's good to see all of you happy. Spirituality is happiness, the happiness to rediscover your Self. So don't be shy to clap your hands when you sing the Name of God. The clapping of the hands is the same whether you understand or you don't understand what you are singing. And you are not clapping for me, you are not clapping for people, you are clapping for God, you know? And He loves it! When you take the *Srimad Bhagavatam*, it says that however you sing the Name of God, whether your voice is beautiful or not, He

doesn't care about it. What He cares about is that it comes from your heart. It is said that even if in anger you use the Name of God it is always positive; because the Name of God carries such vibration that it can transcend everything into positive.

So, don't be shy. Don't think what the neighbour next to you is thinking. The evil thought in your mind, only you know it; nobody else knows about it. So, when these birds fly away, *you* will be free, not your neighbour. By you being free, they will, also, profit afterwards, because when the evil thought has flown away what will take its place is Pure Love. And this Pure Love, that's who you are in reality.

We will sing now. Try to participate. I want all of you to participate. Even if you think you can't sing, just sing. If you can't sing, just clap your hands. I will sing a bhajan, which I always sing in Portugal, actually. It's about a discussion between a Saint named Surdas and Krishna. He asks Krishna "What is the greatest form of worship that will please you? Tell me, what can I do for you, to please you, to make you happy?"

> Surdas is asking Krishna "Tell me which kind of prayer or which kind of service shall I do to make you happy?" So Krishna says, "Just love! Love is the greatest worship."

You see, to love God is to please the Divine. When you love somebody, you do everything to please that person. And here Surdas is asking Krishna "Tell me, which kind of prayer or which kind of service shall I do to make you happy?" So Krishna answered "Just Love! Love is the greatest worship." Everywhere it is said Love is God, no? God is present in the heart of man as Love. So the greatest worship is to offer this Love to the Divine. So this song is about this Love.

I will just explain to you quickly about it. The first verse of it is about Duryodhana. If you have read the *Gita,* there are the good and the bad ones. The bad ones are Duryodhana and his family, the Kauravaswho symbolise negative qualities, and the good ones are Yudhishtira and his brothers, the Pandavas. So this song describes when Krishna was on Earth. , Duryodhana invited Him to have lunch at his place and he prepared lots of delicacies, a great, lovely big feast, but Krishna refused. Instead, He went to a very humble man, called Vidura and at his house he ate just very simple food. It was just because of his Love, because the one that is full of pride is devoid of love.

The second verse is about Sabari. This is from the epic *Ramayana.* There was an old lady who was always waiting since childhood for Rama. She would always recite the Name of Ram – all the time. Every day she would go in the forest, pick all the fruit that she could get and always chose the sweet ones. So, one day Rama came to her and she was so happy that she gave the fruit to Rama, but she wanted to choose the sweetest one. So, she tasted it and gave it to Rama. Rama's brother saw that and said "Oh, how disgusting! You are eating what she has been eating. Look at her mouth, she doesn't even have any teeth." Rama looked at him and said, "You don't understand. It's not the fruit that matters to me, it's about the Love that she is giving to me." And it's all about the Love of God, you know, how different Saints, different persons have expressed their Love to the Divine, how important Love is. You all know how important it is.

So, in the song I will sing *Sabse Oonchi,* and you will sing *Prema Sagai. Sabse Oonchi* means *'the greatest worship is'* and *Prema Sagai* means *'the Love relationship'.*

Look, when you are in love, you can always proclaim your love. You will do anything to proclaim your love. Here you are saying to God "Look, God, I Love You!" Just don't be shy about it, because when He says "I love you", He is not shy about it; He gives Himself completely, fully to you.

The easiest way to calm the mind and attain happiness is through singing, because when you sing, you can't think. You think only about what you are singing, so if you're singing the Name of God, you are thinking only of God. In God you have all the happiness.

You know, God has given so many of His Names to Mankind. You can call Him Allah, you can call Him Krishna, you can call Him Jesus, you can call Him many Names and it's the same. We say there is only one God, but yet, Man always tries to say "Mine is the best." When all are the same God, how can one be better than the other? In the *Srimad Bhagavatam*, Krishna said, "Don't judge anybody. Don't judge any religion. Don't judge anybody by their colour, don't judge anybody by their culture, because they are also loving Me and in all the forms I am present." You will see that Christ has said the same, "Don't judge and you shall not be judged", because our mind is always tempted to judge, always thinking, "I'm the right one; you are the wrong one!" How can they be wrong, when everybody is having the same God? Tell me, can there be something wrong in it? There can't be anything wrong. The paths are different, the ways are different, each one suited to the way they like, but everybody want to attain this eternal happiness, to become *satchitananda* and to attain God-Realisation.

See the world nowadays, how the world is, see how the mind of man is working. I don't say that there is just negativity or just positivity, there is a balance of both, but people who are spiritual, they have the Grace of God. And when you are spiritual, you awake this Divine Love within you. You try to know who you are, because you know the mind is limited by something and the body is limited by something but there is a greater force, which governs everything, which is deep inside of you. This greater force can't be satisfied by anything in the outside, only by Pure Love, only by complete devotion to the Divine. But yet, you always run towards things that have limitation. You bang your head and say, "Oh, I have hurt myself", but you haven't learnt anything. And what is it? God will always give us everything, because God is this Wish Fulfilling Tree. Whatever you wish under this tree He will give you.

There was once a man who was walking in the forest on his way home, but his house was far away. On the way, he felt tired and he saw a beautiful tree and he lay down under this tree. As he was lying under the tree, inside his mind he wished "Oh, how wonderful it would be if I had a beautiful bed", not knowing that he was under the Wish Fulfilling Tree. Suddenly, next to him there was a beautiful bed; it just appeared there. When he saw the bed, he jumped on it, enjoying the softness of the bed. The next thought that passed through his mind was "Oh, how wonderful it would be if there was a beautiful lady massaging my feet." Even this wish was fulfilled: the moment the wish came to his mind, he saw a young lady there, massaging his feet and he was very happy.

Then he started to realise, "Oh all my wishes have been fulfilled, so what about some food, I'm feeling hungry." The moment he wished it, he thought about it, there was a lot of food all around him. He was very happy eating the fruit, all the food and while he was eating, he said "Oh, all my wishes have been fulfilled, so what if, while I'm sitting in this forest, a lion jumps on me and eats me?" So what happened? Eventually, a lion appeared and jumped on him and ate him!

This is the same with men. We are being eaten every day by these lions, but yet, we like it, no? So say to the Divine "We want to Realise You. We want to be free from all the pain. We want to be free from all the worry" isn't it what you want or not? Not everybody wants to be free from pain. Do you really want to be free from pain and worry? Some people like the pain and worry. So you really want to achieve eternal happiness, no? What you have to do is ask God for it! And *really* try your maximum, try your best to achieve it. It's only when you try your best, that God will give you His Grace and blessing. He will say "Look, this one is trying very hard, let me go to him." And for sure you will have the Grace of God, try your best, always. Not that when a small wind passes by, you drop. You have to be strong! Know that God is always with you, wherever you are, whatever you are doing, whether you're positive or negative, He is with you! When you go in the quietness of your heart, through meditation, through yoga, you experience this quietness. All of you have meditated, no? So in this quietness, what do you feel? You feel peace and harmony. And for sure, you can always be in this peace and harmony only by the controlling of the mind. The weakest point is our mind. Our mind always wants to understand things. But in meditation, in prayers, in yoga, what do you do? You calm the mind. You don't want to understand anything; you just want to know your Self. And you will know, not with the mind, but by utilizing the mind and transcending the mind itself and by transcending the physical body. When you have transcended the mind and the body, what is left? The spirit. That's what Christ said "Give what belongs to Caesar back to Caesar." The mind and the body belong to Caesar; give it to him but the spirit belongs to God! Give what belongs to God back to God. So, Realise your Self. When He was saying, *the kingdom of God is not far, it's here*, He means *here* [inside of you]. He has shown the way to Realise it but Many people are looking for Him outside, not within themselves, within their

> Many people are looking for Him outside, but not within themselves, within their hearts. And here He is sitting in the heart of man, knocking. He says, "Open the door. Let Me out"

hearts. Here He is sitting, in the heart of man, knocking, saying "Open the door. Let Me out!"

So, unlock your heart and let Love flow; let unconditional Love flow. This is a Love that will really help you in your path, whatever path you are on, whatever religion, or whatever path you are following, it doesn't matter. Love is Love and that's what you have to understand. If you want the world to change, if you really want peace to reign in the world, change yourself first. By you changing, it will make a difference; by you becoming this pure love, it will make a difference!

But if you always say "Later we shall see," know that time is running, the world is changing. The moment you get the opportunity, take it! Never let go of it, because if you let go of it, you will get another chance, but it will not be the same. So let Divine Love awake and only through that will the world change, only through that you all will change, only through that, pain and worry will disappear from your life-only though Love and devotion!

So, I would like to do a small meditation with you. This is not really a meditation, but you can, wherever you are sitting, just try to centre yourself inside. What we will do is, we'll chant *Om Namo Narayanaya*.

You see, this *mantra* is a very powerful mantra. By chanting this *mantra*, one gets calmness of the mind, the mind becomes calm, it gets rid of all the worries, removing all the pain. It also bestows on you a lot of wealth. It doesn't look after only your spiritual advancement, it also helps you to advance materially, because I know not everybody likes only to focus themselves on the spiritual path, they like also the material path and both are important. When you chant *Om Namo Narayanaya*, you don't need to sit.

Guided Meditation

Close your eyes and visualise a lotus flower in your third eye. So, first, chant *Om Namo Narayanaya* aloud and then secondly, you will hum it: you will just hum the mantra and thirdly you will go into complete silence, but hear the inner sound of *OM Namo Narayanaya*, inside of you. So first is aloud and second is humming. First I will say to chant, then after 5 minutes, I will say to hum it and you will feel the vibration inside of you. By doing the humming, you will feel every part of you vibrate inside. Then when I say 'Silence', you all stop at once and go inside. You will hear the sound that you have been making inside of you even though you won't make any sound. Your mind should always be focused on the lotus.

So, visualise a closed lotus. While you are chanting, the lotus is still closed. When you're humming, the lotus opens, fully opens, like beautiful flowers. And when you are in silence, see the cosmic OM inside of the lotus or see the feet of God inside of the lotus, the feet of Narayana, inside of the lotus.

- Close your eyes and visualize a closed lotus flower in your third eye. Now:
- Chant *OM Namo Narayanaya*. (5 minutes)
- Hum *OM Namo Narayanaya* and see the lotus opening fully. (5 minutes)
- Silence. See the Cosmic OM or the Feet of Narayana in the open lotus. (5 minutes)
- Now slowly open your eyes, but stay still in the calm. Just open your eyes and, with open eyes, enjoy the calmness.

If you practice this meditation for 15 minutes: 5 minutes chanting, 5 minutes humming and 5 minutes in silence, you will have peace. The point of chanting is to control your mind and to make your mind positive. The humming is to vibrate the cosmic energy inside your body. And the silence is to attain the inner calm where the Divine reveals Itself to you. It's only for 15 minutes.

FROM EXPECTATION TO REALISATION

Darshan, South Africa, 23 June 2009

The meaning of the song that we just sang is so beautiful. That's why I chose to sing it today. It's actually about life itself. You will see how many similarities it has with our own life. The first part, *Sukha me sab saathi dukha me na khoi*, means: In prosperity, when you are happy and everything is going well in your life, you will have a lot of friends, but the moment there is pain in your life, people who say they love you very much, people who say that they are always with you, they are the first ones to back out, they are the first ones to run away.

There is also this famous saying "In a well, when there is water there are lots of frogs, but the moment the well gets empty there are no frogs at all." This is how it is. But if you are sincere, firstly towards yourself and then in your relationships – your friendships or any relationships – no matter what comes, nothing will ever move you; because neither your relationships nor what you feel inside depend on anything outside or on anything that you expected.

Expectation, that's the main thing in our life that makes us so unhappy.

Expectation, that's the main thing in our life that makes us so unhappy. Whatever we do we expect something in return; we have expectations in everything. How many times in your life have you done something that was unconditional? Do you remember? Everybody has done it, because that is your true nature; I am not talking about the outer nature that always has expectations.

Of course, we are so ruled by our mind and we expect so many things, but in your life, for sure, you have done something unconditionally, but very often it's easy to forget about it but you will always remember when you do something for somebody and you expect something you will always remember it. Or if somebody has hurt you, you will always remember it. But the good that somebody has done to you disappears [from you memory], also. Time makes everything disappear.

There is one question that we always ask ourselves. In the beginning we were with God, so why do we have to incarnate here? Why do we have to be separated from the Divine? This is a question that everybody asks, no? We have read books and we have seen, probably, many Masters who have said "Yes, the main thing in life is to realise your true Self, to realise your true aspect." But the question, which is still in the mind, is "Why are we separated from the Divine?"

Actually, the Divine is not separated from us, but it's true that our mind perceives us to be separated from the Unlimited One, because we let ourselves be ruled only by the outside. We forget what is inside. The last part of the song that we sang says "We visit holy places, we visit lots of pilgrim places, but one place that we forget to visit is our heart." Why did we get separated? Of course, the Divine in manifest or unmanifest form is present everywhere, in each cell of our body and pervades everything manifest and unmanifest. When we think of the manifestations of the Divine, we only think of Saints and Avatars, but He is, also, in all of you. Of course, these Saints and Avatars are grand manifestations of the Divine where He *has* to come to help humanity.

He always comes to help people, to help Himself, actually, but we are so bound by the outside that we create *karmic* things. Always, in many lives, we have been creating a lot of *karma* and we bind ourselves by that. Some will say "Yes, but we are here to remove the *karmic* things. We are here to Realise our Self." It's very true and this is the purpose of life; this is also the purpose of religion. It's not only waving the light in front of the Deity or singing the glory of God, which is very good, but we have to attain Him.

For that, you have to make an effort from your side. But if you let yourself get caught by the illusion, Maya will get you. Illusion is also the Lord's creation, but He gives us the choice, also, to want *Him* or to want the world. Some people are pretending to be very clever, saying we want everything! We want the world and we want the Lord! But Christ said in the Bible, "Give back to Caesar what belongs to Caesar and give back what belongs to the Spirit to the Spirit." He, also, said that if you think yourself to be Spirit you will be Spirit; but if you think yourself to be human, you will be just human, because you bind yourself.

You all know Shiva and Parvati. Shiva is a renunciate. He renounced the world and He lived like a beggar, going around begging for His food. He was just wearing a tiger skin. And, of course, Parvati wanted so much to marry Shiva. To marry Him was quite difficult, but She did so much penance and through Her *tapo shakti*, which means the *shakti* of the tapasya, the penance that She did, She won Shiva.

When She won Shiva, She said to Him "Lord, let me always be with You. Whenever You meditate, I will sit next to You. I will just look at You." Hearing that, Shiva just smiled. Time passed. Shiva was still in meditation and She was just sitting near Him. But after some time, even the thing that you love starts losing its quality, because it becomes so normal and we always want to experience the same longing and feeling that we had in the beginning.

So the same thing happened with Parvati. She was just sitting, in the Himalayas, in the cold. And as time passed, it became a bit boring for Parvati just to sit there, in the cold. So one day She approached Shiva and said to Him "My Lord, I have been here for so long now. I would like so much to go into the world to see your *bhaktas*, to see your devotees." Shiva didn't say much; He just listened. So Parvati sat there, again, for another month. You know very well with *matajis*, when they have something on their minds, it is very difficult to get it out. And that is not a bad thing. It's a good thing, because like this if you want God no matter what, you will get Him!

So one month passed and Parvati said again to Shiva "My Lord, can I go into the world? I would love so much to see your devotees, to see your *bhaktas*." Then Shiva said "Okay, fine. Go!" Parvati was very happy. She came down from the Himalayas and saw so many *bhaktas* who welcomed Her happily. They were so happy and made big parties and feasts for Her. So She started travelling and many years passed like that. Finally, She arrived in South India and for that great occasion they had built a huge temple for Her. But as She entered the temple, even though they welcomed her with all these grand things, all of a sudden She became very sad. She started to feel the longing for Her Beloved. But, because of all Her travelling, She had lost her way back. So, She searched for it again, but could not find it.

Finally, Parvati turned to the Lord and said "Through all this travelling, I blinded myself, and now I cannot even find the way back home. How will I find You? The only way is that You come and find me." She cried and cried and cried. Shiva was pleased with it and He came to Her and took Her back to the Himalayas.

In the same way, if you sit down quietly and empty your mind completely, through meditation, through chanting, controlling the mind and, especially, knowing that all is One, the Lord will come, because He is sitting always in your heart. We look for Him outside and it's good; outside is very good: we go to the temple and we pray to Him until He reveals Himself from *inside* of us. We say we want God, but yet, in our minds, God has to be *our* way. Of course, we all have a personal relationship towards the Divine and He will always come according to how we call Him. He is not limited, He has millions of forms, but we have to let Him do His Will. That's the meaning of the word surrender.

But very often we pretend to know better. This is the mistake that humans always make, to think that they know better than anybody else. There is this saying "The wise one keeps quiet; the unwise one makes lots of noise." The wise man knows the truth about himself and about everybody else. The unwise one doesn't know much. That's why He wants to have the attention of everybody.

Have you ever sat quietly with yourself? I'm not talking about meditation – meditation is something else – but just to sit and enjoy the moment, quietly, with an empty mind, without thinking of what your husband or your wife is doing or what your children are doing.

I would like to do a little and simple meditation with you. Just sit in a relaxed way. You see, we live in a world of energy, whatever we do is made up of energy. If we don't eat our body will be weak. We need energy and this energy is always flowing, but there is also a greater energy that we always need. And what is that energy? Love. And this energy is always flowing. Whatever we do is just to attain Love, nothing else, because in Love you will have peace, in Love you will find what you are looking for. But to attain this Love you have to make an effort, also. You can't just sit around saying "Okay, I have some love inside of me" and that's it. It's already there, but it can get more intensified. So you can utilise this energy also to awaken yourself. So now I ask you to sit and try not to think. Even if you think, don't hang onto the thoughts. It's not difficult, you know; it's very simple.

Guided Meditation

- Take your hand and place it in front of your heart, but don't touch your chest. Just place your hand in front on your heart level. Close your eyes.
- Concentrate on your breathing – your inhaling and exhaling. Don't hold your breath. Inhale and directly exhale.
- Don't hold onto your thoughts, either. Even if you think, let the thoughts pass and go by.
- Relax yourself. Relax your hands, especially the one that you are holding in front of your heart.
- Now place your hand on your heart without any pressure. Just place it and feel the trillions of bits of energy flowing through your heart, in each part of your body.

Did you feel something? What did you feel? If you have not felt anything, keep trying. It's very simple. You just need to get into contact with yourself. See, we have to awaken the Love that we treasure so much and keep always for ourselves. When you are in love, what do you like to do? To give, right? You like to spread this love. In the same way, when you are awake, His grace will flow through you, you will come out of this dreaming state you always put yourself into.

This reminds me of a story. There was once a woodcutter. One day, after finishing working, he came home, sat down and fell asleep. In his sleep he was dreaming that he was a king who had seven wives and many children. He was enjoying the dream very much. Then, all of a sudden, a friend of his came – not in the dream, but in reality – and said "Wake up!" The woodcutter came out of his dream and started shouting at his friend, saying "I was a king and you came and disturbed me!" Then the friend said "But it was just a dream." But the woodcutter was very annoyed and said "For you it was just a dream, but for me it was reality."

It's the same for us; we are living in a dreaming state. When we become awakened we will see the reality. But this reality is not to be understood with the mind, it's different. And that's what human beings are here for, to attain this reality of who they are, to see that they are not just this... let's call it, bag of bones. We will attain this reality only through Love, unconditional Love, only by loving in the same way that He loves us. Do you think His Love is bound by any limitation of what we understand of Him or how we dress Him? The Love of God is not bound by anything, except by the love of His devotees.

When we look at the life of Krishna, what was binding Him? He was always free, ever free. He was born free. The only thing that binds Him, that limits Him, is the love of His devotees. There was a Swami from Vrindavan last week in the *ashram* in Germany. He told this beautiful story, which is also in the *Srimad Bhagavatam*, of when Krishna was small. You know He was very naughty, always breaking all the butter pots, trying to annoy everybody, because He wanted all the attention to be only on Him and on nothing else. One day, Yashoda had Him on her lap and she had some milk on the fire. Then the milk started to boil and to spill into the fire. This Swami was explaining how great this milk was, it was even crying, because even though the Lord was so near to it, yet, he couldn't come to Him. Seeing the milk boiling, Yashoda put Krishna down and rushed to remove the milk.

There are many great *yogis* who try to attain the Lord through meditation and penance, but they cannot. And there He was playing on the lap of Yashoda, but yet she let Herself be distracted by the outside, forgetting about the Lord. So He went and broke the pots of buttermilk and gave the butter to the monkeys, starting to feed them. When Yashoda came and saw the broken pots and monkeys all around, she knew that it was Krishna. Then she started to look for Krishna and to run after Him everywhere. Of course, Krishna with His little, little legs started to run around and she couldn't catch Him.

But finally, He let Himself be caught by Yashoda. So she tried to tie Krishna with a rope, but every time She tried to tie Him, the rope was short by two inches. Then she would go and get some more rope, but again it was short. And she tried again with more rope, but again it was short. Finally, Yashoda became really, really tired. Then Krishna was looking at how much love she had at that moment, He thought "OK, I succeeded in getting Her attention fully on me." So He let Himself be tied. So, Love is the only thing that binds the Lord.

Love is the only thing that binds the Lord.

When we talk about finding Him inside of us, it's actually finding His Love inside of us, to catch Him completely and when we catch Him, then we can say "Yes, I have Him." Actually, all the Masters from all religions – not only Hinduism – Mohammed, Jesus, Krishna, all have come just to teach mankind to attain this Universal Love, to attain this unconditional Love, because this is your true nature. Apart from that, there is *nothing*. All that you have you will leave here. You took it from here; you will leave it here. Once you have attained this Love, just give, because you become an instrument of the Divine Love and let it flow, always.

Life passes. You were small, now you are grown up, tomorrow you will be old and then you will die. Then you come back again. The same cycle keeps repeating, but you come to a point of saying "Enough is enough!" Or do you always like to be in these cycles? How many of you like to be in these cycles? You see, in life you don't understand these cycles until there is a problem in your life. Then you turn to God and say "Oh, my God, come to my rescue." Then you understand those cycles. When something doesn't go right in your life, you turn towards God and say "Help me." But, first you turn to everybody else. You think that people can help you. Am I right? And then, finally, you say "They can't do anything. Let me turn towards Him only."

All of life is only to attain His Love and the moment you get Him, you get everything! Your prayers and mediation and all your *sadhana* are to attain this Love, to Realise it or to awaken it. If you have a precious stone and leave it inside the safe, it will not shine, but when you have it outside, it will shine more and more. Christ said, also, "If you have a lamp, you don't hide it under the bed. You put it high up that it can shine everywhere." The same thing with what you have inside of you, don't keep it closed inside. You have kept it closed up for *so* many lives. You have darkened it; you have put so many covers around it. Now you have a chance to let it shine, again.

Be sincere towards yourself and do your *sadhana*. You can talk about sincerity. You can be sincere towards God, you can go in front of Him and pray everyday, but *here* [from the heart] you have to be sincere, because it has to come from within yourself. Even the littlest thing, if you ask from within you will get it; even the greatest thing, if you ask from within you will get it.

God is represented in temples, so we have a form outside to concentrate on and it's very good until He reveals His Cosmic Form inside. And once you have found His Cosmic Form within yourself, you will see that He's everywhere; He's in everybody. *You* are in everybody, because at the end it's only Him.

We are ruled by our mind, by our pride and ego. We say "Yes, I, I, I," always, "*I* am doing this." But if you are doing it, why don't you always succeed in doing it? It's because you are so bound by your little pride. It's so little, but yet it seems *so* big. It blinds you so much that you don't see even the reality; but there is an easier way to surrender, to always remember the Divine. Whatever you do, wherever you are, just remind yourself that it's only Him who is doing it, because if He doesn't Will it, nothing happens. It's life, actually, God. There are different ways, but at the end everybody will attain Him, because we all come from one place and we all will go to one place only. The journey can be long, or it can be short, but at the end we will reach Him.

LET GO

Darshan in Steffenshof, Germany, 5 August 2007

Wherever you are to be, it's always through the Grace of God, through the Grace of Narayana, that you reach your destination. You can try your best to do something, spiritual or material, it doesn't matter, but if your heart is not there, you will not have the Grace of God into it and it will never work. You can try as much as possible, but as long as you have not attained the blessing of the Divine, it will always be incomplete.

That's why *bhakti*, devotion, is very important. Devotion, like I said during *Guru Purnima*, is not slavery as some people think, but first of all it's the joy of serving the Lord, the joy of trying to know God. We talk about God and we think about God, but still our mind can't comprehend Him, our mind can't picture Him. Out of His humbleness, He manifests Himself in different aspects, different forms, so that we can focus our minds on these forms. And He has different Names, so that we can focus our intellect on these Names. But man is so absorbed in his learning in order to feed the mind that he forgets about the reality. By feeding his mind, he always stays in the mind consciousness, in the mind level. And don't think that you will ever be able to understand and realise your true Self, Realise God with your mind. It is only when you surrender your mind to the Lotus Feet of God that you will really release yourself from this bondage, from all this suffering. Then you can say "God, here I am. I surrender to You, without anything. Help me; pull me out of this illusion."

There is this beautiful story of Draupadi. She was married with the five Pandavas and she regarded all five equally as her husband. She loved all of them in the same way. One day they were playing a dice game with their cousin, Duryodhan. The Pandavas had put everything they had in this game and they lost everything, because the dice that they were using were magic. So they lost everything. Seeing that, the Kauravas, said to them "What else do you have? Now that you don't have anything left, we want you to bet your wife; put in your wife, also." And the Pandavas agreed. So they even bet their wife in, Draupadi, and they, lost her as well. So to ridicule them, the Kauravas asked that Draupadi be brought to the court and they tried to remove her sari. Of course, when somebody is trying to remove your clothes, if you don't want this, what do you do? You hold onto them, no?

So Draupadi was calling to Krishna "Govinda, help me! Come! Where are you?" but at the same time, she was holding onto her clothes very tightly. She kept calling Govinda, but He didn't come, so she finally felt tired and she let go. She lifted her hands up and again called "Govinda." In that moment, the Lord appeared and the sari started to flow continuously. They pulled and pulled and pulled, metres and metres of cloth was coming off her and still they were not able to remove all her clothes. So they gave up and let her go.

One day Draupadi finally asked Krishna, "Krishna, when I was in the court, I was calling You. Why did you take so long to come?" Krishna said "Well, my dear sister, when you called me and said my name, Govinda, when you said '*Go*', I was leaving my palace to come to you. When you said '*vinda*', I was already there. But when I was there, I saw that you were hanging onto your clothes, so I didn't help you. And only when you let go of things, when you let go of your clothes, did I help."

It's the same thing with people. They want liberation, they want Self-Realisation, but at the same time, they're hanging onto things and they don't want to let go of anything. They want realisation, but they also want everything else. It is not wrong to want something, but you should want in the right way. Wanting and being, at the same time, detached will lead you to God-Realisation, but if you want and hang onto things, you will always be miserable and unhappy. And it is only up to *you* to decide whether you want to let go and surrender completely to the Lord and His Will or not. As long as your mind is judging things "This is like that. I am right. I am the only one who is right," you will never reach that point of Realising God.

Once, there was a very learned priest, a *pundit,* who went to a king and said "I will teach you the *Bhagavatam.*" The king, who, of course, knew about the *Bhagavatam,* looked at the priest and said "No, I don't want you to teach me the *Bhagavatam,* because you yourself have not understood it, so how could you teach it to me? Go back, learn it and when you understand it, come back to me."

The priest went away very angry, because his ego and pride had been hurt. He closed himself in his room, took all the books and started to read, again, the *Bhagavatam.* When he finished, he went, again, to the king and said "King, I have read everything and I am coming to you, again, to teach you the *Bhagavatam.*" The king replied "No, no, no, go back!" So he was sent back for the second time. This time he thought "If the king is sending me away all the time, for sure there is a meaning. Let me study it really carefully." Again, he closed himself in his room and this time he *really* surrendered himself and out of Love, he really opened his heart and read the *Bhagavatam.*

As he was reading the *Bhagavatam,* new knowledge arose in his mind, new wisdom came. Things that he didn't know before arose within him. Then he realised that he had been going to the king for the wrong reasons - for fame and wealth - and that was why the king had been sending him away. When he realised this, he didn't go to the king anymore.

After a few months, the king remembered him and went to see him. He said "I have come to you because I didn't see you coming back, so I was wondering what had happened?" But he saw that the priest was radiating so much light so without asking him anything more he fell at his feet and said, "Now you can teach me. I surrender to you. I take you as my Guru. Now I see that you have understood the *Srimad Bhagavatam*."

Humans always do this mistake of wanting things for the wrong reason. They pray to God, they ask for realisation, but they do this out of selfishness. They ask "God, grant me this, grant me that, give me this." They don't really trust; they just ask. Out of pride, out of ego, one asks always to gain things that will make him happy only for a certain time. When you have enjoyed these little things and the happiness is gone, then you are back again in the same misery.

If you want permanent happiness, it is possible only when you surrender completely to God. When your body, mind and soul have become one and are offered at the altar of the Lord, He will happily give everything to you. He will give Himself to you.

When you give yourself completely to God, God will also give Himself completely to you.

The king surrendered to the priest, who had understood that real teaching is within us, not in books. The same way, when you give yourself completely to God, God will also give Himself completely to you. But if you give Him only half, fifty percent, don't expect Him to give Himself one hundred percent to you.

So call upon the Lord from your heart. When your heart calls Him fully, when your mind is *completely* centred on Him, you will see that He will, also, completely surrender to you. Then you will be in this bliss, in this Love, continuously. You will be continuously in Love with God. You will be continuously in love with everybody and everything around you. This Love, you can't understand it with your mind. It surpasses *all* the love that this world can say about love. You have to attain this Divine Love, this Divine Ecstasy, and it's *only* when you surrender.

Real happiness lies deep inside your heart. So surrender your mind, which is so proud and so egoistic, and don't let it flatter you, making you think that you know a lot of things, when actually you don't know anything. As long as you haven't come to a point of God-Realisation, you can't say that you are realised or say that you know. But keep trying and never lose hope. Know that He is always with you. Whatever form of Him you call, He will be with you.

The *Maha Mantra, OM Namo Narayanaya,* that we always chant, has a lot hidden in it. It's one of the main *mantras* that used to be chanted and it is comprised of the force, the power of God, both materially and spiritually. So by chanting *OM Namo Narayanaya,* you will rise in gaining spiritual benefits and when you have spiritual benefits, the Lord will take care of your material benefits, too. He will sustain you. You have to have complete trust in Him. You have to have complete trust in yourself. So develop this trust. When your mind says "No" about something and when you feel you are right, go with your feeling. Listen to this feeling and say to your mind "Shut down." But the more you listen to the mind, the more it will think "Yeah, I have another victim, I'm very happy." We can see that very often, even with spiritual people who are on this path, they can't really shut their mind down, because when their mind starts to talk, they like to listen to it. And, when they have listened enough, they can't go out of it!

It's like if you're thrown in the sea: you will do anything to go out, you will move. Even if you don't know how to swim, you will try to go out. You know the water is deep but you will try to go up. You keep trying to pull yourself up, knowing that a hand will pull you out. You know that help will come, but if you let yourself drown in the water, you will lose everything. That's what people are doing. They go up and then down. They go up and back down. For how long will you do this?

The *Maha Mantra, OM Namo Narayanaya,* will pull you out of this illusion the same way the Lord pulled out Gajendra, when he was drowning. He asked for help from everybody, but nobody could help him. Then he turned to the Lord and said "Lord, You are the only one who can help me. My friends and my family have abandoned me. They could only do so much. But here I am in this illusion. I have been pulled and drowned in this illusion by this crocodile, by this ferocious beast. You are the only one who can help me." He called to the Lord with his heart full of Love. He turned to Him saying "Lord help me! Pull me out of this illusion." At that moment Narayana appeared and delivered him. The power of the Name of God is very strong, so chant!

You can do a lot of things, but to control the mind is the most difficult of all as long as you haven't surrendered it, as long as you have not given it at the altar of God saying to Him "Here, I surrender my mind to You!" But don't just say it. Mean it when you say it! And the more you mean it, the more you will see that He is right next to you. He is ever ready to pull you out of this illusion and He is giving His hand to you. His hand is always there. When you look at Jesus, His hand is always there and he says "Hey, I am here!" Also, Narayana says "Don't worry, I'm here." But *you* have to give them your hand.

So whatever you do, wherever you are, always chant inwardly *OM Namo Narayanaya.* The more you chant it, the more the power of the mind will decrease, the more you will be in the Divine bliss and the more your heart will open up to this word that we can only call Love, though it's so much more than that.

WHO IS GOD?

Darshan in Boulder, Colorado, United States, 9 June 2007

We often hear people asking the question "Who is God?" I will ask you, now, "Who is God?" Well, it's true, as long as you have not known Him, you can't answer. Love is God, but how many realise this Love? To which religion does God really belong? Is God Christian? Is God Hindu? Is God Muslim? Is God Buddhist? To which religion does He belong? Love.

Wherever you go, you will see that there is only one God and He is the Love in each ones heart, but how to realise this Love? We are so busy with this material world that we forget about the Divine Love. We try to look for this Love in the outside world. We try to look for this Love in other people. We try to look for this Love by travelling around the world, but we forget that we have to travel not outside, we have not to try to find this Love in other people, but we have to find this Love in ourselves. We have to realise the closeness to this Divine Love which is here, inside our hearts. Some people will say that it is very difficult to reach this point, but I say that it is very easy. You just need to want it! People try to find an easy way and if they could buy Love, they would do it. But Love can't be bought. Somebody might come and tell you "Listen, I will make you realise this Divine Love", but only the Guru can do that. Only by the grace of the Master can you do that.

This Divine Love, which is seated deep inside your heart, is like gold. And when gold is found in nature, it is covered with dust. Both gold and diamonds in nature are full of impurities. To get a beautiful jewel, a beautiful stone from a rough diamond, what do you do? You polish it. The same with gold: to get pure gold, you have to purify it, to remove all the impurities from it. It is the same with man. As long as you are stuck in the mind and don't purify the mind, this Love will never shine. You will never realise this Love. Even if you think you know it, because you have read about it or somebody has told you about it or Swami has said it, as long as you don't purify your mind, as long as you don't purify yourself, it will be difficult to realise this Love.

And how is one to purify the mind? The easiest way to purify the mind is to chant, to chant continuously the Name of God. You were chanting the *Mahamantra*: *Hare Ram Hare Ram, Ram Ram Hare Hare, Hare Krishna Hare Krishna, Krishna Krishna Hare Hare*. It is said that just by chanting this *mantra* one can get liberation, but one has to chant it with faith. Mere chanting alone will not help, but chanting with the heart will help. And how is one to chant with the heart? How is one to train the mind to calm itself? It is by forcing it. When you discipline yourself and say "Okay, today I will chant", then you start by taking your *japa mala* or rosary and you chant your *mantra* so you are focusing yourself on it, you are dragging the mind and putting your focus on the *mantra*.

The more you do it, the more you will see that, with time, you will not even need the *japa mala*. You will not need any rosary, because the *mantra* will automatically be chanted inside your heart. When you become the *mantra*, you reach a point of realisation, you reach a point of elevation, but still it's not the final one. There is still more to go. And how do you to get there? It's only when you abandon yourself into the hands of God, when you say "Lord, I surrender to You. I surrender myself - my body, my mind and my soul - completely to You" that you will get there. Don't do it superficially, but sincerely. And how do you do it sincerely? Be sincere with yourself and say "Yes, God, I want You. I'm surrendering myself to

You." When it comes sincerely from your heart, it will happen.

But nowadays in this world people always want quick things. When you tell them to chant ten *japa malas*, they say "Swami, it's *so* long – ten *japa malas*. When will I finish?" And when they start to chant, they are already thinking about when they will finish. So their mind is not really on what they are doing, but on what they will do afterwards.

When you are centred, when you concentrate, when you pray, when you chant the Name of God, that moment is between you and God. Christ said: If you want to pray, don't make it as a show. Run to the darkest corner where you and your Father, you and God are alone, where you converse with the Divine. And this corner where you can be quiet is your heart.

The mind is never quiet. The mind is always thinking and you will make it quiet by chanting. When through chanting you train the mind to go inside your heart in that deep quietness, you will realise that God is sitting there and not because you know it in the mind, not because you have read about it, but because you have realised it, because you feel it.

We are all on the search. Of course, people will go left and right, looking for the truth. As long as one hasn't found the spiritual path, one is never satisfied. It's like a train, which is going, but without knowing the destination. Like this train, people go left and right, but when one knows the destination one goes directly to this destination. When one knows ones path, one goes directly. Take this path and just go and realise your Self!

There was once a saint in India who lived as a hermit in a small hut made with grass. A couple came to him and said "Guruji, we love you so much that we would like to make you a nicer and stronger hut. Please, come with us." The saint answered "No, no, I'm happy where I am. I don't want to come." But after some time he called the couple, again, and said "Yes, I will come with you, but can you do me one favour?" The couple were very happy and said "If you are asking, we will do anything for you." The saint said to the couple "Let me come and live in your toilet." The couple were wondering "We want to build a nice hut for you, so why do you want to come and live in our toilet?" The saint said "I would rather stay in your toilet than among devotees or people who are only looking for fame and glory. These people come to me and they are only looking for how to end their misery, but they are not really looking for God. If I stay in the toilet, I would rather bear the smell of the toilet than the insincerity of those people and also the smell of the toilet will keep them away!" This made the couple realise how people are. People are searching, yes, but they are not sincere towards themselves.

Only when you are sincere towards yourself, you will find your path. When you accept yourself, when you accept the Will of God and whatever He gives you as right, you surrender to His will, you surrender to His Love and then you say "Yes, God, I believe in You and I trust in whatever You are doing for me. I trust in Your Love and I don't doubt You." But when we doubt Him and question Him, we are not truthful. Then we say "God, You have made a mistake." But how can God make a mistake, when He is so perfect? How can Love, which is the purity of your True Self, make a mistake? It can't. It can be a mistake only when there is doubt, when there is fear. But when all these things are clearer, when all of these things are put away by the Holy Names of God - which are thousands of Names - then you will see His glory, you will feel His Love.

While we were singing, some people were dancing. When you are dancing for God, you are doing also a kind of dancing yoga. You are forgetting about your body, you are forgetting about your mind, you are just singing the glory of God, singing the Name of God. In this way you are decreasing the power of the mind. You will notice that after moving, when you sit down and relax, your concentration is much better than if you just sit down. When you just sit your mind is jumping left and right. When you dance in the right way, you are energising yourself; you are calling upon this inner Self to reveal Itself. And when you lift your hand up, you are calling to the Lord, to God, "I'm in this illusion. I'm drowning in this illusion. Here, I'm lifting my hand up to You. Pull me out of this illusion. I'm surrendering." You will notice that in all the Holy Scriptures there is this phrase, which says: "*Lord, I'm lifting my hand up to You. Come to rescue me.*" You will find it in the Psalms, you will find it in the Koran and you will find it also in the *Gita*. So singing the glory of God, transcends all religions, transcends all cultures, transcends all races, transcends all the mind can create and you will find God inside of you.

Man lives in ignorance. Of course, you need a little knowledge of God, a little knowledge of the Divine to get out of it, but at the end, you have to surrender completely. It is neither your intelligence nor your ignorance that will make you realise, but it is your true Self, it is your surrendered-ness. It's like if you are walking barefoot and you get a thorn in your foot: you will need another thorn to remove it. In the same way, when the thorn of ignorance is in your feet, you need another thorn to remove it. But what do you do afterwards? Do you keep both thorns in your pocket and say "OK, I will treasure them"? You don't keep both of them. You throw both of them away. So even knowledge will bring you to a certain level, but for the rest you will have to surrender yourself completely to the Love of God. Firstly, you have to surrender your mind completely, then you have to surrender your body and then you have to surrender your soul.

The power of chanting the Name of God doesn't purify only the mind, it purifies the body and it purifies also the soul. It purifies the mind, which becomes healthy. When your mind is purified, when your mind is positive, eventually your body will also be healthy. How many times do people who are ill, when they surrender completely and say "I'm fed up now. God, I'm praying to You and I surrender to You. Do whatever You want to do with me" what then happens? The miracle happens – the miracle of faith, the miracle of Love, the miracle of surrender. But nowadays people are so scared of surrender. They say "I will surrender, *but...* what will happen? If I surrender, how will I live?" The insecurity is already present. How can they trust when there is insecurity? Only when there is complete trust in God, complete trust in yourself and you ask God for Himself that He will give Himself to you. Trust that whatever He does is right. Even if the mind doesn't understand it, it is right! Once there was a king. This king was very generous and very loving, but he had one fault: he was short-tempered. For that many people were afraid of him, but in his kingdom there was one minister that he loved very much. This minister used to pray every day and he had great trust in God. One day the king went hunting in the forest and, on the way, there was a cobra in front of the king's horse. The horse panicked and threw the king up in the air and the king landed down near the cobra. The cobra bit the king's index finger. The king knew that if he didn't cut off his finger, the poison would kill him. So he pulled his dagger and chopped off his finger. He was in much pain, so the minister rushed to him, took a piece of cloth and bandaged the king's finger. As he was doing the bandage, he said to the king "King, don't worry, it's God's Will that you cut your finger and it's God's Will that you have pain." The king bore this for some time, but the minister was going on and on and on. The king could not handle it anymore, so he said to his soldiers "Take this man and put him in the prison. I can't bear him. I can't listen to him. He keeps on saying it's God's Will, God's Will. I'm in pain and he's saying that it's God's Will." So they took the minister to the prison and locked him inside, but he was happy and said "Thank you God, I am here now, quiet and I can chant Your Name. In the world where I'm so busy, I chant Your Name only when I have a little bit of time, but, now, I'm here and have time to chant Your Name all the time."

A few days later the king went out hunting again, but this time he was attacked by a group of tribesmen. They captured the king and brought him to the chief. The chief was very happy to see the king tied up and said "King, you are so lucky. Today we will sacrifice you to the Goddess Kali." The King thought "Well, I'm not lucky at all. I will be killed!" Then the chief of the tribe said to his tribesmen "It's not every time that the Goddess gets royal blood. Take the king, wash him and dress him nicely. We will offer him to the Goddess afterwards." But as they were removing his clothes to wash him, the tribesmen noticed that the king had one missing finger. They rushed quickly to the chief and said "Chief, chief, we can't offer this king to the Goddess, because he is incomplete. He is missing one finger." The chief thought for a moment and then he said "OK, let him go. You are a lucky king. Because of your missing finger, we can't offer you to the Goddess."

The king was very happy. He rushed back to the palace and he went directly to the jail. He opened the jail and embraced the minister.

> "You should never be scared of surrendering yourself to His Will. You should never be scared of opening your heart and Loving".

As he was embracing the minister he said "Thank you! It's true, you were right. It was God's will! I was saved because I'm missing one finger." Then he asked the minister "But I don't understand one thing. Why did I lock you in here? You are such a good man. You praise God all the time." The minister replied "It's simple. I told you that everything happens through the Will of God. If I had come with you the second time, if you had not locked me up in jail, what would have happened? They would have taken us both. And when they had seen that you were missing one finger, that you were incomplete, but that I was complete, they would have taken me and offered me to the Goddess!"

So, whatever the Higher Consciousness, whatever God, whatever Name you put to Him, gives you, He's always right. If something negative happens, now you may not understand it, but later on in life you will realise that whatever He did was for your own good. You should never be scared of surrendering yourself to His Will. You should never be scared of opening your heart and Loving.

Start to Love now, this moment. Open your heart and love. Let it flow. The more you open up, the more your mind is pure, the more your mind is positive, the more you will become more loving and you will give more Love. And know that whatever you do with this Love, will always be perfect. You will meditate and you will enjoy your meditation. You will do yoga and you will enjoy your yoga. You will chant the Name of God and you will enjoy it. People meditate and chant, but when there is no Love in it, it fades with time. Also, love with limitations fades. But True Love, Real Love, Unconditional Love never fades. So cultivate this Love, cultivate this Unconditional Love and surrender to the Divine.

THE SECRET IS THAT I AM EMPTY

Darshan in Lisbon, Portugal, 12 April 2008

What more is there apart from God? Nothing, no? So what we want is Him, yet we don't want to surrender, we don't surrender ourselves completely to Him. That's why there is always incompleteness inside. But to surrender means to say to God "Lord, I give myself, my body, mind and soul completely to You." Isn't that what spirituality is about? That doesn't mean that you have to leave your family and renounce everything, but live in a detached way. Try to put God always first in your life. Like that, He can work through you.

We all want to be somebody, we all want to realise our Self, we all want to know who we are in reality, but with this mind, we will never be able to. We have to calm the mind. We need certain knowledge, yes, to achieve the Divine, to attain Him, but we need devotion, we need *bhakti*. When *bhakti* arises inside, we give ourselves completely. *Bhakti,* devotion, is when you give yourself, when you are in the fullness of Love.

Like I said when I was in the Algarve a few days ago, when you are in love, you always want to be with your beloved, no matter what. You will leave father, mother, everybody. You will fight for your beloved, isn't that so? The real Beloved is God, because He is the only One who is always fresh. His Love always renews itself. Whereas all the other loves, they start very fresh like a beautiful flower and they also fade the same as the other flowers. You know that, no? How many times in your life have you fallen in love? You *really fall* in love! And then to rise is a very difficult achievement.

About surrendering, there is a beautiful story about the flute of Krishna. You know Krishna always holds a flute in his hand; there is a great story behind it. Everyday Krishna would go in the garden and say to all the plants "I love you." The plants were very happy and responded back and said "Krishna, we love You, too." One day Krishna rushed quickly into the garden, very alarmed. He went to the bamboo plant and the bamboo plant asked "Krishna, what's wrong with you?" Krishna said "I have something to ask you, but it is very difficult." The bamboo said "Tell me. If I can give it you, I will give it to you." So Krishna said "I need your life. I need to cut you". The bamboo thought for a while and asked "You don't have any other choice? You don't have any other way?" Krishna said, "No, no other way." The bamboo then said "OK, I surrender to you".

So Krishna cut the bamboo, made holes in it and each time he was doing that, the bamboo was crying with pain, because it was very painful. Krishna made a beautiful flute out of it. And this flute was with Krishna all the time, it was with Him 24 hours a day. Even the Gopis were jealous of the flute. They said, "Look, Krishna is our Lord, but, yet, we get to spend only some time with him. He wakes up with you, He sleeps with you, you are with Him all the time." So one day they asked the bamboo, "Tell us the secret of it. What is the secret for the Lord to

"The secret is that I'm empty inside. And the Lord does whatever he wants with me, whenever he wants with me and however he wants with me".

treasure you so much?" And the bamboo said "The secret is that I'm empty inside and the Lord does whatever he wants with me, whenever he wants and however he wants."

So this is complete surrender, where God can do whatever He wants with you, whenever He wants and as He wants. For that you don't need to be scared, you know, you just have to give yourself. Who is your Self in reality? It's just Him! In the *Gita,* Krishna said, "Everything is me." In the Bible, Christ said "Give what belongs to Caesar, to Caesar and what belongs to God, to God." But what belongs to God? It is your spirit. It is your true Self and if you want to realise your Self, be like the flute! Say: "Lord, do whatever you want with me, whenever you want with me, and however you want with me" and make this your prayer. And in your mind don't ask any questions. This is poison, because the mind always doubts. The mind always thinks it knows best.

When you surrender this mind to the Divine, *bhakti* will arise, devotion will arise and when devotion arises, the purity of Love will also arise together with it. It's not a love where we just say "I love you. I love you." It's a Love where when we say "I love you" there is no condition in it. It is not "I love you because of something. I love you because of your body. I love you because of your wealth. I love you because you are beautiful outside but if we pull the skin from your body, I don't love you anymore." But it's a Love where you Love the person the way the person is. That's the purity of Love, the Unconditional Love, the way God Loves, the way your heart knows how to Love. That's why you do feel Love, but the moment you start to put conditions to that Love, it fades. But when you stick to this purity of Love, and make this Love grow, it will grow, because Love is like a seed, which is inside the heart of man. The seed has to grow, has to blossom, also. It has to germinate and grow big; the seed can't just stay like that.

That's what Christ said, also. You can see so many similarities between Hinduism and Christianity. Christ said "If you plant a seed on a stone, it will never grow. But if you plant it in the heart of Man it shall grow." This is the Love in the heart of man. When real Love is felt, when real Love starts to grow, it grows in six different stages, which are called: *Sneha Prem, Pranaya Prem, Mana Prem, Raga Prem,*

Anuraga Prem, and *Maha Bhav.* - Of course, I will now not go into detail about it, but these stages of Love grow when purity is there [in the heart], which leads you to complete surrender to the Divine. But, first, what is needed in a normal life is to calm the mind and let Love itself start to grow inside of the heart. Only through this Love will you know who you are. And this is not up to me to tell you, it's up to you to take the first step.

The easiest way to calm the mind is to sing the Name of God, because you can sing the Name of God anytime, wherever you are. So I would like to chant with you *Om Namo Narayanaya,* because this *mantra* is so powerful that it raises you, it raises your spiritual consciousness to a very high state. Also, it helps you in your material life and it calms your mind. This is one Name of God but, of course, there are many Names of God that you can chant that create the same happiness. Just chant these three words: OM Namo Narayanaya. Chant it every day, wherever you are, whatever happens to you, just chant *Om Namo Narayanaya* and you will see how close the Divine is. He is just sitting inside your heart, you know. You just need to bring Him out and let the Divine Love awaken inside of you. Don't have fear. Don't have fear to surrender yourself. Actually, you will not lose anything, but you will gain everything. Because, often, when we talk about surrender, people say "Oh my goodness, what will I lose?", but people forget to say "What will I gain?"

We always like to gain something, no? We pray, we always ask God for something. We do our meditation and we do our yoga, but always to get something. So as humans we always ask, we always like to get something and when we want God, He will give Himself to us. We will gain everything. And in this time, we don't need to sit in caves to meditate like the yogis, because our mind is like a cave itself it's so dark! And we sit always in that cave that is our mind. So like the yogis are always sitting in their cave and meditate, let us chant the Name of God. It's very simple.

SURRENDER

JUST LOVE

GURU

The Guru is no different from
the Self.
This is beyond doubt the Truth,
the Absolute Truth.

Lord Shiva

THE ONE WHO HOLDS YOUR HAND
AND GUIDES YOU

Darshan, Steffenshof, Germany, 2 May 2008

Often, there is a question that we all ask: who is our *Satguru*? Isn't it a good question? Some lucky people know and some, who are to *be* lucky, they are waiting to know. This search, actually, is not only for one life, but has been for many lives. We always search for our *Satguru*, because only the *Satguru* will lead us out of this illusion. Only the *Satguru* can give us the blessing, guide us and make us Realise our True Self. But to find the *Satguru* is very often difficult. We go through many ups and downs. We keep searching, thinking that we will find the *Satguru*. We pray to God "God, send my *Satguru*." But very often when the *Satguru* is in front of the person, the person doesn't know it, because in the mind of man, how he fashions a Guru is completely different to how the *Satguru* is in reality.

Only the *Satguru* can give us the blessing, guide us and make us Realise our True Self.

It's the same when we look at Mahavatar Babaji. We have a beautiful *murti*, a beautiful Deity here. In our mind we have an image of the *Jagat Guru*, but yet, I tell you, He is not like that. When we look at Him He looks strict. He is strict when He has to be strict, but He is the personification of calmness. No matter what, He is always calm and this is the quality of a *Satguru*.

Once there was a man. He was always searching for his *Satguru*. So he went everywhere, but yet his heart was not satisfied. He met many masters, but yet, his heart was not satisfied, because this is also one quality of the devotee that when they meet their *Satguru*, their heart shall feel it. So he went around, but he didn't find his *Satguru*. One day he came across a saint and he asked the saint "Listen, dear sir, I am searching for my *Satguru*. Could you please guide me?" The saint closed his eyes, meditated for a little while and then said to the man "Listen, my son, there are many holy men staying on that mountain that you can see here. Tomorrow is a very good day. Invite all of them to your place. Invite them for lunch. With love and dedication, serve them food and give them respect and when they are eating, ask them a question. Take a twig from a tree, from any tree. Take two twigs, two pieces of branch. And tell them 'Tell me dear sirs, which tree does this twig belong to?" And when they give you an answer, contradict them: When they say it's from a mango tree, you say 'No, it's from a peepal.' and if they get angry, they are not *Satgurus*, but the one who stays calm and says 'Maybe, it is possible that it is a peepal twig', this will be a *Satguru*." So, he did as the saint told him: He invited these saints and served them food with lots of love and respect. He showed them the twigs and he asked all of them "Dear sirs, tell me which fruit tree this twig belongs to." They all looked at it and said "It's a mango twig from a mango tree." But as the saint told him, he started to contradict them and told them: "No it's from a peepal tree!" so, the other gurus got *very* frustrated, even furious, and they said "Why don't you see that it is a mango twig? Why are you telling us all the time this is a peepal twig? We tell you it is mango!" They all got very angry except one very simple man who was among them. He was eating his food and was very calm. So he looked at this man and he asked him: "What about you, dear sir?" With a smile, this *guru* said very calmly and very serenely "Well, it is possible that this is a peepal twig."

You see, the quality of calmness is very important. How can a master guide if he is not calm? And this is the greatness of a *Satguru*. No matter what happens, he will always stay calm. So, now you will all go and test your *Satguru*? Like I said during *Guru Purnima*, the best way is to ask the *Satguru* directly or the *Guru* directly. When you have found your *Satguru*, surrender and you can stop asking questions. The mind, like I often say, is always full of doubt. If you don't give the *Satguru* a chance to hold your hand and guide you out of it [*maya*], you will go away and you will lose a chance. So let the *Satguru* hold your hand and guide you.

The feeling, the joy that you have when the *Satguru* is in front of you is reflected back to you. The *Satguru* will never show this feeling, but *you* will feel it. He knows it, but he wants *you* to know it. The *Satguru* has already found God, has already Realised the Divine and he wants you to Realise, also. That's why you look for him.

Try to always feel with your heart and try to listen to your inner Self, because when your inner Self reveals something, the mind will always say "Oh, no, no, no, no it's not like that. It has to be like this!" The mind will always try to divert you from your path, from the reality. That's why you have to show the mind that *you* are the master. Not the mind is the master of you.

So, how to master the mind? Chant the Name of Narayana. Like yesterday, during the *satsang* I was explaining the power of the Name of Narayana, how powerful this *Maha Mantra* is. If you want to attain Him, chant it. The more you chant it, the more you will draw Him closer to you. When you call somebody, you will not call "Hey, come here." You call the person by name. So the Divine also has many Names and many forms and when you call Him, He will come in that form.

Often people ask me "But if I pray to Shiva, should I change [to Narayana]?" Actually, no, you should not change it, but your love has to grow more and more. If you call Him as Shiva, He will come in that form. If you call Him as the Divine Mother, He will come as the Divine Mother to you. But in reality, you will find Him deep inside your heart as the form of Love, Pure Love, Unconditional Love and it's there that you have to find Him. And the mind can't understand Love, because the mind always has expectations. The mind always has a limit, but when you cross over this limit, then you can't understand.

It happens so much in the life of people that when the grace of God comes upon them, they don't understand anything. They try to understand, but yet, they can't understand. So many people I have met have told me "Oh, you know, I love God, but I don't know, I don't understand Him, I don't know why I Love Him so much." So, you have to come to that state, where even if you want to understand, you can't understand. You see Him in front of you, you want to grasp Him, but you can't.

Imagine what will happen? It will drive you crazy, crazy for Him. It's the best thing. It's a deep longing, yet it makes it sweeter. Our soul is always longing for Him – always! There is not a time when the soul does not long for the Beloved, whether we are conscious, aware of it or we are not aware of it. But our true Self, the soul consciousness is always aware of it. Like Christ always said: He who has eyes to see, let him see, and he who has ears to hear, let him hear.

Try to see with the eyes of the heart and try to hear deep inside of you. It's very simple to know if what you are hearing or what you are feeling is from the heart or from the mind because, whatever is from inside of your heart, there will be no doubt about it, but whatever comes from your mind, there will be lots of questions. Even if the mind keeps thinking the same thing, there will still be lots and lots of questions and the mind will not feel free from it. So that's why in meditation, you try to go into the calmness of yourself and to listen deep inside of you, you try to attain this calmness, to attain this Love that you have inside of you.

RESURRECT WITH CHRIST

Easter Sunday, Chapel Shree Peetha Nilaya
Springen, Germany, 12 April 2009

So in this Holy Gospel that we were reading, you see that this is the beginning of John the Baptist's testimony where he said that he is not the Light, but he came to bear witness to the Light. It's the same for all of us; we are here to Realise our Self, to make ourselves who we are in Reality. You see that Christ came, but yet, people were against him. He came to His own people who did not even recognise Him. It is like it is said: 'no one is a prophet in his own land'. It is always afterwards.

It is the same thing with a Master. When you have a Teacher with you, nobody appreciates it and then, after the teacher has passed on, people say "Oh how wonderful it would have been if we were there!" But know that whatever is written about a Teacher is always good afterwards. Of course, everybody wants to have been around at that time, but when the Teacher is there, nobody wants to be around. And it is always like that. Only 10 years or 20 years after, people say "Oh how wonderful it would have been if we were there." So this is how the mind of man functions. So, if you have the chance to be with the Master, take it, so that one future day you won't be saying "Oh, why when the opportunity was there, didn't I take the chance?"

Like I said about the resurrection of Christ, He is resurrecting inside everybody and He is calling everybody to resurrect with Him and to let the old man, the old one who is inside of you die and to let the new one resurrect together with Him. That is the resurrection of Christ. It is not only by saying "Oh yes, let's praise Him. He has resurrected." Yes, He resurrected 2000 years ago and even if He had not resurrected, He would still be Christ Himself. But he has shown that resurrection is possible, He has shown that Realisation, God-Realisation or your true Realisation *is* possible. He has shown the Way. That is why He said: "I am the Way, the Truth and the Light." So He has shown that if you *really* want God, it is possible to achieve Him, even in one life; but you have to be sincere with yourself, you have to *really* sincerely say "Yes, I want Him!" and not be fake just because you have read about it in a book, and you say "Okay, Realisation is beautiful" or "I want to see God. I want to feel God. I want to have God-Realisation" and you think "It's beautiful just to hear it, because it's nice to the ears." But it's not about that! It's about you being sincere with yourself. If you *really* want it, no matter how you are – you

> He is calling everybody to resurrect with Him, and letting the old one, who is inside of you, die and letting the new one resurrect together with Him. That is the resurrection of Christ.

can even be the greatest criminal – you will become the greatest Saint.

Take Valmiki, he wrote the *Ramayana*. He was the greatest criminal but by the grace of Rama, what happened? He changed to be one of the greatest Sages of all time. Also, take Mary Magdalene, about whom people said so many things, but yet, we praise her and she is the greatest model of women, the greatest model of devotion.

It's not what we see outside. It's not what we judge on the outside with our mind. For once, truly listen to your heart, really listen to the call of your heart. The call of your heart will reflect the call of your soul. Listen carefully, don't listen to the mind, don't say "yes" to the mind when it says "I want Realisation", without knowing what it is. The mind doesn't comprehend certain things. The mind doesn't even comprehend what Love is, so how do you think the mind will comprehend what is greater even than Love itself?

We use the word 'Love' to express God, because there is no other word greater than that to express Him in our language, but if we look deeper inside ourselves, what we feel inside we can't even put a name to it. The word 'love' is just a word, but God is greater. What you have inside of you is even greater than what you can think about! If He is calling 'that' within you and if you are sincere with yourself and cleanse your mind from all impurity, you will have Him, you can have Him even in one second, He can change your life in one second. And it is not about what you practise.

Why do we practise? It is to show that we are interested in Him, we are really interested in achieving something and that is very beautiful. We show our appreciation, we show devotion and we are thankful for what He has given us; but know that everything depends on His Grace and His Grace is within you. When you cleanse everything from your mind, everything from the outside and you *really* reach the depth inside then, you are completely surrendered to Him and He is completely surrendered to you.

Like it is said in the other Gospels, the Father does not exist without the Son and the Son does not exist without the Father. The Spirit does not exist without the Son and the Father; the Father does not exist without the Spirit and the Son. So the Father, the Son and the Holy Spirit exist already within you. They are not separate from you. That is what Christ said: Call upon me to become the sons of God and the daughters of God and to realise your true identity. When you have Realised your true identity of being the child [of God], the Spirit will flow inside each part of your veins and each part of your arteries will radiate the Divine Light, the Cosmic Light. You will see each atom as being the same light.

We look very often only on the outside. Our mind is focus on the outside and we see the duality of the outside. You and 'x, y and z' are different, yes, but in reality we are all one. If we remove all the identities that we have created from many lives, if we remove all the karmic things that we have created around the soul itself, we will see that the light is the same. If you look around, there can be so many lights, with different kinds of bulbs, yes, but there is only one source of electricity that lights everything. In the same way, you can have different bodies, you can have different colour hair, face, clothes and whatever else, but yet, the light that shines inside you, the Light of who you are in Reality is the same one. All of you are One and if you see it in that way, you go beyond the mind.

Christ said: Be humble like a child, then you shall enter the Kingdom of God. When you look at a child, the child doesn't bother about anything. So experiences of life make you become like that. Don't close yourself, rise above everything and you will see God face-to-face, you will see yourself face-to-face. And be humble always, because if you are arrogant, if you have pride, don't think that you will have God and don't think that you will *ever* have Realisation. You can practice for whole lifetimes - I am not talking only about one life, but lives - you can practice thousands of lives if you want but you will not get it, you will not reach this point.

But if you really humble yourself and are really pure in your heart and really cleanse your mind, then you will see that He can remove all the karmic things just like that!! He can change your life, He can change the lives of people in one second, but you can also destroy your life in one second! It's up to you. It is only you who has this choice. If you want to change, you will change. If you don't want to change, you won't change, but *you* have the choice. He will not do this for you. The Master will never do this for you. The Master will show you the way. Like Christ said: "I am the Way, the Truth and the Light." So the Master will show you the Way, but you have to take your first step. If you don't take your first step, then forget it. Like it is said, it is easy to judge but you forget that you have a log in your own eye. It's often like that, you know. You judge others, but what are these judgements that you see in them? Is it not your own reflection? So, be humble like Him. Today you are all celebrating the resurrection of Christ, so let Him arise inside of you, let Him Resurrect inside of you.

Glory be to the Father and the Son and the Holy Spirit, now and to the ages of ages. Amen.

WHAT IT'S LIKE TO FIND GOD

Darshan, Shree Peetha Nilaya, Springen, Germany, 4 June 2009

Today, I wanted to talk about spirituality. We are all spiritual people, no? Yes? How do you know? What qualities qualify you as being spiritual? How do you know that you are spiritual? We like very much to have this title of being spiritual because we like to feel special, but in reality everybody is special, because everybody is unique and *everybody* is spiritual – it doesn't matter which path they follow or what they are doing.

It's true that spirituality is to Realise God, to Realise Love, to Realise the Oneness with the Divine, to attain the Divine *but* when I look at spiritual people, they always think they know better. They think they are greater than everybody else and they always think the best of themselves. It's all right, but the best of oneself is to not criticise others. As Krishna said, the best is to rise above good and evil.

On the spiritual path, everybody tries to purify herself or himself. When I talk about purity, what does your mind perceive? It thinks only about good things. You think that when you are spiritual, when you are purified, you become very good. Whatever you do, your mind perceives you to be always right and that's what you call perfection, but what is perfection? In the *Gita*, Krishna explained what perfection is. He said: If you can rise above right and wrong, if you can rise above good and evil, if you can rise above all duality, then you can say "Yes, I have attained certain perfection." Your mind makes you judge and as long as you have not yet achieved the vision of the Divine and you have not purified yourself, meaning that you have not trained your mind to see the non-duality, to see the oneness, then spirituality is still far away.

In the same way, when you go to school, why do you go to school? You go to learn, no? So, in school you have teachers, don't you? And when you go to school do you know better than the teacher or do you go there to learn from the teacher? Is it really to learn? I don't know, because in the West, I guess it's the opposite, no? You don't know better than the teacher but gradually, little by little, you learn and, probably, one day you will also become a teacher.

It is the same thing on the spiritual path. When you find a teacher, you go to him but you don't pretend to be better than the teacher or to know better than him. You are there to learn *from* the teacher. No matter what kind of learning you receive, it is for your own benefit, for your own growth and for your own advancement towards the Divine. If you succeed, for sure one day you will become a teacher yourself to help others who are going on the spiritual path. Then you can say "Yes, do it like this or do it like that."

So, on the spiritual path we are all learning. We are learning to attain God, but first of all we are learning to rise above our mind. And if you *really* want to be spiritual, be positive. Train yourself to be positive. All the masters who have come, all the teachers who have come, all the *gurus* who have come, they haven't come to collect disciples, you know. They have not come to make people slaves or to use them, like some people say. They have come to help people, to make them masters one day, but for that you have to really surrender yourself.

Once, somebody asked a master "How is it to find God?" The teacher took the disciple by the hand and brought him to the river where he dragged him into the water. When they were in the river, the teacher took the head of the disciple and put it under the water.

After some time the teacher pulled back the head of the disciple and said to him "How was it?" The disciple said "I was trying to breathe but I was suffocating, I was trying to grasp some air but I was battling." The teacher smiled and said "You want to find God? It is this way [with the same yearning]."

You have to try your best. When this longing for the Divine or for God-Realisation or whatever name you put on it, is *really* like you are suffocating, so that you can't even breathe, then you can say "Yes, I'm on the way towards Divinity." But as long as this longing is not like that, you are still far away and that's how it is.

> When this longing for the Divine or for God-Realisation or whatever name you put on it, is *really* like suffocating, so that you can't even breathe, then you can say "Yes, I'm on the way towards Divinity."

You see, in the West people perceive spirituality in a completely different way. It has to be *their* way. It's like with a Christmas tree: you decorate it the way *you* want it and you put whatever you want on it. You do the same thing with the Master, with the teacher; you want the teacher to be *your* disciple, you want the teacher to be *your* student, rather than you being the student of the teacher. That's what people do.

The Teacher knows that the learning never finishes. There is always learning, it never ends. From day one until the end and from life to life, you always learn new things, because the Creator is continuously creating new things. Each individual that he creates is created with new qualities. Even though, we are separate and different from each other, we all have certain qualities within each one of us. A true teacher doesn't think that one is greater than the other. A teacher knows that all are equal, but the disciples don't know about that.

A teacher is happy when one day the disciples themselves become teachers. It's the same thing if you are a teacher and one day you meet the teacher that you had when you were small and tell him that you are now a teacher, he will be happy. This is how it works. Ramakrishna said: "It's great to have a good teacher, but it's very rare to have a real disciple." That is absolutely true.

There was once a Saint; his name was Matsyendranath. He had a disciple named Gorakhnath who had reached such a high level of spirituality that wherever he was, whatever he wanted to know, by the Grace of his Teacher, he would know it. One day Matsyendranath wanted to test his disciple. Gorakhnath wanted to know where his Teacher was, so he sat down and meditated and in his meditation he saw that his Teacher was in Assam, about 5000 kilometres away. He was at a big party and he was having a lot of fun. There were lots of women and he was drinking and everything. Seeing this, Gorakhnath became very restless. So he rushed there with the idea of saving his Guru. He walked and walked and walked – 5000 kilometres and finally he reached Assam. He disguised himself so that the people would not beat him up and went to his Guru. Then he started to sing "Hey, Matsyendranath, don't forget that you are a *Nath* and the Lord of *Nath* can't enjoy all these things. I am your disciple, Gorakhnath, and I have come to save you!" The Guru said "OK" and let himself be taken away.

But on the way Matsyendranath had to take a dip into the Ganges. So he gave his bag to his disciple and said "Hold this for me. I'm going to take a dip in the Ganges." While Goraknath was holding the bag, he felt that it was very heavy. He started to think "What does this old man, who is so detached from everything, carry inside his bag?" So, out of curiosity, he opened the bag and looked into it and he saw two big bars of gold there. He started to think "He can change even stone into gold, why is He carrying two bars of gold in his bag?" Then he thought "I will save him." He took the two bars of gold and threw them very far away.

Then Matsyendranath came out from the river and said "Where is my bag?" Then He took the bag like nothing had happened and they continued their journey. Finally, they reached their town. Gorakhnath said to his Guru "Do you remember who you are? I have saved You." Matsyendranath smiled and just knocked Gorakhnath's head. Then Gorakhnath saw himself back again in his house meditating and he understood that everything had just been an illusion.

The Guru was so pleased with His disciple that He blessed him with a vision of Shiva, because Matsyendranath was a direct disciple of Shankar Bhagavan. Gorakhnath had always wanted so much to have the *darshan* of Shiva and when he got the blessing of his Master he saw Shankar Bhagavan in front of him. Shiva blessed him and said "From now on people will remember you as also being one of my incarnations." So you see how it is. Very often you think things are a certain way, but it's all God's way.

THE SWEETNESS OF *AMRIT*

Darshan, Shree Peetha Nilaya, Springen, Germany, 24 July 2010

It's lovely to see all of you. As you know, tomorrow is a very special day: *Guru Purnima*. One can ask oneself "Why do we need a *Guru*?" Many people say "I don't need one, I don't need a teacher. I don't need somebody to guide me." But if you don't need a teacher, you don't need a guide, how come you are going to school? Why do you go to school? You don't need it! No? It's the same thing on the spiritual path. God created two worlds within this world: one is the spiritual world; one is the material world.

The material world consists of a few things which everybody runs after: wealth, fame, power. They are running after all the things which can exist *only* in this world and which are limited only to *this* physical plane. So when these few things are removed from the people who are running after them, what is left? Nothing, zero! And when you ask these people "What have you achieved in life?" They will say "Nothing" or they will talk about something which is within this limitation.

Whereas the spiritual life, the spiritual world is the opposite of all this, because one craves to know the Divine, one craves to understand the Divine, one longs for the Divine *but* it's just not enough, because without an objective, without knowing where one wants to go, it's difficult, and nowadays, not many people know about it. This knowing, only the teacher, only a *Paramguru*, a *Satguru* can give to you. The rest will bring you to a certain point only, to certain limitations and then what happens? One always stays in this circle.

Imagine the Grace that God has given, firstly, for you to have been born into a human form and also to be spiritual, to search for the goal in life, to search to attain the Divine. How special it is! Of 8.4 million species of life on Earth, you have been gifted with this human body. It is said that within all these 8.4 million species of life, the human being is the highest. Why? Because human beings can reason; human beings have the capacity for reasoning. Sadly to say, nowadays, human beings are even losing that. This capacity for reasoning is given *only* to Mankind.

If you take, let's say a cow, it is considered one of the highest forms of animals in the species. After being a cow, the cow can take a human birth, but yet, it can't attain the Divine. I understand more in this way: Even with bhakti and devotion, a cow is limited to its duty. The capacity for reasoning is only for Mankind. If you use this reasoning and analyse yourself, you will know your objective in life, you will know where you are heading. Otherwise you will just be a marionette, like a small puppet and whatever people want you to do, you just do it. That is how the societies in the world function. When one becomes a slave of society, one becomes this marionette. If society wants you to move right, then you will move right and, if it wants you to move left, then you will move left, but what about you? You will lose yourself into that.

As you are all sitting here, singing *bhajans*, for sure people outside are saying "These people are crazy, they are nuts!" When you go on the spiritual path, people point a finger at you and say "What are you doing on this path? Come with us, we will enjoy life outside!" When you are in the outside world, you have many friends, but once you become spiritual, you see how many so-called friends stay. Why? It's because there is this rumour that people on the spiritual path are a bit nuts. They put the spiritual path as the fourth grade but actually, it's the opposite. The spiritual path is the highest. That's why only a *few* attain it. Only a few can be blessed with that. The rest of the people have reason, but yet, they are not using it. It is said in the *Vedas* that people who don't use their reasoning are the same as animals. So even their life is wasted, the purpose of incarnating as a human being gets wasted. Then if you ask these persons "Are you happy?" They say "No, I'm not happy", because they don't know what they really want, because they have been listening to what people have been telling them. You know how rumours begin? Imagine if at the beginning of your spiritual path, somebody starts telling you lots of gossip and telling you that your path is not right. Of course, at that moment the mind takes over. There's this beautiful story about a King called Kandhalsena. One day the King went to war and while the war was taking place, a sub-minister came and told the Chief Minister of the King "The King has died" and, of course, the chief minister became very worried. So then a *rishi* coming from the palace announced "The King is dead" For 3 days, the people went on mourning the death of the King. They cried and cried and cried. But, on the third day, the King came back. The King came back and saw everybody in white clothes. (White clothes are used in the Hindu tradition when somebody dies and we wear white clothes also on the spiritual path because the old you is dead. You wear white clothes because you are advancing towards the Divine.)

He saw everybody in mourning clothes and everybody was crying so he said "Why are you all crying?" and he heard that the Chief Minister had said that he was dead, so he went to the Chief Minister and said "I heard you said that I am dead. Well, I am still here. Who told you that I am dead?" The Chief Minister said "It's the sub-minister who told me that." So they called the sub-minister and the sub-minister answered: "I heard a group of people in a certain village were saying 'Kandhalsena is dead." So they went to the village and enquired, going from one to the other, and finally they reached a potter who was crying. They asked him to come to the royal palace and he came in front of the King and was crying. The King said "How do you dare to say that I am dead?" He said: "But my King, I didn't say that you are dead!" the King said: "But everybody says that you said that Kandhalsena is dead!" The potter answered: "Yes, I did say that Kandhalsena is dead, but Kandhalsena is my donkey and my donkey is dead!" So, the King asked: "But why did you name your donkey Kandhalsena?" The potter replied: "It's a long story. One day I was going through the jungle, I saw this donkey and the donkey spoke to me in human language and told me 'I am Kandhalsena and I would like to go home to your place. Take me and I will fulfil all your wishes.'" So the potter took the donkey and the donkey died. The King and the donkey had the same name, so the potter was crying for the donkey, but when the people heard "Kandhalsena is dead", they thought it was the King.

This is to show you how one can fool oneself with certain rumours, certain gossip. One fools oneself and loses reasoning without knowing the truth, without knowing what one really wants. Learn to listen to your heart, because whatever people say, there is a certain degree of untruth in it, but whatever you hear from inside of you, there is certainly a degree of truth in it. That's why it is said that following one's intuition is very important on the spiritual path. Developing the capacity of intuitiveness inside oneself is very important and will lead you to your objective in life.

In order to develop that quality, you need somebody who has already mastered this. You always need a teacher; you always need a *Satguru*. If you take any Deity – take Rama, take Krishna – they all have a *Guru*, they all have a teacher to guide them. They are the embodiment of the Divine fully and they could have said we don't need a teacher, finished, but yet, they show that in life, one needs the blessing of a *Guru* and the way to receive it is through *satsang*, through gathering.

In general, why do people go to a Master and receive what the Master is giving? It is because, you see, the Master carries the *Amrit*, the nectar. Even though you don't perceive it with the mind, you do receive it. Through *satsang*, through our talk, you are receiving something and what you are receiving is contributing to your advancement. What you are receiving, even without knowing, is the *Amrit*.

It's this nectar that bees fly from far away to come and collect from the lotus flower or certain flowers. Not all the flowers have the same capacity of honey inside of them. Not all the flowers have the same capacity of sweetness inside. And who knows that? Only the bees know that, not the frog – the frog, or the stupidity that is always thinking it knows everything. It will jump up and down on the flower, but it will not know what sweetness is inside. To know that, one has to dig deep inside oneself, dig deeper and deeper, where one gets this *Amrit*. Through the help of the teacher, the *Guru*, you receive this *Amrit* so that at the end of life, you can say "Yes, I have achieved the purpose of life."

> The master carries the Amrit, the nectar. Even though you don't perceive it with the mind, you do receive it.

As for change, very often people say "I can't change." They say "Later on in life I will change, now I am young, I want to enjoy life." No, life is running! You don't know when you will die. Who knows when death comes? You don't know! Maybe, a meteorite will fall and everybody will be finished! So, the moment to change is always the present moment. This is a great gift. If you want to change, change now! Don't say tomorrow, don't say that you already changed and it's finished. Past is past. Past is dead, finished! If you want to do something, only now can you do it. You can't do it for the future; it's only now!

So if you want to change, it's now that you have to change. If you take a certain resolution, it's now that you have to take the resolution. Being in the *now* is the greatest gift. Being in the *present* moment is the greatest gift. So, enjoy the nectar, enjoy the sweetness, even if, as I said before, you don't perceive what you are receiving. You are receiving something which will contribute to your awareness and to your advancement, to attaining the Lotus Feet of the Lord, the fulfilment of the human life, fulfilment of why you have incarnated here. Otherwise life is wasted.

Always use your reasoning to understand things. Don't use your reasoning to judge, because whenever you judge it is the stupidity inside. If you follow the path of Love, if you follow your heart, you will grow. As the Master is, you shall be also! You shall become a part of this Divine Nectar and you will be able to spread it and give it to many people. That's what Christ said to his disciples: "Go and make disciples; grow and help people." In the same way you will also grow by helping people.

RECEIVE EVERYTHING

Gurupurnima at Shree Peetha Nilaya
Springen, Germany, 25 July 2010

Today we are celebrating *Guru Purnima*, also known as *Vyasa Purnima*. On this day, all the Gurus, all the teachers, are remembered. Some are worthy to be praised and some not. Why do I say some are worthy and some not? It is because there is a difference between a *Siksha Guru*, which is a teacher from the school and a spiritual teacher. They are two different types. The teacher from the school gives you a certain kind of knowledge, which will make you a better person, which will make you understand how to live here. But a spiritual teacher, a Guru, a *Satguru*, gives you not only the purpose of life, but also the direction in life: how and where one sets life. That's the difference. We also say that the first Guru in one's life is the mother; the second is the father and it is very true. The *Vedas* talk about the Guru being the mother and the father, but yet the *Vedas* proclaim that the mother and the father give only the physical to the child, they give the body to the child, but the Guru gives spiritual life, which is a second birth. And how does this happen? If you remove certain qualities from humans, from people who are not on the spiritual path, like pride, the sense of living in the material world, wealth and enjoyment, it's the end for them! They become zero. Whereas from a spiritual person, you can't remove the spiritual qualities because spirituality is endless, knowledge is endless. When you have knowledge, it should not just stay as knowledge, it should transcend to wisdom.

Actually, all this happens through Grace. We can say that you can do certain things, but long before you incarnate on Earth, it's already said where you have to be, who will be your guide and when God will make everything possible for you to achieve Him. Actually, you can say it is you, but it is not you at all. It is only Him, because in the core of everything, your *Atma* is only Him. In this process, we want to attain the Grace of God, we want to attain the Love of God and we want to purify ourselves. For Mankind to do this on its own is very difficult. It's only when the urge of these spiritual qualities awakens inside of Mankind that God will provide everything and prepare one to receive His Grace.

There is a Sufi Saint who said "When I got enlightened, I realised I had made three mistakes in life. The first mistake I made was that I always thought that I was taking the first step towards God but, actually, after I had enlightenment, I realised that it was not me who had taken the first step but God, long before I had taken that first step, had already taken more than one step towards me. The second mistake was that I thought that I loved Him immensely but afterwards, I realised that when I thought that I loved Him immensely, my love was just a drop compared to His ocean of Love. And the third was when I attained Him and realised Him, actually, it was Him that realised Himself". So, try to understand these three things. These three things show that all is the Grace of God. And, of course, to attain this Grace, one can't just sit around. Do your *sadhana*, try to prove yourself, to make yourself ready.

One may say "Well, I don't need to have a teacher. I don't need to have a Guru." But you see, you can receive knowledge in books, but you will not receive wisdom in books. The knowledge will transform itself into wisdom only when the Grace is flowing through the teacher to the disciple. So when you are ready, you manifest yourself as a human being here. Of course, just to stay a human being, a mere human being, is a bit boring, no? How do you know it is boring? You don't know anything else. You do feel it, because you feel this dissatisfaction. Whatever you do, you don't feel happy. So there is an urge to search, an urge to look for something that will make you *really* happy, not just simple happiness, but pure happiness, *shuddha* happiness inside of you. When this urge arises, of course, the Guru comes. And it can take lifetimes, you know, it is not only in one life, it can take several lives. Don't think that in every life, one will have the same urge. It is not like that. It can take thousands of lives. It can take thousands of years.

So, firstly, when you manifest yourself and you have the urge to search, the Divine manifests itself as *Prereka Guru*, which means the first thing that happens when you come across your Guru is that Love gets ignited inside. There is an urge to be near the teacher and it is like this: once you have tasted nectar, nothing else in the world tastes the same. In the same way, once you are near your Guru the world changes. That is why when you become spiritual the world lets go of you, the world sees you differently. Some say you are crazy, because your actions don't suit them, because, deep inside you, Love starts to awaken. The first meeting of the Guru is called *Prereka*, which is the awakening of the Divine Love inside the heart of the disciple. This is how you know who is your Guru, because there will be an irresistible pulling, like a magnet which attracts.

Secondly, the Guru takes the aspect of *Sachaka*, which means the one who purifies and cleanses the *bhakta*, the devotee. In that process, you can say the Guru is wrong, you can say the Guru is bad, you can say all bad things about the Guru, but know one thing: who will understand a Master? Until one becomes a Master, one will not understand a Master. That is why, sometimes, when one looks at a Master and says "Oh, you know, this one is a bad one!" or "This one is a good one!" How do you know what is good and bad? You are just seeing the actions on the outside, but you don't know what lies behind them. So, this is the purification aspect of the *Guru: Sachaka* - to purify, to cut down all the impurities. And in the cutting down, sometimes he can be very cruel, very tough. Like that, you know a Guru is a Guru, because if a Guru is soft, soft, soft toward whatever you come with and he says "Ah, yes, yes, yes", it does not work.

If you see diamond or gold in nature, diamond looks like a normal stone. But when the expert has seen the stone, takes it and starts polishing it, the polishing is not soft. The polishing is very, very difficult, but then you have a beautiful stone afterwards. It is the same thing with gold: when you find some gold with a lot of impurities, it has to go through fire. When it goes through fire it is very cruel, because to melt the gold, to purify it, it has to burn in thousand degrees and finally you can get beautiful jewellery. This is *Sachaka*. In that process many will go, because they cannot bear it, but when this has happened and when this has manifested in the *bhakta*, in the devotee, and strong faith and determination are still there, if one stays, one will shine.

After that process, the Guru takes the aspect of *Vachaka*, which means that the Guru gives the glory of the Lord to the disciple. He reveals the stories of the Lord, the manifestation of the Lord to the disciples, telling them beautiful stories, so that when all impurity has gone away, it fills the *bhakta* with the Divine, with the glory and the shine of the Divine. Of course, this is only knowledge.

After some time, the Guru takes the aspect of *Bhodaka*. *Bhodaka* means that he transforms this knowledge into *wisdom*, so that the *bhakta*, the devotee, can understand everything. Lots of people in the world have knowledge about many things, but the knowledge of the soul, the knowledge of who you are in Reality is not called knowledge, it is called wisdom. When you have wisdom, you see the world completely differently. This is called *Bhodaka, Bhodaka* Guru. After that, when you have wisdom, what will manifest itself is pure Love. When you have wisdom you become wise. You are not ignorant anymore and when you are wise, you Realise that the Lord resides everywhere.

Then the Guru takes the aspect of *Darshaka*. *Darshaka* means that the Guru manifests Himself into the Divine Form, the Guru reveals the Divine to the disciple. So you see, within this whole process there are five stages, five steps and you don't go through these five stages quickly. The Guru tests you. You go through *Prereka, Sachaka, Vachaka, Bhodaka* and *Darshaka* is the final one. When you reach *Darshaka* you see the manifestation of the Lord everywhere, you Realise your Self fully. Whatever you are looking for is just at the feet of the Master. And He has given it to you.

In the *Shiva Purana*, Shiva said to Parvati: "One can attain all knowledge of this world, but if one is ignorant about the Teacher, all the knowledge is meaningless." Krishna said the same thing in the *Gita*: I clothed Myself in this human form and then the ignorant think I am just human, because they just see the outside. Who can understand a *Satguru*? No one! So when the disciple is ready, the *Satguru* manifests Himself and He comes to the disciple. He doesn't come to take anything, because the Guru already Realised the Oneness with the Divine, you know? So what does the *Satguru* need in this world? *Nothing!* He comes to give, always to give, even if it seems that He takes, actually, what you are getting is just what He is giving.

He gives in three forms. The first form is when he gives as *Sankalpa*, which is through thought. The second form is when he gives as *Drishti*, which is through vision, sight. The third one, he gives through *Sparsha*, which is touch. So, the Guru gives through these three forms. The first one, *Sankalpa*, is through thought, through the mind, through the transfer of the *Shakti*, this is like a mother turtle. The mother turtle lays her eggs into the sand, but the mother turtle does not need to sit on the eggs. She lays the eggs and, from far away, her thought is always like a wave of warmth towards the eggs, so that the eggs get hatched. This is done through waves, through thought [waves]. One, who has given blessings in this way, is Shirdi Sai.

The second form is *Drishti*, through sight. To give the blessing through sight is like when a fish lays its eggs in the water, the eggs are inside some transparent bubbles. The mother fish always stays by and focuses on the eggs. Just by this mere focusing of vision the eggs get hatched. This is *Drishti*.

The final form is *Sparsha*, which is through touch. You go to the master, you bow your head, you offer the *sahasrara* and the teacher touches you on the head. He gives you the blessing that says not to worry, the Divine will look after. And if you have faith, you receive the blessing. Even if you don't have faith, you receive the blessing, but it takes longer to manifest.

So, we can say that Shirdi Sai was giving through the first form, through *Sankalpa*. Ramana Maharshi gave through *Drishti*, through sight. He was giving His *darshan* through sight. And Sri Ramakrishna gave His *darshan* through *Sparsha*.

Through these three things, the Master transmits this energy, this Divine energy, which is inside of Him to the *bhakta*, to the disciples. Why did I say disciples and I didn't say devotee? Because, after you have passed through all these purifications, you become a *bhakta*, you become a *true* disciple. You don't stay only a devotee, but you become a disciple. A disciple is the one who has received the Grace of the Master and the Grace of the Master is the same as the Grace of God within. If you graft a small plant with another, for example, you take two roses, two different kinds of roses and you graft them together, when you water, you water only the main one, no? So the teacher is the main plant and whatever passes through the teacher, that which is grafted to the teacher will receive everything. That is why I said yesterday you become the pot of *Amrit*, also. You don't just stay as you are, but you attain the fulfilment of the goal of life.

This is how the Grace of the Divine manifests Itself into the Guru. As we say, *Guru Brahma, Guru Vishnu, Guru Devo Maheshwara. Guru Sakshath Parambrahma, Tasmai Shri Gurave Namaha.* The *Vedas* proclaim the *Guru* as Brahma, Vishnu and Shiva. Even in the *Gita*, Krishna said: Whoever will need Me, I shall come, and I shall be manifested as the *Guru*.

So the greatness of a Master, the greatness of knowing a Master and receiving the *Shiksha*, receiving the Blessing and Grace from the Master is rare. And once one has it, one carries it with him, one carries this Blessing always. It is not that one day you say "Ok, today I am with this master and tomorrow I am with that master." There are many people who do Guru hopping, you know. Well, it's normal, because one is on a search. Until one feels this Love, this attraction, this pull, one will always search, no? And once you have felt it, you have to grow into it and then you know "Yes, I am at home. I belong there." You don't say "I go to this Guru" no, you say "I am going home, I am going where I belong, where I long to be." You go there where you feel the Love of God inside of you and where you will achieve the purpose of your incarnation.

So this is, in short, how the Guru works. He gives through these three forms - through thought, through sight and through touch. He gives Himself fully to his disciples. He gives Himself fully to the devotees. What the devotees have to do is to be like an empty recipient and receive everything.

You see, the rain falls everywhere. The rain does not have enmity toward anyone. It falls on the mountain; it falls on the hill slope. But can the mountain hold the water? No it cannot: it flows. When can it hold the water? When there is a hole in it, then the mountain can hold this water. People who are not searching for the Divine, not searching for the purpose of life, they are like the mountain: when the Grace of God flows from the Divine to them, it just flows out, whereas, you all who have really the Grace of God - I should say the blessing of God, not yet His Grace, but the blessing of God to have the urge to search, the urge to look for Him, the urge to practise your *sadhana*, the urge to feel a Love greater than what the whole world thinks of as love. So, don't waste time! There is one thing that a lot of people are wasting and that's time. They think that later in life they can do everything, whenever they have time they will do everything. But you see, one thing is that if you do not make time now, you will never make time - later never comes. Like somebody was

> The Guru gives Himself fully to his disciples. He gives Himself fully to the devotees. What the devotees have to do is to be like an empty recipient and receive everything.

saying "Tomorrow never comes." It's true!. You have many excuses for not doing your *sadhana*, but know that what you are doing now is very important and contributes a lot.

So take every opportunity to be near the master, to be near a teacher, to receive the Grace is a must in life. Like I was just saying, you all are very lucky for Mahavatar has Graced all of you, the Divine has Graced all of you, God has Graced all of you, so that you may search, you may look for the greater purpose in life. I am sure you will achieve it and I am sure you will get what you are looking for. One thing only that I ask is: just be sincere with yourself, open your heart sincerely to yourself and let the Divine do the rest. You will see that you are full with this nectar, which we call Love. Even if your mind does not feel it, if you are looking at yourself and you do not feel it like that, actually, each part of your body is full of this. You are sitting here, you are receiving the Grace; you are chanting the Divine Name, you are singing the Glory of God, and you are receiving the Blessing. Even though you do not know about it, you are receiving it!

There was once a criminal, a murderer who asked for a *mantra* to his Guru, but he didn't want to chant the Name of God, so he said to his Guru: "I don't believe in any God, just give me something to chant so that I can make my mind, calm." The Guru was very happy and told him: "Chant *Maramaramaram.*" The murderer was very happy and he was chanting *"Maramaramaramararamaramaramaram."* Can you see what is he chanting? *Rama, Rama Rama, Rama, Rama, Rama, Rama, Ram.* So, ignorantly, he had been chanting the Name of Rama and at the end of his life he was fully Realised, He attained God, He attained Rama.

When you go to *satsang*, when you go to pilgrimage places, it is always you who receives, it is always for your benefit. So surrender to the Guru's feet. As it is said: When one meets one's Guru, the world becomes the feet of the Master. And the Guru's feet are everything. That is why in the Hindu tradition, we worship *Vishnu Padam.* Why do we worship the Feet of Maha Vishnu? When we say feet, we don't mean the upper part, but the down part. That is why when the Guru places his feet, he does not put the upper part on it but he puts the down part, because under the soles of the Feet of the Master is *Vishnu Padam.* Under the feet is All, the Feet of Maha Vishnu Himself. That is why in the *Gita* it is said: "Guru Govinda". Krishna manifests Himself as the Guru and the Guru is Govinda, is Krishna. Service to the Feet of the Master is equal to thousands of pilgrimage places. So do your service to the Feet of the Master and surrender.

Adi Shankaracharya said: "I received everything only by surrendering to the Feet of my Master." But sadly, nowadays, when we say "Follow and do this", what does the disciple say "*Why* should I do this?" It is normal because the difference between the times before and now is that nowadays the mind has taken over. And when the mind takes over, of course, there are lots of questions, lots of doubt, a lot of unreasonable thinking in the mind and then, one loses certain opportunities. That's why Mankind always goes in the circle of birth and death, even though they can achieve everything in one life. So surrender to the Lotus Feet (*Charanasparsha*).

So, I wish all of you happy *Guru Purnima*. As the Divine resides in all of your hearts, may the Divine put His Lotus Feet in your heart. And, as all the saints and all the masters and all the spiritual seekers, may you always be in the Love of the Divine. May you always feel the Divine. Whatever you are doing, wherever you are, know that God is close to you as ever.

You know, in the Hindu tradition we have a prayer, we say: Karaagre vasate Lakshmi, karamadhye Sarasvati karamuule tu Govinda, prabhaate karadarshanam samudravasane Devi Parvata stanamandale, Vishhnupatni namastubhyam paadasparsham Kshamasva me. [Oh! Mother Earth, who has the ocean as clothes and mountains and forests on her body, who is the wife of Lord Vishnu, I bow to you. Please forgive me for touching you with my feet]

Adi Shankaracharya said "I received everything only by surrendering to the Feet of my Master"

Do you know this prayer? This prayer is a prayer which one does before getting out of bed. One puts one's hand touching the fingers tips saying Goddess Lakshmi is there, the middle of the palm is Goddess Saraswati and down is Govinda - Maha Vishnu. This is the first thing people used to do before getting out of bed. They would remind themselves that in their hands there are Lakshmi, Saraswati and Govinda. So, like that, they would never forget that the Divine is always with them. But nowadays, when one gets out of bed, the first thing one says is: "What will I do today?" instead of thinking of God, one thinks of everything else except the Divine. So make it a habit, the first thought when you rise in the morning, just think of any Divinity that you feel close with. If ever you know your *Ishtadev,* think of your *Ishtadev.* If you have your *Guru mantra,* just chant one time your *Guru mantra.* And if your Guru has told you who your *Ishtadev* is, build up the connection between you and your *Ishtadev.* Like that the Master will do His work wherever you are. Even if you are not near to the Master, even from far away, He will do his work.

Don't forget that God is form and formless at the same time. He is *Nirgun Brahma* and He is *Sargun Brahma.* He is *Nirgun* as formless, as Omnipresent everywhere and He is with a form as *Sargun,* where one has to concentrate oneself on [the form]. So the Guru is also the same, I mean the *Satguru* because there are different Gurus and the difference between a *Satguru* and a Guru, is that a Guru, is just in one place and he is just sitting and delivering discourses, but the Omnipresent aspect is not present in him. Whereas a *Satguru* or *Paramguru* has this Omnipresent quality inside. Whatever the disciple is thinking, the Guru is connected to.

It is the same as what I was saying before: When one surrenders, sincerely, to the Master, it is like one is grafted to the Master. It's like with a rose bush: whenever the bush receives the Grace, receives the water, of course, the grafted part also gets the water. The same thing is when one is surrendered to the Guru. Whatever flows through the Guru, whatever energy, whatever *Shakti* is flowing through the Guru, the disciple, wherever he will be, will receive also the same Grace. Do not think where you are or how you are, just *be* how you are. *Jai Gurudev! Sat Guru Maharaja Ki Jai!*

CHRIST REVEALS HIMSELF

Liturgy in the Chapel of Shree Peetha Nilaya,
Springen, Germany, 2 October 2010

This Gospel, the *Transfiguration* is actually one of the most beautiful Gospels because Christ reveals Himself. Usually, like all the Masters, He never reveals His true aspect. People always pretend to know or think they know who the Master is. Even if the Master says it many times, they don't hear who He is, because the mind always plays its game of judging and thinking that it has understood.

Christ said: Don't try to understand me, because you will not. Where I come from, you will not be able to understand with the mind, because you can only understand with the heart. I am from above, I am not from this world, but you all are from beneath. It's like children in the kindergarten. The Lord said: Don't try to understand what is from university or higher than that, because you will not. Even if you try your best to understand a Master, you will not understand. That's why a Master is a Master and you are *you*.

Here, Jesus is saying to his disciples: "Why do you try to understand me, when you can't understand me? The only thing that you can do is just to accept. And don't create things, because your understanding is bound by your perception from the outside, but you also have a heart that can make you feel and give you an inner perception. So, Christ said to his disciples: "I come from God", but you see, men always hear what they want to hear! They always hear only what suits them or what pleases the ears. That's why they didn't hear that He was from God; they heard only what they wanted to hear even though He said it so directly. But anyway, Man is like this.

From 2,000 years, until now, humans have not changed. And I think in the next 2,000 years also they will not change much. That's why He said: "If you have ears to hear, then hear". Yes, people have ears, but they try to stay deaf always. They try to hang onto their limitations and they are happy with their limitations, they don't want to see more than that, because people like to build up their own world, sit in that world and say "That's it, that's my world." It's like, the fish in the pond doesn't know that the pond exists. It doesn't know how big the ocean is or how big the lake is, because it knows only the small part where it always stays and the memory of the fish knows only that.

Grow! The world is moving. Change! Grow! And move forward! Move forward! Move and rise!

You know there is a Saint who said: "You have a mind like a fish" Why? It's because the fish already forgot what happened just before.

The same thing is so with men. They like to build up their own limited corner, limited image and limitation of who they are in Reality and they like to hang onto that part, because they feel good, they feel secure in that. But when something new happens, they don't want to understand, when something is challenging for the mind, they don't want to understand and what do they do? They pull back, because it's not in their mind-set, it's not in their little world that they have built up. This is where they judge and criticise, because they don't understand anything. Even if they try [to understand], they will not, because they are stupid. And they want to be stupid, they want to be limited. They forget that the greatness of the heart is also there but they don't want to see. That's why they choose to be blind always; they choose to be deaf.

But when this veil is removed through prayer and through serving, when this Love gets awakened inside the heart, then they see the Reality. Then they see that Love is endless. Even if you think yes, I have loved a lot, no, love is endless and you will always grow, it will never finish. And that's what Christ said: "I came. I told you who I am. But yet, you choose to be blind, you choose to be deaf. You choose to be in that limitation, you choose to be in this world that *you* create." Grow! The world is moving. Change! Grow and move forward! Move and rise! Don't choose only to be down, but rise, also. Rise, so that you really can say to God: "Father". If you call God 'Father', but you choose to be the limited one, then this doesn't make sense. So, this is the Gospel.

FROM DARKNESS TO LIGHT

Guru Purnima Retreat, Steffenshof, Germany, 29 July 2007

As you all are well aware, today is a very special day. It's the day where all the Masters, all the Gurus are venerated around the world, wherever there is knowledge of the importance of a teacher, of course. So the importance of a teacher, the importance of a Guru arises when one has the desire for God. The Master or the Teacher comes to one's rescue when one really wants to know God, when one really wants to Realise one's Self.

But before that, let's see in our lives how many teachers we have. You see, there are a lot of teachers. At the beginning, as God was the Unmanifest One, as God was unknown to the mind of Man and without Names, all the greats Saints, all the rishis perceived the teacher in nature. It is said that there are twenty-four teachers in nature.

Once somebody went to a Master and he saw that the Master was so blissful. So, he asked him: "Tell me, who is your teacher? Why are you radiating so much light?" Then, the Master said "I don't have one teacher. I have twenty four teachers." So the man asked "Who are these twenty-four teachers?" The Master said "First, above all the teachers, I've learned from my parents and above all, first, I have learned from my mother, who held my hand and made me walk. So, my mother has shown me how to stand on my feet. Secondly, I have learned discipline from my father, who disciplined me, who sustained me and showed me how to sustain myself."

He never mentioned anybody else apart from the mother and

father. The rest he mentioned was about everything that he had seen: the plants, the animals, he learned from every small insect and all together, he had twenty four [teachers]. He had learned humility, patience, joy, happiness – all these qualities just from nature. So, if you observe nature carefully, you will learn a lot! This was when there was not yet the Name of God, when there was not any specific form that we now give Him. Of course, when one is centred and trusts oneself, trusts one's feelings and knows that the inner Guru which is seated in the heart will reveal Himself, the inner Guru will reveal Himself!

As the world progresses, so man falls. So, there is a need for this Higher Consciousness to keep appearing. That's why, like I said the day before yesterday, the Lord incarnates thousands of times to help people. Even if I'm sitting up there (on an armchair), don't think that a Guru is just somebody to be put up [on a chair]. To be put up like this is something else, this happens because of the love of the devotees. But actually, the Gurus are a servant of the devotee. They have come to serve the people, they have come to help, not to be helped!

People always ask me "What can I do for you, Swamiji?" I don't need anything from anybody! If I need something, I will get it from Him. I have come to help you, so what I need is that you all rise. Like Narayana came to sustain one's spiritual path, when the mountain was sinking from the churning of the Ocean of Milk, He will also come and sustain you. Such is the help of the Master. A Master is just a guide who will sustain you on your spiritual path. That doesn't mean that you have to cast everything on the Master and say "OK, he will do everything. I don't do anything!"

That's what the whole concept of Christianity nowadays is about because Jesus said: "Cast upon me your burden, I shall carry it for you", people don't want to change. They say "I cast everything on Him. If I do lots of bad things, I will go confess and then He will forgive." So, what then is the use of changing? You are here to *rise* in spirituality, you are here to *Realise* your Self, not to be static, not to be just on the same platform all the time and that's the mistake that the world makes. People didn't understand what Christ really meant by that. Yes, it's true, He will help you, He will pull you out of this, but then, it's up to you to carry on, also. He will not do it for you but that's what people think. Because He said: "Cast upon me all your sins, all your negativity", they think "OK, I'll carry on doing the same thing; I will not change," but this is wrong. The Masters suffer for that; that's why Christ went through this suffering, because He took on karmic things from people. Such is also the Master, the spiritual guide or whatever name you want to call it, because in the West, people don't really like the word 'Guru'. Maybe they prefer to say Master or spiritual guide, but it's all the same thing! The words change but it's just the words that change, the guide is still the same.

So, as I was saying, when one comes into the guidance of a Master, it becomes the responsibility of this spiritual guide to guide this person and if ever there is something negative that the disciple does, don't think that the disciple will suffer. It's not the disciple that suffers, it's the Master that suffers, because the disciple is under his guidance. It's like with a child; when a child hurts himself, who suffers more? The parent, the mother does. When a child is sick, it's the parents who suffer most. Yes, the child suffers from the pain, but it's the parents that suffer most. It's the same thing for the Master. When the disciples start messing up, when the disciples start doing their own thing, of course, it's the spiritual guide, the Guru, that really suffers.

When one takes the spiritual guidance of the Master and surrenders to what He says, of course, one will be pulled out of this illusion, but as long as one doesn't want to take the guidance of a Master, one will always be in the ignorance. You will see this is the same in all religions. Take Christianity, Hinduism, Islam, Buddhism or any other religion, and you will see that there is always a hierarchy. You don't even need to go that far; let's take for example the hierarchy among the angels and you will see that there is this obedience. Of course, they all obey God but there is this obedience within the hierarchy of the angels itself. The angels are bound to listen and to serve the archangels, because this is very important [to obey].

If one just thinks that one *knows* something, it's pure ignorance. The word *guru* is in two parts: *gu*, which means dispeller, and *ru* is darkness, so it's *dispeller of darkness, dispeller of ignorance in man*. So when one comes into the guidance of a spiritual Master, the Master takes on the responsibility of getting the ignorance out of the disciple. The ignorance means all the negative things. Also, in the word Guru, *gu* means *the ultimate fulfilment, r* is *remover of sin, remover of ignorance* and *u* is Narayana – Maha Vishnu. So the Guru is the one who gives spiritual knowledge which illuminates the mind of the disciple and He is the Ultimate One, because He has already Realised the Oneness with God and He has these three [qualities] together in Him.

So when the disciple comes into contact with the Master, the disciple has to be loyal. Loyalty not only to the Master, but loyalty also towards oneself! Only when you are loyal towards yourself will you be able to be loyal towards the Master and towards the outside. Also, the disciple must have obedience. Obedience doesn't mean slavery. Often people think that to be obedient is just to become the slave of the Master. No, it's the opposite, actually. Like I said before, it's not you who are slaves of the Master, but the Master who is the slave of you. But as in the mind you have ignorance, you have pride, ego, all these things, you have to listen to the one who has already overcome it.

When you go to your work and your boss gives you a job, do you say: "Ok, but I will do it my way!"? Who knows better, you or the boss? The boss knows better what he wants! It has nothing to do with what *you* want. So it's the same thing when you come into the discipline of a Master, it's not about you, it's about what your Master is telling you to do, because He knows the Way and if you surrender to what He says, all your work will be fine. You will not be thrown out of your job! But then, if you start doing your own stuff, with your own mind, then what's the use of obedience? And this you will see everywhere.

There is a book I was reading once, it's about the Desert Fathers and it gives the guidelines of obedience. This is from a Christian point of view. Because here, we live in a Christian country, I will be happy just to give it in the Christian way. But *actually*, it has nothing to do with Christianity or Hinduism or Islam or any other religion. Obedience is obedience! It's when one closes off one's mind and surrenders. But I will just read the five points that they give and you will see by yourself that there is no difference between Christianity and Hinduism. People shout that there is a big difference and of course, the rituals, the deities are different, but the ultimate goal is the same thing everywhere.

The Desert Fathers said about faith in one's spiritual guide "The disciple must have perfect trust in the spiritual guide, the same as they have in God, the same as they have in Christ. Let there not remain in his heart any doubt or hesitation about whatever the Master says, whether what the Elder, the Master says is right or not, unless it contradicts the law of God."

So, in that part, it is said that whatever the spiritual guide says, one should never contradict, one should never question, one should close off one's mind to one's own egoistic thinking and just accept what the Master says. But, nowadays, what do you do? When the Master says "Turn right", you say "No, I will turn left" and if he says, again, "Turn right", you will again say "No, left looks more beautiful. Let me turn left." He will again say it, another time, but then he will say "OK, you want to turn left? Turn!" Then *you* take your own responsibility for that! Of course, like I said, the Master will suffer, yes, but you will also suffer because you didn't listen to his directions.

The second guideline that they give is about truth: "He [the disciple] should speak the truth in everything, without twisting things. And let him not make up stories to tell the spiritual guide, so as to hide something in his thoughts. It is necessary to tell the facts exactly as they are, in all truth."

So, you have to be truthful towards your spiritual guide, you have to be truthful towards your Guru, your Master, because when you don't surrender towards your Master, when you are not truthful towards your Master, you can't become truthful with yourself. If you are false towards your Master, you will always be false towards yourself. And when you are false towards yourself, of course, God will never reveal Himself.

The third guideline is "The disciple should cut off his will, not deviate from his spiritual Master in his intent. He should offer up his own desire, inclination, inspiration and talents as a sacrifice and should do everything in accordance with the opinion of his spiritual guide. The disciple should not have an opinion about anything. The spiritual guide will judge how the affair must be conducted; the disciple should mortify his own judgement and follow the judgement of the spiritual guide."

Again, it's saying that your own judgement, what you think, you have to keep it and mortify it. You have to let go of it. You should never question what your spiritual guide is asking from you, what he is telling you to do, but just do it. This is the whole concept also in Hinduism: When one comes under the direction of a Teacher, a Master, one has to surrender not to his own will, but to the Will of the Master. Whatever one does is to please the Master, whatever the Master says. But above all, know that you're not pleasing only the Master, you are pleasing God, because the Master doesn't need your pleasing. Even God doesn't need your pleasing, but *you*, out of Love, out of surrender, out of joy, you're offering everything.

The fourth guideline is: "He [the disciple] should neither quarrel, nor contradict at all, but should have reverence for his spiritual guide." Again, it's the same thing!

The fifth guideline is "He should clearly confess his fault to the spiritual guide, for it is a joy for evil, the demons, when the disciple hides the fault."

Like I always said, the spiritual guide is the one who is seated with the people. So, whenever there is a question that arises that the disciples can't answer, they have to turn to the Master and say: "Can you help me?" and the disciple has always to be ready to listen to the Master. It's not that the spiritual guide is far away from the disciple.

As long as you have not reached a level of really connecting spiritually and inwardly with the Master, be near him. And when you are near the spiritual guide, when you are in the vibration of the spiritual guide, the more you are in it, the more it will benefit you. The more you are in it, the more the delusion of darkness will be removed. But the more you are far away, the more you will be in your ignorance and the more difficult it will be. This is the role of a spiritual guide. This is the role of a Master.

The Desert Fathers said "These five mighty weapons are indispensable for the disciple. He must always follow his conscience and carefully examine it in regard to these commandments." They say it's so important to follow these guidelines. It's very important to follow what one's spiritual teacher is saying, because if one just thinks blindly "OK, I feel something" and one thinks it's right, without asking the Master, it can be that you are wrong! How do you know that your feeling is right? Most of the time, people feel things only according to what *they* want. One's pride and ego are so strong, what one wants will always be placed in front. So what in reality has to be, is covered up. So the Guru, the spiritual guide, the Teacher, the Master will remove one from this illusion, from all this illusion only when one surrenders completely, because if one doesn't surrender completely to the Master, if one doesn't surrender completely and become obedient to the teaching of the spiritual guide, one will always be in ignorance.

Once, there was a tiger, a female tiger. She was pregnant and she attacked a flock of sheep and when she jumped over the sheep, she gave birth at the same time to a small baby tiger, a cub. When she gave birth to the cub, she died on the spot. So what happened? The small cub grew up with the flock of sheep and became a huge tiger, but he would bleat the same way as the sheep would do and would eat grass the same way. One day, another tiger from the forest jumped out and started to run towards the flock of sheep. As he was running towards them, he noticed that there was another tiger, but this tiger was also running away!

The tiger stopped and wondered: "What is this? Why is this tiger running away from me?" So he ran faster, jumped over the other tiger that was bleating, and said "What are you doing?" The other tiger started grazing like a sheep. Then the tiger from the forest said "You're eating grass! You are not a sheep! You are a tiger like me! You should not eat grass. Here, take this piece of meat, eat it!" The other tiger, who was eating grass, said "No, no, no, I don't want to!" Then the other pushed the piece of meat into his mouth and when he got the taste of blood, eventually, he realised that he was not a sheep, but a tiger.

So, do you get what is behind this story? Men in this illusion think they are just human, mortal, but when the Preceptor, when the Teacher comes and says "Hey, it's time for you to wake up, now", of course, the mind will rebel against it and it will say "No, no, no! He's not right, I am right!" The mind will say "Follow me", but the teacher will say "Look, you are not a sheep, you are a tiger!" The Guru will say: "Look, you are not just human, you are Divine and if you want to realise it, follow me, follow my advice." But as long as you want to stay as sheep, as long as you want to stay just as normal human beings, you will just stay like that. Only when one surrenders to the Master, surrenders to the spiritual guide, will it lead one out of this illusion. But if one wants to live in this illusion, one will run away from the spiritual Master, one will not be disciplined. So, this is the role of a Master: to serve the disciples, to serve them, so that they can achieve a higher state.

Today is the day where you have great reverence to the Master, to your mother, to your father, to your teacher in school, to all your teachers that you have been following, because they have done their work. It's like school, you go through many different stages until, finally, you reach university, and after university, you can go to work. When you have reached university and you have finished and passed your exams, the world opens up. You have good jobs, everything. In the same way, when you have reached the Master that will guide you, the spiritual Teacher that will lead you out of ignorance, out of illusion and once you have passed a test, he will say "Go and work now! Go, bring this light, bring this Love, bring what you have got to others and help them." This is again through the Grace of the Master.

Only when you start to desire God, only when you start to want God, He will send the right person to you. He will send your spiritual guide that will guide you out of this illusion. When you have been guided out of this illusion, He shall reveal Himself. When all the signs of ignorance, all the pride, all the ego inside of you is erased, what stays is the surrender to the Divine, surrender to the Higher Self.

Last week somebody asked me to talk about *brahmachari*. A *brahmachari*, whether it is a monk or nun, [the word] *brahmachari*, when people will just literally translate it, means celibacy. This is the official translation of *brahmacharya*. But, actually, the *Veda* gives another explanation of *brahmachari*. *Brahmacharya* means inwardness, not celibacy. Celibacy is one part of it, but what it means is inwardness. This word *brahm-acharya* is composed of two words: *brahm*, which means *the Ultimate Self* and *acharya*, which means *the one who lives in*. So *brahmacharya* means the one who is attuned, who is living in the Ultimate Self, who is living for the fulfilment of one's True Self. This is a *brahmachari*.

Of course, celibacy is very important because this is a way to self-discipline. You see, as long as there is no self-discipline, you will always go left, right, left, right, left, right, left, right; but you have self-discipline, when you say: "This is my path, and I want to fulfil it. I want to Realise God, I want to Realise my Self, I want to have Self-Realisation." and you are dedicated to this path. Whether Hinduism, Christianity or Islam, all paths are the same thing, when you are dedicated to one path and are clear on that path, you will reach the goal of life.

> The Guru is the one who gives spiritual knowledge which illuminates the mind of the disciple and He is the Ultimate One, because He has already Realised the Oneness with God.

And this is how it is: Self-discipline, self-discipline in your life will help you to calm the restless mind, will help you to go out of this ignorance. Otherwise, if one is not disciplined, if one does not have discipline or have self-control over the senses, what will happen? They will get attached to this world, they will get attached to this illusion. Again, as I said, it is not wrong to be in the world. God has given the world for humans to enjoy it, to profit from it, but one has to be detached from it. One has to have discipline and know what one can do and what one can't do. Otherwise, the more you do things that will drag you deeper and deeper in illusion, the more you will be far away from reality. That's why the chanting of God's Name can help you on your path, help you to surrender, help you to calm your mind. When you chant God's Name and ask God "Please, guide me", like I said before, He will send the right teacher that you need.

Lord Chaitanya Mahaprabhu who was living in the fifteenth century chanted Hari's Name all the time, chanted the Name of Krishna all the time, but nobody listened to Him, nobody really followed what He said. They thought that He was mad, they thought that He and His brother had gone crazy. So, do you know what He did? He said to the people "Come, my dears!" He knew that the people were after food and women. The men were after food and women, because you see, in India, the women listened to the husbands, but the husbands were always running after women. So, He would say "My dear fellow, sing the Name of Hari, sing the Name of Krishna, sing the Name of God and you shall get a bowl of soup, fish soup, and you shall get embraced by women. The more you chant the Name of God, the more you will embrace women and the more you will have fish soup to eat."

Then, when they heard this, they were very happy. The mind was thinking "Oh, we'll have lots of soup and lots of women! Of course, then let's chant!" So they started chanting Hari's Name, they started chanting God's Name. Of course, they did get the soup; they did get the nectar. The soup was the nectar, 'the soup' was the bliss that they got and 'the women' was earth, because in this Divine Ecstasy, they would go into rapture and roll around on the earth in great Love. In surrender, they would roll on the ground. So these were the women, the embrace from the women, from the earth. So you see, sometimes the Master has to do things to bring the disciple on the right path, you know?

Like I said, one can't question. If someone is a Master, He knows what is best. Then one just needs to surrender. Even if one's mind is saying "no, no, no!" to it, it's only by being humble, only by humility, by humbling yourself, by putting aside what your arrogant and prideful mind says, that you can really surrender. And once you have surrendered, the Divine will shower His Love upon you. God will shower you with His Grace and Love and you will feel His Love continuously, you will feel His joy continuously – a joy which doesn't have any limit, a Love which doesn't have any limit. And this Love, once you have Realised it, once you have treasured it inside your heart, once you have treasured it in each part of your body – in your mind, in your heart, in your soul – you also have become a master, you yourself will spread this Love, you yourself will spread the Name of God, because this is how it is with the Name of God, this is how it is with the Love of God. The more you have the Love of God, the more it will spread out, the more you will not be able to keep it, the more your heart will explode to let it out. But the more you try to close it, the more you try to put a barrier around it, the more the mind jumps around, the more you don't surrender; the more problems you will have, the more you will see that it's far away to achieve[God], far away to gain Him.

When you look at somebody who is in Divine Ecstasy, you will

> When one really lets go of everything and surrenders, one gets everything, one gets the real thing: why one has come here, one gets Self-Realisation, God-Realisation, one rises in the Divine Love.

say "Oh my goodness, look at this one. He is crazy!" You will judge everything around you. This is how the mind is, but when you have Realised this Love, all becomes the same! You will see somebody crying out of joy for God, you will see somebody laughing out of joy for God, but your mind will be still. Your mind will not have any judgements on anything. Christ said: "Don't judge and you shall not be judged." As long as one judges, one becomes negative and cultivates this quality of negativity.

I tell you something: it's not really a Christian virtue to do that. You see it in early Christianity, the saints were so much surrendered to their faith, they had so much trust in their faith, they even accepted death for that. They never rebelled, they knew God was with them and they happily accepted it. They had surrendered to the path. And this is not only during that time, you know, it's always. Through thousands of years it was like that and even now it's still the same. Whenever it's needed, it is said that God Himself manifests as a Teacher. I explained already before about the several incarnations of the Lord but it is said also that when one becomes a disciple of a Teacher, a true Teacher, who has overcome all these things and knows how to guide the people out of it, one has to surrender. And to know that this is the right Teacher, one has to feel, one has to follow one's heart. And when one follows one's heart, one has to surrender completely.

Nowadays, there are a lot of teachers; there are lot of masters because everybody wants to become a master. But as I said, everybody can become a master, everybody can become a spiritual guide, but as long as there is no ego in it, as long as the guide, the spiritual teacher realises that he is the servant of the disciples, he is the servant of his devotee, then we can say that he is a true Guru, he is a true Master. But as long as one doesn't realise this and thinks "OK, I am a guru!" and very proudly puts himself up, forget it! No matter how big the teacher can be, how great he can be, how many millions of disciples he can have, if the Master, if the head himself is corrupt, nothing works. So if the teacher himself thinks and says proudly: "I am everything", then there is no humility. The Teacher has to always think that he is the servant.

If ever you become a master, a teacher, always put that in your mind: you are the servant of the devotee. And *whatever* the disciple's faults are, you will have to deal with God afterwards. It's your responsibility, it's not the disciple's responsibility. Then God will ask you "I sent you on Earth to guide these people, I have sent you on Earth to bring these people [to Me], to make these people Realised, what have you done?"

What will the master say? "Think well, disciple. Think well people!" Take a Master, a Guru but know that you have also not to hurt the Guru, not to do anything that will contradict the Guru or will hurt him or make him sad or whatever. So this is the relationship between the disciple and the Guru. It's actually a Love relationship. In this relationship, the disciple surrenders.

It's the same thing when you fall in love or I mean, rise in Love, we will put it like that. When you fall in love, you fall down and break your head! The world is always constantly falling in love and going out of it. But with the Divine Love, you rise in Love, because Divine Love is not falling, but rising. And this is the Love that one cultivates when one surrenders to a Teacher, when one surrenders to a Guru, one cultivates this Divine Love that will raise one from the human to the Divine.

Amongst all the gurus, when you find your spiritual Teacher, when you surrender completely to your Master, your Master becomes everything for you. Your Master becomes the mother – He will shower the Love of a mother on you. He becomes the father – He will be disciplined with you. He becomes everything. Then the world dies, He becomes the world. The Master becomes the path. That's why you will see in *ashrams*, in monasteries, one lets go of everything. One lets go of family, one lets go of children, one lets go of husband, wife, one lets go of mothers, fathers, and lives for God. There is the same thing everywhere. In the *Gita,* you will see something similar, when Krishna explained that to Realise God, to Realise who one is in Reality, one has to let go of everything. Christ said: I have come not to make peace, but to separate the daughter from the mother, I have come to separate the father from the son, so that one doesn't get attached, so that one detaches and Realises who is the real Father and who is the real Mother. Otherwise, one stays always in this illusion.

The Guru will say: "Look, you are not just human, you are Divine and if you want to realise it, follow me, follow my advice."

When one enters the spiritual life, one always says "Oh my goodness, I have to let go of this, I have to let go of that. There are so many things to let go of, it's too boring, it's too much!" Whereas, when one really lets go of everything and surrenders, one gets everything, one gets the real thing: why one has come here, one gets Self-Realisation, God-Realisation, one rises in the Divine Love.

So, this should be your ultimate goal if you are on a spiritual path: to have Self-Realisation, to Realise God's Love continuously inside of you. And whenever your mind is jumping, your restless mind, calm it by chanting God's Name. He has millions of Names, He has thousands of Names, so chant! Sing His Name. Sing and dance in ecstasy. When you sing, feel Him with you. Don't just sit and chant because it becomes boring. If you just sit and chant, you will do it for one week, two weeks, one month, two months, maybe, then you will drop it, because when you sit and chant only, you start to expect something. So, keep chanting whatever you are doing.

When you are walking, when you are working, when you are taking your shower, chant! The more you chant, the more the mind will move away from the unreal to the Real.

THE OCEAN, THE BOAT
AND THE BOATMAN

Guru Purnima Retreat, Steffenshof, Germany, 29 July 2007

You see, very often men have an arrogant attitude. They always think they know better. They will always talk loudly of what they know little. It's said that the one that talks less knows much and the one that talks a lot knows less. That's true. You see, when people don't know much, they want to be heard, so they raise their voice very loudly. But when you look at a Master, you look at a spiritual guide, they talk when they have to talk, but they keep quiet most of the time. Like I explained in the morning, they analyse everything and they have a solution for everything because *only* in quietness will you get a solution.

Solutions are here, but the mind is too busy to see them. When you have a problem, you look for a solution. You keep looking, looking, looking, you fight and you go crazy about it, but at the end, when you say "I am tired of it!" you see that the solution was here, but you didn't see it. Why didn't you see it? Because your mind was busy, your mind was too much in action. When the mind is in deep action like that, one will always think that they know better, even when they don't know much.

Then where is the quality of humbleness? Where is the quality of obedience? Where is the quality of surrender? Where is the quality of Love? There is none! That's why even sometimes you will hear that there are certain Masters who are really, really bad to the disciple. You see, like I said in the morning, when you desire God,

God will send you the Master. And, if you desire God, but have a lot of work to do on yourself, of course, you need a Master who is sharp like an arrow to put you in your place, otherwise you will not [do it].

So, coming to the point of obedience, like I said, the saints say that obedience is to crush one's pride and ego. As long as one doesn't have obedience, one will fantasise lots of things in the mind and the fantasies of the mind like to put one very high, even if it is not so, these fantasies like to make someone seem much grander, but the more one thinks of oneself as being grand, being more than others, the more one is going away from the reality, going away from the path, going away from the true identity, because your true identity is humility.

God manifests Himself to teach humility. There are, like I said, so many manifestations of God. For example, we can take Jesus: He humbled Himself so much! You see how humble He was. He was always with the people. He was always there, ready to help them, even people who were not listening to Him, people who were coming to Him because of miracles, to get healed and just to see some miracles, but it was not His purpose. His purpose was to imprint Love and He showed this – He showed this humility He had by washing the feet of His disciples, by surrendering to God's Will when He was crucified.

You see the same humility in the *Mahabharata*, when Krishna accepted to be the one driving the chariot. I will tell a little bit of the story for you to understand a bit more why Krishna was on the side of Arjun and not the side of Duryodhan. When Sri Krishna went to Duryodhan, to the Kauravas, and said to them: "If you don't accept Arjun and his brothers as your brothers and give them half of the kingdom, for sure there will be a fight." Duryodhan, who was very egoistic, very proud of himself, said "OK, we will not give anything. We would rather fight!"

As the time for the war was arriving, they had to decide which side Krishna would be on, whether with the Kauravas or with the Pandavas. The Pandavas are Arjun and his brothers. The Kauravas are Duryodhan and his family, the bad ones. So, Arjun from the Pandavas and Duryodhan from the Kauravas went to Krishna and Krishna told them: "Listen, I know why you are here, but know one thing: I am not going to fight in this war. I am not going to be on anybody's side. I am ready to give 30,000 of my soldiers to one of you and for the other one I will come. If one wants Me, I will come, but I will come only as the charioteer. I will come to drive the chariot only. I will be the driver." When Duryodhan heard that Krishna was not coming to fight, He would just be the charioteer, he said "No, no, no, no! Go with Arjun and give me 30,000 men, 30,000 of your soldiers. It's better." So he took 30,000 soldiers. He forgot that Krishna is God.

> Christ said:
> For real Love, you can also give your life happily. If somebody has real Love for someone, he can give his life for this person. And that's how it is for a Master. A Master can give his life for his disciple.

This is what we do every day in our life. We would rather choose something opposite than our own path; we would rather choose something that will make us unhappy than choose something that will make us happy. So, Arjun took Krishna as the charioteer and, of course, where there is Krishna there is victory. When one walks on the right path, there is always victory. When one walks on the right path, for the right reason God will always be by his side. Krishna humbled Himself and became the charioteer of Arjun on the side of the Pandavas and of course they won.

After the war, the Kaurava's mum came and cursed Krishna. He happily accepted it! Even being a Divine Incarnation, He accepted the curse of Gandhari, the mother of Duryodhan, because the mother of Duryodhan said, "Lord, You are the Lord of the Universe, you know everything. You could have stopped everything, but yet, because it's your own play, you have let everything happen! Because my heart as a mother is paining, I curse you." And Krishna said "OK, I accept it."

What the great Masters, the *Paramgurus* - the *Jagatgurus* teach us is that only by humbly surrendering to one's Master, to one's spiritual guide, will one be relieved from suffering. As we were just singing before - *Sat Ki Nava Kevatiya Bhava Sagara Tara Ayo* - meaning: In this illusion, in this world of *Maya*, this ocean of illusion, we are all passengers on a boat and the boatman is the Satguru. The boatman knows the way. Only the spiritual guide knows the way out of *Bhava Sagara*, out of this ocean of illusion; knows the way to liberation. So, when you hold onto your spiritual guide, when you hold onto your *Satguru*, your *Satguru* will lead you to Self-Realisation.

I also said in the morning not to think that the Master, the *Satguru*, needs anything from anybody. They have everything; they have Realised God. The only thing that they want is that all of you Realise God. They humble themselves to be your servant, to serve you and lift you, so that you can hold the hand of God, so that you can Realise the Divine. But, nowadays, often, when the *Satguru* says something, of course, one has to contradict the *Satguru*!

Once, there was a man who went to his *Satguru* and the *Satguru* said "My dear fellow, now it's time that you renounce the world and fully dedicate yourself to Self-Realisation and Realise God. I will help you." The man looked at the *Satguru* as if the *Satguru* had gone crazy and said "But, Guruji, you know, I have a lovely wife, I have two lovely children, of course, they are grown-up but I also have my mum, I have my dad, I have my friends, so I can't because they love me so much! They show me their love so much!" So, the *Satguru* said "But my dear child, this all is just illusion that you see, it's not real." But then the disciple said "But Guruji, their love is so real. I can feel it, they love me so much!" The *Guru* looked at him and thought "My goodness, hard head, hard nut to crack."

So, he said "OK, here are some pills that I have made. On a fine day, just take one of these pills. You will not die, because it's not poison, but you will go into a state where you will be completely relaxed. You will be in a sleeping state, but your consciousness will be working. You will hear everybody, you will feel what they are doing around you, but you will not be able to react. You will just be completely paralysed, like a dead person and as long as I am not at your house, you will not get up." The disciple said "OK, I will try and I will wait for you" The day came, the man took the pill in the morning and, of course, he lay down on his bed and could not move. He could not make any movement - even the breathing was reduced completely.

He was lying down in bed and sleeping and when his wife called him, he didn't react. So she went there and looked at him and called him: "Swami, wake up!" (This is how the wives in India call their husband!) But he didn't wake up and she thought that he was dead and started screaming, pulling her hair, throwing herself on the body of her husband, screaming, crying and wailing.

The children came rushing "Mum, what happened?" "Your dad has left us! I have become widowed; you have become orphans!" There was lots of crying, the mother [of the man] came, all the neighbours rushed from everywhere. When finally, one of the neighbours said, "Let me see if he is dead." He checked the pulse and said "No, he is not dead!" The wife said, "Noooo, he is dead!"

At the same time the *Guru* came and said "Why are you crying, my dear children?" the wife said: "He has left us! He died!" The *Satguru* said "Listen, I have a pill. If you take it, he will live, but you will die in his place." So much love they had for him, they were all crying. When they heard that the pill would give back life, they were very happy but the moment they heard that the person who would take the pill would die, they stopped crying. The wife who was crying so much, at once stopped and was quiet.

Then the *Guru* said to the wife "You were just crying and wailing so much. This is an expression of your love. So, take the pill and your husband will live!" The wife said "No, no, no Guruji. He's dead, he's dead; let him be. So the *Guruji* turned to the mother "This is your son, no? You take the pill." The mother said "Me? Look, I am already old! Why should I take the pill? Very soon I will die myself. Let me enjoy [life] a little bit longer. He is dead; let him be." It was the same thing with his father, same thing with his children. Everybody refused; everybody had something to enjoy!

Then the *Guru* went near the disciple took his pot of water, threw a little bit of his water on him and said "Get up!" He got up and without saying a word to the family, he said "Guruji, take me. Let's go." So, you see, that is how much love they had for him!

Christ said: "For real Love you can also give happily your life. If somebody has real Love for someone, he can give his life for this person. And that's how it is for a Master. A Master can give his life for his disciple. To save his disciple, He will do anything, but people run blindly. People are like blind men. They think they know better and start talking loudly about big, big things, but really, it is only by asking, by surrendering to the Master that one will really be free.

Once there were five blind men. They would sit under a tree all day and talk and talk and talk. One day, as it was very hot, a huge elephant came and stood under the tree. They were blind but they could hear that somebody had come. So, all five got up and started walking around. They could feel there was something in front of them. The first one said "What is this? This is a huge wall made of mud, but I don't understand how this wall has moved here?" The second one was holding the tusk. Feeling it, he said "Oh, these are two spears made out of ivory." The third one was holding the tail at the back and said "No, no, no, you are wrong. This is a rope, a big, huge rope."The fourth one was holding the trunk of the elephant and he said "No, no, no, this is nothing that you have said. This is a snake hanging from the tree." And the fifth one said, "No, you are all wrong! This is the trunk of a tree."

So there was a big discussion, everyone was fighting and each one was proclaiming "I am right, I am right, I am right!" At the same time a small boy passed by. Looking at them, wondering why they were fighting, he said "What are you quarrelling for? Why are you hanging on this elephant like that?" And, when they heard an elephant, they all got shocked, they said: "an elephant!" After some time, when the boy had gone, the first one said "We are not just blind. I think we are, also, stupid!" The second one said "No, no, no. I was a bit confused when I said what I thought." And the third one said "I thought it was something like that, but I didn't say." So the fourth one said "Well, we were just talking loudly whatever was passing through our minds" and the fifth one said "You know, I feel so foolish. We could have just asked someone and it would have been much faster."

It's the same thing: humanity is blind to God-Realisation. Only someone who has Realised the Divine can really guide you. Only someone who knows the path can really lead you. Otherwise, you will be like these blind men – you will be touching everything, left and right and it will not lead you anywhere. So, just ask; just surrender.

GLOSSARY

Abhayahasta: *Abhaya* means helping and *hasta* means hand; a gesture of encouragement. Sri Swami Vishwananda has said it is "a blessing received from the Guru. ... You go to the Master, you bow your head, you offer the *sahasrara (crown chakra)*, and the teacher touches you on the head, no? He gives you the blessing that says not to worry, the Divine will look after. (Gurupurnima, Shree Peetha Nilaya 25ᵗʰ July 2010)

Amrita: The nectar of immortality that emerged from the churning of the Ocean of Milk. (see Churning of the Milk Ocean)

Asana: A body posture or pose that is done as part of a spiritual system called Yoga.

Asura: Demon (*a-sura = without light*)

Arjuna: A hero in the *Mahabharata* war in the Bhagavad Gita; the archer in the chariot with Sri Krishna who humbled Himself to be Arjuna's charioteer and teach him about his *dharma* and *Bhakti* Yoga.

Atma: Soul that is supreme and super conscious; the individual soul, known as the living entity; Jivatma.

Atman: The individual Self or eternal soul; true Self.

Atma Kriya Yoga: *Atma* means Self, *Kri* means action and *ya* means awareness, thus a series of yogic techniques given by Mahavatar Kriya Babaji to his disciple, Sri Swami Vishwananda, who has given it to the world, that helps one Realise one's True Self – Divine Love. Techniques in this Kriya Yoga system include the OM Healing technique, asanas , japa, meditation, mudras and pranayama.

Balaram: The elder brother of Krishna who incarnated with Sri Krishna and was carried in the womb of Vasudeva's, first wife, Rohini, much to her surprise, since she was beyond child-bearing age when He appeared there. He was so powerful that He single-handedly, at a very tender age, killed the great demon, Asuradhenuka, who had the form of an ass.

Baptism: Baptism is a sacrament (sacred secret) common to all Christian traditions. Practiced by religious traditions worldwide, it became associated with the early Christian movement following the baptism of Jesus of Nazareth by John, called the Baptist or the Baptizer. Jesus would later issue a Great Commission to his church: Go ye into all the world and preach the Gospel, baptising them in the name of the Father, the Son and the Holy Spirit. (Matthew 28:19) [1]

Bhagavad Gita: In it's own words, the Gita is described as "the scripture of yoga and the science of God-Realisation" (brahmavidyayam yogashastre). *Bhagavad Gita* means *Song of the Spirit...* and consists of 700 verses in which Bhagavan Krishna's intent in the dialogue between Him and Arjuna is to overthrow the usurping psychological forces of the body-bound ego and material ignorance and reclaim his eternal spiritual identity – one with Spirit." [2]

Bharata: Second brother of Lord Rama whose mother wanted him to rule in Lord Rama's place, so their broken-hearted father acquiesced to her wishes, because of a promise he had made to her. Bharata was mortified when he came back to Ayodhya and found this out and tried to persuade (to no avail) his brother, who was devoted to Dharma, to return from exile in the forest to his rightful rule of Ayodhya.

Brahman: According to the Vedantins, the *Brahman* is both the efficient and material cause of the visible Universe, the all-pervading soul and spirit of the Universe, the essence from which all created things are produced and into which they are all absorbed at dissolution. The *Brahman* is not generally an object of worship, but rather, it is an object of meditation and attaining it is the ultimate aim of knowledge. [3]

Bible: A collection of writings that comprise the main Christian teachings.

Buddhism, Tibetan: A type of Buddhism whose main Buddha is Padmasambhava.

Buddhism, Zen: A type of Buddhism that is practiced extensively in Japan and includes the incorporation of Taoism.

Buddhism: A religion or philosophy founded on the teachings of the Indian teacher Siddhārtha Gautama.

Chakras: Chakra = wheel. "The seven centres of life force and consciousness in the spine and the brain that keep the physical and astral body of Man alive. The seven centres are divine exits or entrances through which the soul has descended into the body and through which the soul has to ascend, again, by meditation. The soul reaches cosmic consciousness through seven consecutive stages. By consciously ascending through the seven opened or awakened cerebrospinal centres, it begins the path to infinity – the true path, which finally leads to confluence with God." [4]

Chanting: Repetition of a mantra or Divine Name.

Christianity: A religion in which followers see Jesus as the Christ, the Son of God.

Churning of the Ocean of Milk: It is said [in the Vedas] that the demigods and the demons assembled on the shore of the Milk Ocean that lies in the celestial region of the cosmos. The demigods and the demons made a plan to churn the Milk Ocean to produce the nectar of immortality. They then agreed to share the nectar equally once it was produced.

For the task of churning the Milk Ocean the Mandara Mountain was used as the churning rod and Vasuki, the king of serpents, became the rope for churning. As the churning began the Mandara Mountain began to sink deep into the ocean, at which time Sri Vishnu incarnated as a great tortoise [Kurma Avatara] and supported the mountain on His back. With the demigods at Vasuki's tail and the demons at his head, they churned the milk ocean for one thousand years.

At last Dhanvantari [Sri Vishnu Avatara, physician of the gods and father of *Ayurveda*] appeared carrying the pot of nectar of immortality in His hands. Seeing Dhanvantari with the pot of nectar, both the demigods and demons became anxious. The demigods, being fearful of what would happen if the demons drank their share of the nectar of immortality, forcibly seized the pot.

Wherever the demigods went with the pot of nectar, fierce fighting ensued. ...In an endeavor to keep the nectar from falling into the hands of the demons, the demigods hid it in four places on the earth, Prayag (Allahabad), Hardwar, Ujjain, and Nasik. At each of the hiding places, a drop of immortal nectar spilled from the pot and landed on the earth. These four places are since believed to have acquired mystical power. Eventually, the demons overpowered the demigods and took possession of the nectar of immortality. To rescue the demi-gods from the hands of fate, Maha Vishnu incarnated as a beautiful woman, Mohini-murti, and approached the demons. ...While the demons were thus bewildered by Her beauty, Mohini-murti seized the nectar and returned it to the demigods, who drank it immediately. [5]

Darshan: literally *sight* or *seeing*. *Darshan* is the sight of a holy being as well as the blessing received by such a sight.

Devi / Deva: (sometimes called a Demi-God) Literally, shining one. A Divine Being, a celestial. [3]

Devaki: Birth mother of Bhagavan Krishna and wife to Vasudeva (see Vasudeva), who had done much tapasya (penance) to have the boon of being Sri Krishna's mother. Sri Swami Vishwananda has said: "...Narayana... chose the right time and manifested Himself into the womb of Devaki. ..... in one of their past incarnations, Devaki and Vasudeva had been a king and a queen who had wanted so much to have God as their child. They had done penance for thousands of years. Mahavishnu was really pleased with them and had promised to them: Whenever I will incarnate myself next time, it will be through you." (*Krishna Janmashtami*, Shree Peetha Nilaya, Springen, Germany, 13th August 2009)

Devotee: One who is ardently given (devoted) to a Guru or Master.

Dhanvantari: In the *Hindu* tradition, an incarnation of *Narayana*. He appears in the Vedas and *Puranas* as the physician of the Gods (Devas) and the giver of *Ayurvedic* medicine.

Dharma: The eternal rules of righteousness that keep up the whole universe; the innate duty of man to live in harmony with these principles. [4]

Disciple: A devotee who is completely surrendered to his or her Guru.

Divine Mother: Devi is the Divine Mother of Hinduism. Her name means goddess. All Hindu goddesses may be viewed as different manifestations of Devi. In some forms she is benign and gentle, while in other forms she is dynamic and ferocious, but in all forms she is helpful to her devotees. Her main Scripture, adored by Hindus, is the *Devi Mahatmyam* (also known as *Chandi Path* and *Durga Saptashati*), in which an allegorical telling of the binding force of *Maya* and ego is represented through devotional stories about the Divine Mother slaying demons which afflict the world.

Divine Names: The Names of God.

Draupati: The wife of the five Pandavas (see *Mahabharata*).

Durga Devi: *Durga* in Sanskrit means "She who is incomprehensible or difficult to reach." Goddess Durga is a form of Shakti worshiped for her gracious as well as terrifying aspect. Mother of the Universe, she represents the infinite power of the universe and is a symbol of a female dynamism. The manifestation of Goddess Durga is said to emerge from Her formless essence and the two are inseparable. Durga, a beautiful warrior seated upon a tiger, was the first appearance of the great goddess. The circumstance of her miraculous arrival was the tyranny of the monster-demon, Mahishasur, who through terrific austerities had acquired invincible strength. The Gods were afraid of this shape-shifting water-buffalo bull, because neither Vishnu nor Shiva could prevail against him. It seemed that only the joint energy of *Shakti* was capable of vanquishing Mahisha, and so it was the eighteen-armed Durga who went out to do battle.

Duryodhana: The eldest of the Kauravan brothers who was the enemy of the Pandavan brothers in the *Mahabharata* war see.

Ganga Devi: The name of *Ganga* appears only twice in the *Rig Veda* and it was only later that Ganga assumed great importance as a goddess. According to the *Vishnu Purana*, she was created from the sweat of Lord Vishnu's Lotus Feet. Hence, she is also called

Vishnupadi - the one flowing from the foot of Vishnu. According to *Devi Bhagavata Purana*, Sri Vishnu has three wives, who constantly quarrel with each other, so that eventually, he keeps only Lakshmi, giving Ganga to Shiva and Saraswati to Brahma.

Gadha: Mace

Ganesha: The elephant-headed son of Parvati Who is the remover of obstacles; Lord (Pati) of the Ganas (spirits that always accompany Shiva); God of wisdom; the granter of success is spiritual and material life. In pujas and yajnas he is worshipped first and is, therefore, known as Adideva, the First God.

Gopis/gopas: "Bhagavan Krishna's childhood companions, who with Him tended the village herds of cows in the sylvan environs of Vrindavan and who shared with him the purity of divine Love and friendship that bears no taint of carnal expression or desire."ii

Guru: *Gu* means darkness and *ru* means the act of removal; the teacher, the Spiritual Master one who dispels darkness (ignorance) of the mind (ego/personality).

Hari, Lord: (*Om) yam brahma vedanta-vido vadanti, pare pradhanam purusham tathanye. vishvodgateh karanam ishvaram va, tasmai namo vighna-vinashaya* meaning Obeisances unto Him who is the destroyer of all obstacles, who the knowers of Vedanta describe as the Supreme Brahman, and who others describe as the *pradhana*, or totality of mundane elements. Some describe Him as the supreme male person, or *purusha*, while others describe Him as the Supreme Lord and the cause of the creation of the universe." (Vishnu Purana)

Hanuman: Sri Swami Vishwananda has said about Hanuman: "Hanuman is considered to be the model of *bhakti*. ...As you know, Hanuman is an incarnation of Shiva. When Rama came down, all the Deities manifested Themselves in the form of Monkeys – *Vanara Sena*. And Hanuman is Shiva Himself, actually. .....You know, Hanuman is considered as the Ocean of Wisdom..." (*Hanuman Jayanti*, Shree Peetha Nilaya, Springen, Germany, 30 March 2010)

Hinduism: With about 900 million followers (over 13 % of the world population) Hinduism is, after Christianity and Islam, the third biggest religion on Earth and it has its origin in India. The followers are called Hindus. Hinduism is composed of different streams that influence each other and sometimes overlay each other, but have differences in the Holy Scriptures, the dogma, the Gods and rituals.

Hindu-Trinity: Creator-Brahma, Preserver/Sustainer-Vishnu, Destroyer-Shiva

Hiranyakashipu: Hiranya = gold; Kashipu = soft feathers or bed; the one who loves gold and soft beds. He is a demon (*asura*) who was slain by *Narayana* in his *Narasimha* (man-lion) incarnation and who was the father of Prahlad.

Holika: "Holika is the sister of *Hiranyakashipu*... and she was blessed for so many years of penance with a shawl. If ever she wore this shawl, fire couldn't burn her."* She tried to use this shawl to keep herself safe from the fire in an attempt to burn Prahlad for her brother. *(Sri Swami Vishwananda, *Gaura Purnima* at Shree Peetha Nilaya, Springen, Germany, 2 March 2010.)

Hrdaya Mudra: *Hrdaya* means heart; a *mudra* for opening the heart (see *Mudra*).

Incarnation: When a Deity or soul takes an earthly form.

Islam: A religion in which there is one God, Allah, and in which

Mohammad is seen as the main prophet or Saint.

Japa Mala: Chanting the Name of God or a mantra is Japa. A mala is generally a 108 beaded necklace used to count as one chants which collects the vibration produced by one's chanting the sacred mantra of Divine Name of God, hence it becomes a source of healing, so should always be kept safe in one's Mala bag.

Jaya: Victory; hail; salutations.

Jesus: Son of God, Christ, who came to redeem the world and bring new ways of seeing it.

Jivan Mukta: *Mukti* means release; a liberated sage living in the world but being not of the world.

Judaism: A religion whose main teachings are found in the Torah and whose worshippers, the Jews, are descendents of Abraham.

Kalash Puja: A *kalash* is a copper pot and *puja* means worship or a ritual in honour of the Gods; a coconut is placed on top of the *kalash* during the ritual representing the heart of the Deity; the kalash, also, represents the perfection of the devotees' heart.

Kalki Avatara: The future tenth incarnation of Maha Vishnu in the form of a rider on a white horse who will restore *Dharma*. He will come to end the present age of darkness and destruction known as Kali Yuga. The name Kalki is often a metaphor for eternity or time. Further meanings are destroyer of foulness, destroyer of confusion, destroyer of darkness or annihilator of ignorance.

Kali Ma: Kali, the Dark Mother, is one such Deity with whom devotees have a very loving and intimate bond, in spite of her fearful appearance. In this relationship, the worshipper becomes a child and Kali assumes the form of the ever-caring mother. Kali is the fearful and ferocious form of the Mother Goddess. She assumed the form of a powerful goddess and became popular with the composition of the Devi Mahatmya, a text of the 5th - 6th century AD.

Kamsa: Brother of Devaki (see *Devaki*), who imprisoned her and Vasudeva (see *Vasudeva*), her husband, "because an *Akashvani*, a celestial announcement, had said to Kansa that the eighth child of Devaki would kill him." (Sri Swami Vishwananda, *Krishna Janmashtami*, Shree Peetha Nilaya, Springen, Germany, 13th August 2009.)

Karma: From Sanskrit *kri=to do*. Effects of previous actions from this life or preceding lives, the redeeming law of *karma* is, according to the scriptures of the Hindus, the law of action and reaction, of cause and effect, of sowing and reaping. The natural justice causes that each human being becomes the creator of his fate by his actions and thoughts. [4]

Kauravas: Descendents of Kuru; refers to the descendants of the legendary King Kuru who was the ancestor of many in the Mahabharata war (see *Mahabharata*).

Kirtan: devotional chanting, singing the Names and praises of God.

Krishna: Krishna is the eighth incarnation of Narayana and was born in the Dvapara Yuga. He is the embodiment of Love and Divine Joy who destroys all pain and sin. He is the protector of sacred utterances and cows. Krishna is an instigator of all forms of knowledge and born to establish the religion of Love. Sri Swami Vishwananda said about Sri Krishna: "...the most beautiful of all the incarnations of the Divine...is Sri Krishna Himself. The Name, Krishna, just by reciting this beautiful Name, one awakens peace and love. The Name means the one who attracts everyone. Krishna is the one who destroys all the sin, who cleanses and purifies everybody. Actually, His life is a mystery itself. It's one of the greatest mysteries, because His life deals with our spiritual life, to attain Him." (Krishna Retreat, Los Angeles, California, USA, December, 2007)

Kurma: (literally turtle) Is considered in *Hinduism* as the second incarnation of *Narayana*. According to several *Puranas*, the old books about the *Devas*, Maha Vishnu incarnated after his form of a fish (*Matsya*) in the form of a turtle. Kurma lifted the mountain, Mandara, onto his back out of the mystical ocean during the Churning of the Milk Ocean by the *Devas* and *Asuras* in search of the *Amrita*.

Lakshmana: Lakshmana is the twin brother of Shatrughna and third brother to Lord *Rama*. In *Puranic* Scripture Lakshmana is described as the incarnation of Anata Shesha, the thousand-headed Naga upon whom rests Lord *Narayana* in the primordial Ocean of Milk, Kshirasagara). He is said to be an eternal companion of Sri Vishnu in all incarnations.

Lakshmi: The consort of Narayana; the Goddess of wealth and prosperity, good fortune and spiritual abundance.

Lakshmi/Narayana: Like Shakti/Shiva, an expression of the female and male principle of God; Goddess of spiritual and material abundance. *Narayana* is the One who pervades all things. Literally, God in humanity.

Lanka: Sri Lanka, formerly Ceylon, where the demon *Ravana* took *Sita* after he kidnapped her from Lord Rama.

Lila: Divine play; the cosmic play; the concept that creation is a play of the Divine, existing for no other reason than for the mere joy of it.

Mahabharata: India's great epic poem made up of eighteen books recounts the history of the descendants of King Bharata, the Pandavas and Kauravas, cousins whose dispute of a kingdom was the cause of the cataclysmic war of Kurukshetra." [2]

Mahavatar Kriya Babaji: Maha means great, Avatar means Divine Manifestation and *babaji* means revered father; around 5000 year old yogi from the Himalayas and *Paramguru* who has given Kriya Yoga to the world.

Manifest/unmanifest: *manifest=obvious, cognizable*. The manifest universe is absolute and as perfect as the non-manifest, because it comes from the non-manifest. The appearance of the manifest from the non-manifest does not influence the wholeness and perfection of the non-manifest.

Master: A great spiritual guru.

Matsya: In his first incarnation, Maha Vishnu has the lower part of his body like that of a fish (Matsya) and the upper part like that of a man. He has four arms. With two he holds a conch-shell and a *chakra,* while the other two are holding a lotus and a mace or are in the protection and boon giving mudras.

Maya: Illusion, that which prevents us from realising our true Self. Sri Swami Vishwananda said about Maya: "Maya Devi is very powerful, because She traps everything. .... Once you step in the world, you get trapped in the grip of Maya and it's quite difficult to get out of Her grip. Her grip is so strong that once She grabs you it's only by chanting the Name of God that you can get yourself released; only by saying, truly from your heart "'God I want you. I surrender completely to you. Do what you have to do with me.'" Then She will let go of you." (Darshan, Kiel, Germany, December 2006.) Paramahansa Yogananda wrote: "The Sanskrit word Maya means *the measuring one*; it is the magic force which is innate in creation, which causes in the unlimited and undividable, virtual limitations and fissions. [4]

Mecca: A holy city in Saudi Arabia that is the most important pilgrimage site for Muslims.

Meditation: Practices that help one to control the mind. Sri Swami Vishwananda had said it is: "...something, which is very simple, for attaining this state of Bliss. .... It's through meditation that one can really come to the power of complete fulfilment. ..... when one is concentrated, when one is focused on God, when one is in deep meditation, one is not affected by anything around, by any noise, by any touching." (*Darshan*, Mumbai, India, 10th February 2006)

Mohammed: The main prophet in the Islamic religion.

Mohini: In *Hindu* mythology the name of the only female incarnation of Maha *Vishnu*. Mohini is mentioned in the narrative epic of the *Mahabharata*. Here she appears as a form of *Vishnu*, which acquires the pot of *Amrita* (elixir of immortality) from thieving *Asuras* (Demons), and gives it back to the *Devas* (demi-gods), helping them retain their immortality.

Moksha: Liberation from the cycle of birth and death.

Mount Meru (Mount Kailash): A mountain of supreme height on which the Gods dwell or the mountain on which Shiva is ever seated in meditation; the centre of the world, supporting heaven itself; the Olympus of the *Hindu* gods and goddesses, *Mount Meru*, or sometimes Sumeru or Mandara is, according to the *Mahabharata*, a golden mass of intense energy. Brahmā's golden city is at its summit. It is the *axis mundi* for both Hindus and Buddhists. [6]

Mudra: A gesture usually done with the hands that focuses and directs energy. Twenty of these ancient mudras have been given by Sri Swami Vishwananda to his disciples and are available through His teachings to all who wish to learn them.

Nanda: Foster father and uncle of Sri Krishna.

Nada Kriya Yoga: *Nada* means sound. A meditation focused on sound that is one of the *Atma Kriya* techniques.

Narad Muni: Spiritual Master and son of Lord Brahma's Mind who was directly initiated by Lord Brahma, who eternally sings hymns, prayers and mantras to Sriman Narayana and who is always traveling throughout the Three Worlds; author of Pancharatra, the Vaishnava "Vaishnava Sanskrit texts dedicated to the worship of Sriman Narayana.

NARAYANA, SRI; MAIN INCARNATIONS: (see also *Vishnu*) Is said to have manifested himself in various incarnations, called Avatars, for the destruction of evil or restoration of faith and justice in the world. These incarnations have been in the human form, in the animal form and in the combined human-animal form. Though popularly believed to be ten in number, the Bhagavat Purana mentions twenty-two such incarnations with innumerable more to follow.

The ten main avatars are:
1. Matsya
2. Kurma
3. Varaha
4. Narasimha
5. Vamana
6. Parasurama
7. Rama
8. Balarama
9. Krishna
10. Kalki (yet to come)

Narasimha: Nara=man, Simha=lion, the fourth incarnation of Maha *Vishnu*, whose form is half-man and half-lion. The *Puranas* tell about the demon king *Hiranyakashipu*, who once was reigning almost over the whole universe, but who finally was killed by Sri Vishnu in his form of Narasimha. Lord Narasimha is the fiercest incarnation of Maha *Vishnu*. He came to protect His pure devotee *Prahlada* against the tortures of his evil father Hiranyakashipu. While He is feared by the demons and non-devotees, He is worshipped with love and reverence by His devotees.

Padma: Lotus flower or Padma, held by the lower right hand of Sri Vishnu, represents spiritual liberation, Divine Perfection, purity and the unfolding of Spiritual Consciousness within the individual.

Pandavas: The sons of Pandu; Arjuna and his four brothers who, with their allies, formed one side in the Mahabharata war (see *Mahabharata*).

Paramatman: The supreme Being; *the Brahman.*

Paramguru: *Param* means supreme and *guru* means remover of darkness; the guru's guru.

Parashurama: Rama with the axe – Sri Vishnu in a human form, the sixth incarnation of Narayana.

Parvati: Consort of Lord Shiva. "Parvati is the Mother of the Universe. She is *Parashakti*." Sri Swami Vishwananda, *Kartik Purnima*, Springen, Germany, 2 November 2009.

Pentecost: It is the day when the Holy Spirit came upon the Disciples after Christ Jesus had resurrected. It is now celebrated 50 days after Easter Sunday.

Prahlad: A great devotee of Krishna even from birth, having been taught by Sage Narada while still in the womb of his mother. As a small boy of five he would preach about Sri Vishnu to his school friends any time the teachers left the room. This preaching infuriated his father, Hiranyakashipu who was determined to deny Sri Vishnu's existence.

Puranas: A classic set of sacred stories and legends written in simple Sanskrit; belonging to the past, ancient; an ancient story or legend.

RadhaKrishna: "It is Krishna Himself in the form of Radharani. When we talk about Radha, we always put Her first and then Krishna. We say *Radhe Krishna, Radhe Shyam*, because She is the *Shakti* of Krishna." Sri Swami Vishwananda, *Radhastami*, Springen, Germany, 27 August 2009.

Ramakrishna: (1836-1886) Great Indian Saint born near Calcutta who taught the universality of religions; a great *Bhakta* who worshipped Divine Mother in Her form as Maha Kali.

Ram, Rama: According to the teachings of Hinduism, the seventh incarnation of Sri Vishnu. He is described as educated, beautiful and endowed with all royal qualities. His story is told in the heroic epic Ramayana. It deals with Rama's banishment to the woodland solitude and the victory over *Ravana* after he had kidnapped his wife, *Sita*, to Lanka. An essential helper in this battle was the greatest devotee of Lord Ram, *Hanuman*.

Ravana: Evil demon King who abducted Lord *Rama*'s wife *Sita* and took her to *Lanka*.

Reincarnation: When the soul is born again in a new body; the cycle of birth, death and rebirth; reincarnation ceases when one's karma is resolved.

Rishi: Great seers who revealed the Vedas; *Rishis* can speak only truth and have provided much knowledge to the world.

Sabari: Great devotee of Lord Rama. "...she waited her whole life for Rama. Every day she would chant Ram names continuously. Deep inside of her, she knew that one day she would meet her Rama." Sri Swami Vishwananda, *Darshan*, Steffenshof, 2nd May, 2007.

Sage: A wise person venerated for experience, judgment and wisdom.

Saint: One who lives in God or the eternal; custodian of super divine wisdom, spiritual powers and inexhaustible spiritual wealth who is free from egoism, likes and dislikes, selfishness, vanity, lust, greed and anger, who is endowed with equal vision, balanced mind, mercy, tolerance, righteousness, cosmic Love and has Divine Knowledge.

Samadhi: A yogic trance (state) where the mind has withdrawn from limited working activities into freer, higher states of God; a state where the seeker and the process of seeking merge into one single continuum and no separation remains between them; when applied to worship, the state where there is no difference between the devotee, God and worship.

Sannyasin: One who has given up a normal or worldly life to become an ascetic.

Sanatan Dharma: Literally, The Eternal Religion. This term describes the codex of different Vedic sciences, which was called Hinduism after the Greeks had called the people at the banks of the Indus River Indus or Hindus (see also *Dharma*). [4]

Shankha: Conch, conch shell horn.

Saraswati: Goddess of knowledge and the arts, represents the free flow of wisdom and consciousness. She is the Mother of the *Vedas* and chants to her, called the *Saraswati Vandana* often begin and end *Vedic* lessons. It is believed that Goddess Saraswati endows human beings with the powers of speech, wisdom and learning.

Satguru: *Sat* means true; guru the true teacher; highest spiritual teacher; ones primary or main spiritual teacher (see also Guru).

Self: The Atma; who one truly is – Divine Love.

Self-Realisation: Transcending the misidentification with the mind and body that happens to the embodied *Atma* here in the *Maya* and becoming aware of one's true nature; Union with the Divine.

Shiva: Part of the Hindu trinity; aspect of Dissolver and Liberator.

Shiva Shakti: "...the whole universe is governed by these two cosmic energies, which are the female energy and the male energy. That is what makes everything into manifestation. ..... which you can call Shiva Shakti,..." Sri Swami Vishwananda, *The Significance of the Two Hiranyagarbalingams*, 2nd March 2011.

Sita: Consort of Lord Rama. Sita Devi is a manifestation of Lakshmi.

Spirituality: Latin, *Spiritus, spirit, breeze, or spiro, I breathe,* spirituality in a specific religious sense stands for the idea of a mental (spiritual) connection with the transcendent or infinity.

Srimad Bhagavatam: (Bhagavata Purana) This purana (storybook) is the most important sacred book of stories in India, arranged in twelve so-called cantos and is comprised of 335 chapters with about 18,000 verses that stress the prime importance of the maintaining (preserving) aspect of God personified by the transcendental form of Sriman Narayana, Lord Vishnu.

Sri Lahiri Mahasaya: A householder and spiritual Master who was the first person to receive Kriya Yoga from Mahavatar Kriya Babaji who then shared it with other householders.

Sri Shirdi Sai Baba: A great Master (1838-1918) from India whose teaching combined elements of Hinduism and Islam. He constantly chanted *Allah Akbar* and was known for many divine miracles.

Sri Yukteshwarji: A disciple of Lahiri Mahasya and the guru of Paramhansa Yogananda.

St. Panteleimon: 284-305 A.D from Nicomedia; Physician and Patron of midwives and doctors and one of the fourteen Holy Helpers. Known for miraculous healings. An incarnation of Dhanvantari, physician of the Gods and Father of Ayurveda. (see Churning of the Milk Ocean); one of the patron saints of the chapel at Sri Swami Vishwananda's international Ashram Shree Peetha Nilaya, Germany.

Surdas: 15th century devotional saint of Lord Krishna; a poet, saint and musician who taught *Bhakti*.

Subhadra: Sister of Sri Krishna.

Surrender: In spirituality meaning giving everything completely to God. Sri Swami Vishwananda has said:"... to surrender means to say to God, "Lord, I give myself, my body, mind and soul completely to You. ..... So this is complete surrender where God can do whatever He wants with you, whenever He wants, as He wants. And for that you don't need to be scared, you know, you have just to give yourself. And who is your Self in reality? It's just Him! In the *Gita*, Krishna said: Everything is me." (*Darshan* in Lisbon, Portugal, 12 April 2008)

Tulsidas: 16th century great devotee who, also, wrote the *Ramacharitmanas,* an epic poem devoted to Lord Rama.

Tulsi Devi: See *Vrinda Devi*.

Upanishads: Meaning the inner or mystic teachings; refers to over 200 texts which are considered to be an early source of the Hindu religion.

Vaikunta: The celestial abode (*loka*) of Sri Vishnu and His devotees.

Valmiki: A sage and poet told by Narad Muni to write the Ramayana.

Vamana: Is described in the texts of *Hinduism* as the fifth incarnation of Mahu Vishnu and the first incarnation of the Second Age or the Treta Yuga. He is the first incarnation of Sri Vishnu which appears in a completely human form, though it was that of a dwarf Brahmin. He is, also, sometimes known as Upendra.

Varaha: In Hinduism the third incarnation of Sri Vishnu in the form of a boar. In the form of Vahara he fulfills his reputation as the preserver of the world. According to the Varaha Purana, when a new age had begun the Earth was sinking in the primordial waters. Like a mother who does not hesitate to jump after her child when it has fallen into the water, Sri Vishnu's first thought was to preserve the world. He took the form of a boar, the mightiest swamp animal, and dived into the Primordial Ocean. There he killed the dangerous Demon *Hiranyaksha* (the brother of *Hiranyakashipu*), lifted the Earth up with his colossal tusks and saved Her from drowning in the primordial chaos.

Vasudeva: The son of Shoorsen of the Yadu and Vrishni dynasties, husband of *Devaki* and father of Sri Krishna and his sister, Subhadra. Vasudeva was a partial incarnation of Rishi Kashyap. According to *Harivansa Purana,* Vasudeva and *Nanda*, Sri Krishna's foster father, were brothers.

Vasuki: The King of the Serpents. He assisted at the churning of the Milk Ocean. In one of the most famous episodes in the Puranas *(Bhagavata Purana, the Mahabharata* and the Vishnu Purana), the Devas (Demi-Gods) and the Demons (Asuras) had lost their immortality at that time. According to Sri Vishnu's advice, they bound the snake, Vasuki, around the mountain and started – Gods at one side and Demons at the other side – to pull back and forth on the snake. In that way they churned the Milk Ocean in order to gain *Amrita*, the nectar of immortality. In memory of that a festival is celebrated in a major way every twelve years known as Kumbha Mela.

Vedas: Ancient Indian texts and the oldest Sanskrit literature written in Vedic Sanskrit and compiled into four sections by Krishna Dvaipayana Veda Vyasa, a sage considered in some Vaishnava traditions as an Avatar of Maha Vishnu who later incarnated as Sage Kapila to teach the Bhakti Yoga of the Shrimad Bhagavatam written by Sage Vyasa at the suggestion of the son of Brahma, Rishi Narada.

Vijaya: Victory

Vishnu: Literally, all-pervading; God as the Preserver; part of the Hindu Trinity.

Vishwamitra: Was the first saint to have received the *Gayatri Mantra* and who, subsequently, taught it to his Disciple, Sri Rama, who then used it to defeat the great *asura*, Ravana, and rescue His wife, Sita, from the demon; an author of the *Rigveda* known for enduring many austerities and who underwent many trials.

Vrindavan: Vrindavan (also Brindavan) in Mathura district, Uttar Pradesh, India, is a town on the site of an ancient forest where Lord Krishna spent his childhood days and where He was cared for by His foster mother, *Yashoda*, and His foster father and uncle, *Nanda*. It lies in the Braj region about 15km away from Mathura, the city of Lord Krishna's birthplace, near the Agra-Delhi highway. The town hosts thousands of temples dedicated to the worship of Radha and Krishna.

Vrinda Devi: *(Vrindavana)* "The Sanskrit word *vana* means forest. *Vrindavana* is the name given to the forest where Srimati Vrindadevi (Tulasidevi), grows abundantely."

Vyasa: Often regarded as an Avatar of Vishnu, he is sometimes referred to as Veda Vyasa, the compiler of the Vedas; composed *Puranas* and the poetic work *Mahabharata*.

Yagna: Sacrifice of pride and ego; a fire ceremony where one gives up the self, what one wants for the benefit of others getting rid of pride and opening the heart through mantras and offering back what the Divine has given us.

Yamuna: Like the Ganges, the Yamuna, too, is highly venerated in Hinduism and worshipped as Goddess Yamuna, throughout its course. In Hindu mythology, She is the daughter of Sun God, Lord Surya, and sister of Yama, the God of Death, hence, also, known as Yami. "Vasudeva entered the water of the Yamuna carrying the baby Krishna and, as he was going deeper and deeper into the Yamuna River, Yamuna wanted so much just to touch the feet of the Lord. And the moment the feet of the baby Krishna touched the water of Yamuna, she became very calm." Sri Swami Vishwananda, *Krishna Janmashtami*, Springen, Germany, 13 August 2009.

Yashoda: Foster mother of Sri Krishna and wife of His uncle, *Nanda*, his foster father. "So as Narayana had said to Maya Devi 'Incarnate Yourself in the womb of Yashoda', Maya Devi manifested Herself inside of Yashoda. On the same night she was born in Gokul, Narayana was born in Mathura [as Sri Krishna]. ...Bhakti, in the form of Yashoda and Nandadev enjoying the Lord." Sri Swami Vishwananda, *Bala Krishna Retreat*, Los Angeles, California, USA, December, 2007.

Yudishtira: The eldest Pandava; also known as Dharmaraja – the righteous king (see *Mahabharata*).

Zamzam: A well in Mecca where Ishmael, Abraham's infant son, cried for water and kicked the ground and God responded by generating water.

[1] Douglas, J. D., ed. The New International Dictionary of the Christian Church. Grand Rapids, MI: Zondervan Publishing, 1974.

[2] From *The Yoga of the Bhagavad Gita* by Paramahansa Yogananda published by Self-Realization Fellowship, Los Angeles, California, USA in 2007

[3] Srimad Bhagavatam 10th edition English translation by Smt. Kamala Subramaniam, Bharatiya Vidya Bhavan, Kulapati Munshi Marg, Mumbai, 400007 India, glossary pg. 762

[4] Paramahansa Yogananda: The Eternal Search of Man. Collected Talks and Essays – To Realise God in Daily Life. Volume 1. Self-Realization Fellowship Publishers. Printed in USA 2005.

[5] hindupedia.com

[6] Oxford Dictionary of Asian Mythology

SRI SWAMI VISHWANANDA

Sri Swami Vishwananda is a spiritual master from the island of Mauritius. For some years he has been visiting numerous countries in Europe, North America, Africa and Asia to convey his message of universal Divine Love.

Swami Vishwananda inspires people to open their hearts to the Love of God. He teaches to go beyond the boundaries of religions and to experience the all-connecting unity behind the conceptual differences. He encourages people to deepen the individual path to God and supports them in their personal beliefs and religious heritage.

The Essence of Everything

is just

LOVE

29090829R00190

Made in the USA
Middletown, DE
06 February 2016